# STARTING
# STRONG

# *STARTING* **STRONG**

## Evidence-Based Early Literacy Practices

### Katrin Blamey
### *and*
### Katherine Beauchat

**Stenhouse Publishers**

Portland, Maine

**Stenhouse Publishers**
www.stenhouse.com

Library of Congress Cataloging-in-Publication Data

Names: Blamey, Katrin L., author. | Beauchat, Katherine A., author.
Title: Starting strong : evidence-based early literacy practices / Katrin
  Blamey and Katherine Beauchat.
Description: Portland, Me. : Stenhouse Publishers, 2016. | Includes
  bibliographical references.
Identifiers: LCCN 2016001216 (print) | LCCN 2016014733 (ebook) | ISBN
  9781571109309 (pbk. : alk. paper) | ISBN 9781625310569 (ebook)
Subjects:  LCSH: Language arts (Early childhood)
Classification: LCC LB1139.5.L35 B53 2016 (print) | LCC LB1139.5.L35 (ebook)
  | DDC 372.6--dc23
LC record available at http://lccn.loc.gov/2016001216

Cover and interior design by Lucian Burg, Lu Design Studios, Portland, ME
ludesignstudios.com

Manufactured in the United States of America

PRINTED ON 30% PCW
RECYCLED PAPER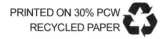

22 21 20 19 18 17 16      9 8 7 6 5 4 3 2 1

# Dedication

We dedicate this book to our families,

who inspire us to always do our best,

and to the many hardworking teachers

who educate our children

and children all over the world.

# Contents

# Acknowledgments

We want to extend sincere thanks to many people who helped support our work with this text. Our thanks to our students at DeSales University and York College of Pennsylvania, who challenge us to think critically every day, and to the administrators of those institutions, who encourage our scholarly endeavors.

Many classroom teachers have inspired us to think harder about engaging students in literacy instruction. We want to thank several teachers for inviting us into their classrooms, including the preschool teachers of the Early Learning Center at the University of Delaware, the Head Start teachers in Newark, the Head Start teachers in Allentown, the preschool teachers of Chesterbrook Academy, the kindergarten teachers and administration at Windsor Manor Elementary School, and the elementary teachers at Arrowhead Elementary School.

We also need to thank our own teachers and mentors—Dr. Sharon Walpole, Dr. David Coker, Dr. Rachel Karchmer-Klein, and Dr. Charles MacArthur—all at the University of Delaware. Without your help and encouragement, we would not be where we are today.

And many thanks to Mr. Bill Varner and his amazing team at Stenhouse. We are honored to be working with you and are ever grateful for your expertise and guidance.

# Chapter 1

# Early Literacy Targets

As former preschool educators, we are in awe of the work that early childhood educators do every single day with our youngest students. We remember days when there was so much pressure to get a number of observations done in time it seemed like we just could not keep up. We remember morning meetings when every child in the room was sick or tired or both. We remember excitement-filled days when a class visitor was coming to teach us about a job in the community and we just could not seem to settle down enough to listen. We also remember the joy that came when a child who really struggled with the letters of the alphabet proudly identified his name in a book. We as teachers play a critical role in children's motivation, skill development, and ultimate success in the process of becoming a reader. The role comes with quite a lot of stress!

The pressure we put on ourselves stems from the knowledge that all children who begin the primary grades with a solid beginning in oral language and vocabulary, phonological awareness, alphabet awareness, concepts of print, comprehension, and writing are able to apply these skills with improved academic outcomes (Adams 1990). The stakes are even higher for children living in poverty, who experience multiple disadvantages when it comes to preparation for and attainment of knowledge and education (Dickinson, McCabe, and Essex 2006; Hart and Risley 1995; Neuman 2006). Further, low-income children who do not attend preschool or attend low-quality preschools are more likely to experience higher high school dropout rates, decreased job opportunities, a lower quality of life, and a higher probability of becoming involved in crime (Schweinhart and Weikart

1997; Schweinhart et al. 2005). Thus, it is not an exaggeration to state that early childhood education has consequences throughout one's lifetime.

The good news is that although teachers are under an incredible amount of pressure, many resources exist to help them with their important work, including this book. Drawing from our personal experiences and conversations with colleagues, we address each of the components necessary to lay a solid foundation for all students' literacy development. We hope that you are able to make connections between our classrooms and yours in order to find practical tips for literacy instruction.

In this book, we think about four types of instruction that can help you educate successfully in your classroom, whether you are a preservice teacher in a teacher education program or an inservice teacher reflecting on your practice and pursuing a professional development plan. Four types of instruction contribute to our thinking about teaching: (1) standards-based instruction, (2) evidence-based instruction, (3) assessment-based instruction, and (4) student-based instruction.

In today's context of the Common Core standards movement we cannot escape, nor should we, the influence of standards on our teaching practice. We feel grounded when we align our instruction to standards, confident in the knowledge that we are teaching something meaningful. Evidence-based instruction refers to teaching methods that have a track record of research to indicate effectiveness. When there are so many instructional activities available online, it is important to be a critical consumer, using scientifically based reading research as a litmus test for use in our classrooms.

We also believe in using informal assessment as a tool for guiding, planning, monitoring, and reflecting on student learning. In our own work, we use assessments to tell us what students know, how much they have learned, what they still need to learn, and how we can best help them reach their learning goals. Finally, student-based instruction reminds us to engage students in learning by considering their interests and motivations. When planning high-quality literacy instruction for our students, we juggle our knowledge of standards-based, evidence-based, assessment-based, and student-based teaching to inform our work. Let's show you what we mean about how each type of instruction can serve as a resource to you as you build children's literacy foundations.

## Standards-Based Instruction

In this era of high-stakes testing and accountability, teachers must base their instruction on standards. This seems like a straightforward statement; however, it becomes infinitely more complex when considering the number of standards that exist in education today.

Historically, teachers have had to most closely address the individual state standards adopted by the department of education in the state in which they teach. States have the prerogative to adopt their own standards and develop assessments around them in order to measure student outcomes. We say historically because recently the Common Core standards movement is veering away from a model in which individual states set their own standards and toward a common set of standards that states can opt to adopt. At the time of this publication, the Common Core standards are still optional, with many states choosing to adopt them as a replacement for their state standards. The Common Core standards are in many cases more rigorous and demanding than previous state standards, causing heartache and frustration as teachers and schools make changes in instructional practices to meet the new demands.

Within each content area or discipline, professional organizations also publish content standards for educators (See Figure 1.1). While you as a teacher may not be required by your school or district to address standards of professional organizations in your teaching, we believe that they offer a wealth of knowledge. Since the standards are developed by the leading researchers and educators in a specific field, they often represent the most well-researched and reasoned standards in the content area. For literacy education specifically, we look to the National Council of Teachers of English for specialized content standards to inform our work.

| Professional Standards | Professional Organization |
|---|---|
| Principles and Standards for School Mathematics | National Council of Teachers of Mathematics (NCTM) |
| Next Generation Science Standards | National Science Teachers Association (NSTA) |
| NCTE/IRA Standards for the English Language Arts | National Council of Teachers of English (NCTE) |
| National Standards for Social Studies Teachers | National Council for the Social Studies (NCSS) |
| National Standards for Physical Education | National Association of Sport and Physical Education (NASPE) |
| Developmentally Appropriate Practice | National Association for the Education of Young Children (NAEYC) |

Figure 1.1 Professional Educator Standards

When we use standards-based instruction, the standards tell us *what* to teach. This is comforting because we do not have to make anything up. At the same time, it can be overwhelming to look at the standards to see all that we are responsible for teaching in the scope of a grade level or one school year.

## Evidence-Based Instruction

If the standards tell us *what* to teach, then the evidence base tells us *how* to teach. As educators today, we are lucky to have billions of teaching ideas at our fingertips on the Internet. By simply googling a concept you need to teach, you can instantaneously find hundreds of ideas that can be adapted to meet your needs. Our preservice teachers are simply enamored with Pinterest and Teachers Pay Teachers, finding cute and creative ideas to engage students in learning. However, this tremendous resource can also be a pitfall. Just because an instructional idea exists does not mean that it is good. We constantly have to remind our students that while the lesson activity they found may be cute, it may not be instructionally sound. Nothing can replace evidence-based practices for developing students' understanding.

Evidence-based instruction is that which has proven itself effective in teaching children based on the outcomes of experimental research. We were introduced to this concept as graduate students in education. Our mentors, experts in their fields of education, led us to read and then conduct our own research in evaluating the effectiveness of different instructional methods. A well-designed experimental study can inform practicing educators, helping us to make decisions about which methods are most effective in accomplishing our work in the precious amount of time we have children in our classrooms. In our minds it is clear—why would we ever use untested methods when teaching our students? We are unwilling to take the chance of using a teaching method that may not work.

Thus, the question for us quickly became: where do we find evidence-based practices? Figure 1.2 summarizes several useful resources for locating best practices in literacy instruction for primary grades. Of course, the main reason for writing this book was also to serve as one of these resources. It was our aim to identify and describe for you the evidence-based practices we ourselves have had success using in the classroom. We look to this book as a summary of many evidence-based practices that are effective in developing students' early literacy.

## Assessment-Based Instruction

While the standards base and evidence base exist independently of our students, the assessment base is intimately connected to them. Assessment is the root system of effective instruction. Teachers who use assessments to determine instructional needs, create instructional groupings, and reflect on what is and is not working to revise instruction know how useful assessment-based instruction can prove. Indeed, in today's classroom, it is hard to imagine a teacher who is not in some way using data from assessments to plan his or her instruction.

In literacy education, we use several types of assessments for instructional decision making (Walpole and McKenna 2007). First, screening assessments can be useful at the beginning of the year to determine if there are any general reasons to be concerned about an individual student's literacy development. If the screening assessment results in no red flags, then the teacher proceeds with normal instruction. However, if the screening assessment indicates that the child may have a deficit in one or more areas of literacy, then the teacher will need to use a diagnostic assessment to determine the specific skills that the child needs to develop. This information can be invaluable in planning targeted instruction to meet the child's literacy needs.

| Resource | Description |
|---|---|
| **Report of the National Reading Panel (National Institute of Child Health and Human Development 2000)** | The Reading Panel was commissioned by the federal government and the Department of Education to study and report on what was known at the time to be effective in teaching children to read. The panel's report is available online and summarizes research-based practices that have sufficient evidence to suggest to teachers in the areas of phonemic awareness, phonics, fluency, oral reading, vocabulary, and comprehension strategies. |
| **The International Reading Association** | A professional organization of researchers and teachers of literacy, the organization hosts an annual conference in the area of literacy education; publishes several journals, including *The Reading Teacher* and *Journal of Adolescent and Adult Literacy;* and moderates the website www.ReadWriteThink.org, which archives literacy lesson plans. |
| **The Literacy Research Association** | A professional organization of leading literacy researchers, the organization hosts an annual conference, maintains an active online presence, and publishes the *Journal of Literacy Research*. |
| **Florida Center for Reading Research** | A center that summarizes and disseminates information to reading teachers about research-based practices working in a range of grade bands. |
| **Reading Rockets, www.readingrockets.org** | Funded by a federal grant, WETA public broadcasting sponsors this education-focused website that houses resources for parents and educators in the field of literacy. |

Figure 1.2 Resources for Identifying Research-Based Literacy Methods

As children are introduced to new literacy skills in whole or small groups, teachers use progress-monitoring assessments to evaluate the effectiveness of their instruction. Progress-monitoring assessments can be used frequently to determine whether children are learning what is being taught. Data from these assessments can be used to regroup students by moving those who are making progress in one literacy area up to a higher group or moving those who are falling behind their peers to a group receiving more targeted instruction. Data can also be used from progress-monitoring assessments to determine whether children are making progress toward individual literacy goals and then to create new goals once initial goals have been met. This process of assessing and reassessing to plan instruction is the heart of differentiated instruction (Walpole and McKenna 2009).

Finally, teachers also use outcome assessments to determine whether the literacy program meets students' needs. Typically, these measures are useful in their ability to provide a big-picture view of the program's effectiveness. Results of outcome assessments may lead you to question the core reading program your grade-level team uses or the structure of your literacy block.

Because a variety of assessments tell us different things about students and their literacy learning, assessment-based instruction can tell us both the *what* and the *how* of teaching (see Figure 1.3). Data can tell us the specific literacy skills that students still need to develop, making up the *what* of our instruction. Data can also indicate whether our instruction is effective before we have wasted too much time using something that is ineffective for a particular child or group of children. Thus, we see assessment-based instruction as an invaluable piece of our thinking about teaching.

| Assessment Types | Description |
|---|---|
| Screening | Determines if there are any general concerns in students' literacy development |
| Diagnostic | Determines deficits in students' literacy development |
| Progress Monitoring | Determines if students are learning what is being taught during instruction |
| Outcome | Determines if the literacy program is effective for meeting students' needs |

**Figure 1.3** Four Assessment Types Informing Literacy Instruction
Adapted from Walpole and McKenna (2007)

# Student-Based Instruction

The last piece of the puzzle is specific knowledge about our students. We tell our preservice teachers that this is the human element that makes it so that teachers cannot be replaced with robots in the future! In order to be an effective teacher, you need to engage students in the learning process. Engagement and motivation require capturing the hearts of our students. Teachers do this with their enthusiasm. They read aloud from their favorite books. They are excited about learning new words. Teachers also do this with their knowledge of individual student interests. We know our students. We know who likes reading fiction and who prefers reading informational texts. We know the student who likes sports stories and the student who is captivated by poetry. We know which authors all students will fall in love with. We also know which instructional methods will work with students this year versus last year.

As much as we rely on standards, research, and data to inform our practice, we also believe in teachers' professional expertise and knowledge of their students. This personal understanding makes teaching a profoundly human process. Without the human element in teaching, you cannot capture your students' attention and engage them in the process of learning.

## Early Literacy Components

We have just outlined the four principles of instruction that we adhere to in our practice. You will see us discuss these principles as we progress through the book. We have organized the remaining chapters around the major skills that children must develop in order to become successful readers and writers (See Figure 1.4). The structure of each chapter includes discussion of the standards base, evidence base, assessment base, and student base that inform our thinking of the specific literacy skill under consideration.

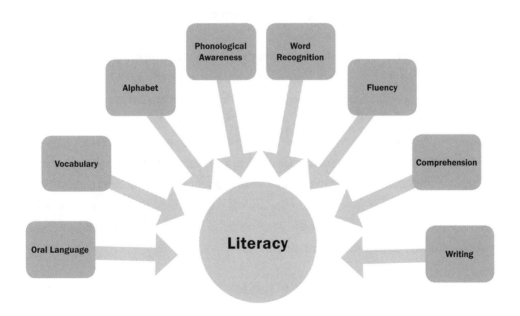

Figure 1.4  The Components of Early Literacy

Chapter 2 describes the need for children to develop a strong foundation in oral language, a skill that helps with later word recognition, vocabulary knowledge, and writing. Within the chapter we discuss components of oral language, teaching methods for developing it, and ways to assess students' progress learning it.

Chapter 3 considers vocabulary, or students' understanding of the meaning of words. In this chapter we discuss types of word knowledge, how to select words for instruction, methods for instruction, and informal assessments of vocabulary knowledge.

Chapter 4 explains the importance of alphabet knowledge and phonological awareness. Children must have a well-developed understanding of the letters of the alphabet and the sounds they make in order to learn to read. In addition, students who have the ability to manipulate the sounds in oral language can apply this skill to decoding words encountered in print. In this chapter we discuss several instructional methods for building children's understanding of the alphabet and the sounds in language.

Chapter 5 describes word recognition, specifically how students begin reading by sounding out words phoneme by phoneme and slowly transition to fluent reading. Within this chapter we discuss the phonics knowledge students need to apply while reading and how teachers can teach this knowledge in engaging and effective ways.

Chapter 6 tackles reading comprehension strategies. The reason we teach oral language, vocabulary, alphabet, phonological awareness, word recognition, and fluency is to build successful text comprehension. Thus, in this chapter we focus on how to help readers understand what they are reading.

Literacy also includes learning to write. Chapter 7 summarizes what we know about how children learn to write and how we as teachers can support students' work as developing writers. Reading and writing instruction work well when the connections between the two processes are apparent.

Chapter 8 takes a step back from the individual components of literacy to examine global classroom routines and schedules for fitting all your instruction within a reasonable time frame. We are aware of the incredible pressures teachers are under to make it all fit! Therefore, in this chapter we illustrate the logical connections that can exist within the components. We hope to leave you feeling reenergized in your understanding and passion for teaching literacy in the primary grades!

## The Structure of This Book

Within each content chapter we follow a consistent format to help us organize our information on the literacy skill under consideration. First, we think it is important to begin with a brief description of what the literacy skill is and why it is important in the process of creating a reader and writer. Next, we present multiple research-based strategies for targeting the literacy skill in the preschool or primary grade classroom. When we selected instructional methods for inclusion in this book we made every attempt to include instructional activities for a variety of classroom contexts, including whole-group and small-group settings, play-based centers, and independent practice opportunities. While the list of instructional methods is not meant to be exhaustive of all the possibilities, our goal was to present the strategies with the most evidence from research to recommend to teachers. In order to facilitate your use of many of the instructional resources, we have recreated the figures in larger format in the appendix.

In order to bring one of the instructional activities to life for the reader, we have included within each chapter a classroom vignette. Our vignettes are based on our own classroom experiences developing literacy skills with preschool and primary grade students. The created dialogue in the vignettes is to serve as a guide for what the instructional method might look and sound like when used in a real classroom setting.

It would be impossible to teach the skills we have outlined in this book without a collection of high-quality children's fiction and informational texts. Each of our chapters includes a table of suggestions for the books we use to target each skill. For example, we love using the Elephant and Piggie series by Mo Willems to develop students' oral reading fluency. At the same time, we would never attempt to model comprehension strategies without a copy of *Owen* (1993) by Kevin Henkes. We could not possibly list all the great children's books we know and love. However, we did try to include a collection of books that represents a variety in old and new and fiction and informational texts.

In today's modern classroom, technology integration is also an important aspect of instructional decision making. Therefore, within our discussion of each literacy skill we have included suggestions for meaningful use of technology to develop students' knowledge and skills. We have included a variety of web-based technologies, including games and educational apps for use on computers or tablets. We see many of these technologies being useful as additional forms of practice developing a literacy skill either in the classroom or at home.

We know literacy development takes time and repetition. Therefore, our instruction cannot simply be confined to the classroom alone. Instead, we need to engage parents and caregivers in the work of fostering their child's literacy in the home. Each chapter includes ideas for meaningful homework activities and routines that are engaging and productive.

Lastly, each chapter also includes discussion of informal and formal assessment techniques for each literacy skill. Part of planning deliberate and focused instruction is knowing the needs of our students. This knowledge can only come from assessment data. However, assessment need not always be formal and standardized. Indeed, some of the best assessments for instructional planning are informal and curriculum-based. We hope in our discussion of assessment to explain some methods for quickly determining your students' understanding and progress.

## Summary

Literacy is reading and writing; it is communicating; it is understanding and interpreting and creating. Becoming literate involves the development of a network of skills, including oral language, vocabulary, alphabet awareness, phonological awareness, word recognition, fluency, comprehension strategies, and writing. Therefore, teaching literacy is a complex business of juggling students' development in a range of interconnected skills.

A good literacy teacher must be knowledgeable in the standards that shape what students need to know about literacy. A good literacy teacher must also know and use a variety of research-based instructional methods for developing students' abilities in each skill. A good literacy teacher must be able to assess students' knowledge and progress in each literacy component in order to plan for future instruction. In addition, a good literacy teacher must know his or her students in order to engage, motivate, and inspire them to enjoy reading and writing.

We know you have the challenging work of teaching ahead of you, so let's get started!

# Chapter 2

# Developing Oral Language

*O*nce, when my son was about three years old, he was talking on the telephone with his grandmother in Denver. Since we live far apart, he had a lot he wanted to tell her. He started by answering her questions. Listening to only his side of the conversation, I heard "yes," "no," and "good." Then, when it was his turn to share, he said, "Today I made this," and held up to the telephone a drawing he had made earlier in the day. It never occurred to him that his grandmother could not see what he was holding in a room thousands of miles away. This is a logical mistake for someone who is still learning about how communication works, since he did not yet understand that nonverbal communication requires that the recipient see you. Even though oral language develops naturally, it is a complex business.

## How Do Children Develop Oral Language?

Talking is a milestone in oral language development, but communication happens long before children say their first words. Young children are exposed to words in their parents' native language as early as the womb. Neonatal response indicates that the second-trimester fetus in uterus can hear and respond, through movement, to voices and sounds that have become familiar (Berk 2012). At birth, children begin a natural process of experimenting with the sounds of language. Infants are fascinated with sounds, turning to pleasing sounds and away from alarming sounds, repeating interesting sounds, and quickly using different sounds to express different needs and desires. Exposure to musical rattles, mobiles, and toys as well as interaction with parents and caregivers continues the process of communication. Toddlers explore language in their environment through play with games such as peekaboo, nursery rhymes, music, repeated exposure to favorite books, and beginning use of high-utility words, such as *drink*, *snack*, and *no*. By the time children get to preschool, they can carry on conversations with teachers and friends.

As children develop oral language, they are confronted with four major tasks: phonology, syntax, semantics, and pragmatics (Clay 1991). Phonology is the understanding of the sounds in language. Toddlers hear the sounds of their native language in the home through exposure to adult models, siblings, and various modes of media, such as television, computers, and cell phones. Syntax refers to the rules of the language that dictate word order, sentence creation, and grammar. For example, a preschooler beginning to learn that some verbs are made past tense by adding *–ed* while other verbs are not is confronting syntax. Semantics is the knowledge of word meaning. Toddlers rapidly add to their word knowledge in periods of vocabulary growth, where they map new words to the experiences they have in their environment. The last language task, pragmatics, is the ability to know when to use specific kinds of speech depending on the social context. For example, there are certain words and familiar phrases that you may use at home that you do not use in the classroom; while *BFF* and *LOL* are appropriate for text messages, they are not typically used as part of oral conversation in class. As preschoolers and kindergartners develop language, they are confronted with each of these four tasks. Children's knowledge and skill with each of the tasks is largely based on experiences and exposures in their social environment.

## Instructional Methods

In many ways, all that you do in the classroom can be a method for developing children's oral language. By talking with your students, engaging them in conversations, reading to them, and writing on the board, you are modeling oral language and communication skills. However, just because oral language is integrated across subject areas does not mean that it is already covered. Indeed, it is important to include intentional instruction specifically planned to target children's oral language and speaking skills. While some students' oral language will develop from incidental exposures, other students' oral language will not. The stakes for children's overall literacy development are too high to leave oral language development to chance.

In this chapter we discuss methods appropriate for developing oral language and speaking in preschool through second grade. Figure 2.1 previews the methods we have selected to help you plan intentional instruction for oral language development. Language modeling and dialogic reading are primarily teacher-led activities; dramatic

| Instructional Method | Format | Characteristics | Strengths |
|---|---|---|---|
| **Language Modeling** | Whole Group, Small Groups, or Individuals | Teacher engages students in conversations throughout the day in various contexts, including Morning Meeting, transitions, and Afternoon Closure | • Many children enjoy talking about themselves or being asked to be a part of an expected classroom routine<br>• Can serve multiple purposes in the classroom |
| **Dialogic Reading** | Whole Group, Small Groups | • Teacher encourages conversation while conducting a read-aloud<br>• Teacher asks a variety of questions designed to get children talking about the book | • Books provide engaging contexts for basing conversations<br>• Targets vocabulary, oral language, and comprehension simultaneously |
| **Dramatic Play** | Small Groups | • Teacher helps set up a play context based on theme or unit, including props, to encourage role play<br>• Teacher coplays to help encourage children to use oral language to communicate during play | • Highly engaging for young children<br>• Develops oral language and vocabulary |
| **Author's Chair** | Whole Group or Small Groups | Teacher sets up a designated place in the classroom for children to share their own writing with the class when they elect to do so | • Children are highly motivated to talk about their own work<br>• Allows children the choice to share in a safe space |
| **Creative Expression— Art, Music, and Game Experiences** | Whole Group or Small Groups | • Teacher allows children to share and talk about their art work with one another<br>• Teacher encourages children to sing songs and perform fingerplays | • Children are highly motivated to talk about their own work<br>• Allows children the choice to share in a safe space |
| **Technology Integration** | Small Groups or Centers | Various websites and apps designed to target oral language | • Good review activity<br>• High student engagement<br>• Potential to foster twenty-first-century technology skills |
| **Connecting with Families** | Multiple | Parents reinforce oral language at home | • Fosters home-school connection<br>• Boosts oral language outside of classroom context |

Figure 2.1  Preview of Instructional Methods in This Chapter

play, author's chair, and creative expressions are child-led activities that require active teacher participation and scaffolding for support. The methods we have selected can be implemented in a variety of instructional formats, including whole groups, small groups, and one-on-one. We also include ideas for using technology to support meaningful oral language development and parents' work at home with their children.

# Language Modeling

Children need models of language to absorb, process, and eventually utilize in their own speech. While language acquisition is a natural process, we cannot assume that all children have good models of language in their home. We know, for example, that low socioeconomic status puts children at risk for having less exposure to language in the home (Hart and Risley 1995). We also know that while some children may have good models of language in their home, these models may not be speaking the predominant language of school in the United States—English. In order to support all students, you can be a model of language in the classroom by fostering a classroom in which you are talking and encouraging students to talk whenever possible (Hart and Risley 1995).

When modeling language in the classroom there are several types of language that you can use effectively (Bardige 2009; Pianta, LaParo, and Hamre 2008). *Self-talk* occurs when you describe your own actions in words. For example, if you state, "To write the letter *A*, I am going to start at the top of the line, write a line down diagonally to the left, pick up my marker, go back to the top and make a line down diagonally to the right, and then put a short line in between the two lines," then you are putting words to your own actions. *Parallel talk* occurs when you put words to someone else's actions. For example, when you say, "I like the way that Kelly is sorting all the puzzle pieces by color first before she puts them together," you are putting words to the strategy that Kelly is using to help put a tricky puzzle together. Both self-talk and parallel talk are good methods for adding oral language models to the classroom and can be used at any time of the classroom day to support oral language development.

Children also need to practice their own talk. A conversation requires two or more speakers to have several back-and-forth exchanges. Thus, asking a question and listening for one answer per student does not count. To truly have a sustained conversation with a child to develop oral language speaking skills, you will need to take advantage of all transitions, routines, and teachable moments in the classroom. Depending on the number of students in your classroom, it may not be possible to have a real conversation with each child every day. We know teachers who give themselves a whole week to reach their goal of having a meaningful conversation with each of the twenty or more students in their class. To make sure no one is missed, one teacher we know keeps a little checklist on her desk and checks off students as she engages each one over the course of the week (see Figure 2.2). A different teacher we work with keeps a ring of index cards in her pocket with students' names on them in order to keep track of conversations as well as other literacy skills. With a quick glance, she knows with whom she needs to speak, with whom she needs to review specific letters of the alphabet, and which phonological awareness skills need more practice.

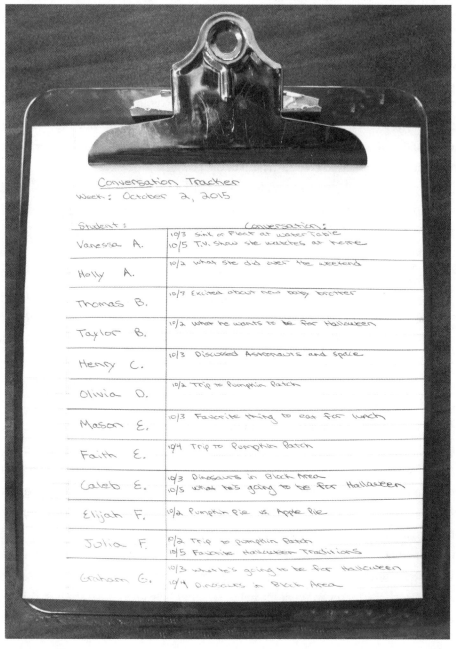

Figure 2.2  Teacher's Conversation Tracker

Peers can also be a great source of oral language modeling. In many of the routines and structures of the modern elementary school, children are asked to be quiet if not silent. For instance, walking down the hall, seatwork, morning work, and even lunch in some schools are silent activities. In terms of oral language practice, it is a shame that students do not have more opportunities to talk with their peers. Creating talking buddies can be one strategy for getting students to talk in meaningful ways in the classroom. Consider pairing students as talking buddies to brainstorm before a science experiment, think about what is happening in a book during a read-aloud, or conduct research on an extra-credit assignment. We have used talking buddies during read-alouds in order to encourage everyone to share ideas. When reading *How Many Seeds in a Pumpkin?* (McNamara 2007), I asked a class of second graders to turn and talk with a talking buddy to predict which pumpkin would have the most seeds. This enabled the whole class to share ideas without taking away too much time from the read-aloud. When students who do not interact that much outside class get paired as talking buddies, they may be surprised to learn something they did not know and make a new friend in the process.

Beyond occasional instructional opportunities, perfect times of the classroom day to model language and encourage peer conversation consistently are during your morning meetings and afternoon closures. There are many different activities that can be incorporated into your morning or afternoon routines that help develop oral language. Figure 2.3 provides a summary of several of these possibilities, which can be combined in different ways to help build language and literacy skills while also creating classroom identity and community. Whether you have fifteen minutes or five minutes at the beginning or end of the day, making deliberate activities part of your daily routine helps set a schedule for students to expect and also targets oral language.

## Dialogic Reading

Dialogic reading (Lonigan and Whitehurst 1998) occurs when you engage students in conversations as you conduct your read-aloud. The term *dialogic* derives from the word *dialogue*. We have worked with plenty of teachers who prefer students to be quiet as they listen to a read-aloud; however, when children are not talking, they are also not actively practicing oral language. There are times during read-alouds—for instance, when modeling comprehension strategies or targeting phonological awareness—when children need to actively listen. At other times, however, it is appropriate and even essential that children are invited to talk about a book during reading in order to build their oral language. As you read for this purpose, there are several reading behaviors that help encourage student conversation. Figure 2.4 summarizes storybook reading behaviors designed to get children talking.

| Routine Component | Description | How Children Practice Oral Language |
|---|---|---|
| Calendar | Children review days of the week, months of the year, numbers, holidays, and special events. | The class chants or sings the elements of the calendar. |
| Word Wall Review | Children review target vocabulary words on a word wall. | Children chorally read the word wall words, review definitions, discuss connections, or segment syllables. |
| Morning or Afternoon Song | Children select and sing a song of the day or week. | The teacher posts the song lyrics and children learn to sing a song as a group |
| Morning or Afternoon Poem | Children select and read a poem of the day or week. | The teacher posts the poem and children chorally read the poem as a group. |
| Weather Report | A rotating class job; a child delivers a weather report to the class. | The weather reporter practices oral language by giving a minireport about the weather. |
| Current Events Report | A rotating class job; a child delivers a current events report about a topic of interest that either the child or the teacher brings in. | The current events reporter practices oral language by giving a minireport on a topic of interest in the local community, nation, or world. |

Figure 2.3 Classroom Routines to Foster Oral Language

As you read, model rich language by talking about what you see in the illustrations or by adding to the written text. You can always use words to describe what is happening in the illustrations on the cover or inside a book. Since children's eyes are drawn to the beautiful illustrations in picture books, it makes sense to talk about what they are seeing. When you describe the colors, lines, shapes, and artistic medium used by the artist, you are adding descriptive language to the read-aloud. You can also add new vocabulary words to describe what is happening and being discussed in the text. For example, after reading about a cactus growing, you may add language by saying, "I think this story is going to take place in a desert. We just read that it is hot during the day and cold at night. It is also really dry without a lot of rain. I know these things are true about a desert climate." Anytime you can add more language to the read-aloud text, you are serving as a model of oral language.

During the read-aloud, you can encourage children's oral language by asking open-ended questions. Open-ended questions typically require more than a one-word answer, prompting children to use more language in a response. Open-ended questions include: "What do you think is going to happen next?" "Why do you think the character did that?" "How do you think the character feels? Why?" "What would you do if you were in the same situation? Why?" In contrast, closed-ended questions have a correct response based on the text and target children's comprehension rather than oral language. Examples of closed questions include: "What color is the boy's shirt?" "Where is the girl?" "Who is knocking at the door?" A well-planned read-aloud includes the kinds of questions that foster the language and literacy skills chosen for development. In many cases, this means the teacher includes a balance of both open- and closed-ended questions (Layne 2015).

Repeating and expanding on what children say when asked a question also provides an opportunity to model oral language. Repeating what a child says helps all children in the class hear the original response. Once you have repeated the response, you have a great opportunity to rephrase it so that it is grammatically correct. Rather than scolding children on the incorrectness of their grammar, simply rephrasing and gently modeling the correct grammar can effectively teach or reteach young children. You can also expand on the response by offering further explanation or adding vocabulary to the idea expressed in the response. For example, if a child states, "He runned home after school," you can rephrase the response when repeating as, "Stanley explained that he ran home after school."

Sometimes it is appropriate to ask a follow-up prompt to a child who answers a question. If a child responds with an incomplete answer or if there is a logical second question to ask, then it is a good idea to stay with the same child to ask a second question. For example, you ask a child, "Which character do you think is the happiest about the new puppy?" When the child replies "the sister," a logical follow-up would be to ask, "Why do you think the sister is the happiest about the new puppy?" Anytime you have the opportunity to ask a follow-up question that gets children to explain their own thinking, take it. This not only allows an opportunity for the child to practice oral language, but also develops comprehension and metacognition.

Finally, it is also important to model being an active listener. Communication requires two participants who listen and respond to one another appropriately. If one participant in a conversation does not listen, then he or she will respond inappropriately, and communication breaks down. Thus, it is important for children to see the importance of active listening. When you as the teacher actively listen and respond to what children say, it sends the message that what they have to say is important and valued. This acknowledgment of students' ideas goes a long way toward building their confidence and motivation to want to speak out again. Using these five reading behaviors in combination during a read-aloud fosters students' oral language and understanding of communication (see Figure 2.4 and the appendix).

| Behavior | Description | Example |
|---|---|---|
| **Model Rich Language** | Add rich language by describing the illustrations or adding more sophisticated vocabulary to describe what is in the text. | "When I look at the cover of this book, I see three children holding pumpkins. There is a large pumpkin, a medium-sized pumpkin, and a small pumpkin. I think this book is going to be about comparing these three pumpkins." |
| **Ask Open-Ended Questions** | Ask questions that do not have a correct answer and require more than a one-word response. | "Why do you think the largest pumpkin will have the most seeds?" |
| **Repeat and Expand** | When a child answers a question, repeat his or her response and add language by rephrasing the response using correct grammar or more sophisticated vocabulary. | Child: "I have ate seeds before." Teacher: "Oh good, Sam has eaten pumpkin seeds at home before. You can toast pumpkin seeds in the oven and eat them as a healthy snack." |
| **Ask Follow-Up Prompts** | Stay with the same child for more than one question if a follow-up question is appropriate to get a more detailed response. | Teacher: "Which pumpkin do you think has the most seeds inside?" Child: "The small one." Teacher: "Why do you think the smallest pumpkin has the most seeds?" |
| **Actively Listen** | Listen to children's responses so that you can phrase appropriate follow-ups and repeat what they said. | "I just heard Mary say that she thinks the medium-sized pumpkin will have the most seeds. That is an interesting prediction. Let's keep reading to see if Mary is correct." |

Figure 2.4 Behaviors to Boost Oral Language During Dialogic Reading

## *Selecting Books for Developing Oral Language*

Success with dialogic reading can be bolstered with the right book selection. When selecting children's books for targeting oral language, we suggest books that give your students something to talk about. Beautiful or unique illustrations provide opportunities for discussion. Similarly, books with interesting or mysterious characters often attract students' attention. Settings that are well described with rich detail can be discussed and

## Let's Take a Book Picture Walk

A picture walk helps develop your children's language and pre-reading skills.

- Have a conversation with your child around a book before you read it.
- A picture walk is not reading the book. It's talking about the pictures - getting to know the book together.
- Speak in the language that is most comfortable for YOU!

**What to do:**
- Look at the cover.
- Point to and say name of author and title.
- Looking at the cover, ask your child what he thinks the book will be about.
- Without reading the words in the book, encourage your child to turn the pages one at a time.
- Allow time for your child to respond to what you say - 5 seconds.
- Point to a picture and ask "what" questions- "What's this?" "What do you think is happening?"
- Follow your child's lead.
- Repeat what your child says and wait. This is one good way to encourage them to speak more.
- Remember to take turns talking.
- Ask questions to discuss what your child thinks is happening. Examples:
  - What is happening on this page?
  - Where do you think they are going?
  - What might happen next?
  - What do you think . . . ?
  - I wonder what would happen if . . .
- Acknowledge what your child says.
- Introduce or explain words and what they mean.
- Add a bit more information to what the child says.
- Help your child make connections to past experiences and future events.
  **Examples:**
  - When did you . . . ?
  - How did you feel when. . . ?
  - How would you feel if . . . ?

Figure 2.5 Steps for a Picture Walk

compared, as well as books with engaging story lines. One format that is particularly well suited for oral language is wordless picture books. Since there are no words in these books, the pictures and the students' own words are needed to tell the story.

If you have never read a wordless picture book to a class before, the first time may feel a little awkward. A good way to think about the read-aloud is that it is just like conducting a picture walk (see www.readingrockets.org)—you go through page by page and discuss what you and the students are seeing in each illustration. Figure 2.5 outlines the steps for a picture walk (also in the appendix). We begin a picture walk by sharing the cover of a book with children. We ask them to comment on what they see on the cover. After children share their observations, we share our observations, pointing out anything students miss related to characters, setting, plot, or theme. This discussion continues on every page of the book. In this way, we create the words that narrate the story. We have seen teachers successfully use wordless picture books for oral language activities with students from preschool to third grade. There are an increasing number of wordless picture books available on a range of topics, with several illustrators such as David Wiesner, Bill Thomson, and Barbara Lehman specializing in the format. Figure 2.6 provides a list of some of our favorite wordless picture books for read-alouds planned to target oral language.

# Dramatic Play

Sociodramatic play, dramatic play, imaginary play, and pretend play all refer to times in the classroom when children explore new settings, new roles, and new props. These are time when children use their imaginations to become firefighters, astronauts, deep-sea fishermen, or veterinarians. There are multiple educational benefits to this type of play, including cognitive growth, abstract reasoning, social and emotional growth, and language

| Title | Illustrator | Description |
|-------|-------------|-------------|
| *Chalk* | Bill Thomson | Children playing with chalk in a playground are astounded when their creations begin to come to life! |
| *Zoom* | Istvan Banyai | The viewer moves from scene to scene and in and around perspectives as if through a camera lens. |
| *Journey* | Aaron Becker | A little girl with a red marker draws an adventure to pursue. |
| *Pancakes for Breakfast* | Tomie dePaola | A lady goes through the steps of making pancakes for breakfast. |
| *Rainstorm* | Barbara Lehman | A little boy stuck at home on a rainy day discovers that his house is far more exciting when he uses a mysterious key. |
| *The Red Book* | Barbara Lehman | A little girl discovers a mysterious book that leads her to make a new friend in a faraway place. |
| *Mr. Wuffles* | David Wiesner | A cat discovers an alien ship to play with, and the aliens may not know what they are up against. |
| *Flotsam* | David Wiesner | A boy discovers a camera that is washed up on the shore during his family vacation. The photographs on the film tell of magical events under the sea. |
| *Tuesday* | David Wiesner | An ordinary Tuesday becomes extraordinary when frogs begin to fly. |
| *Yellow Umbrella* | Jae-Soo Liu | Children walk outside to school on a rainy morning. |
| *Wave* | Suzy Lee | A little girl confronts a wave when she is at the beach one day. |
| *A Boy, a Dog, and a Frog* | Mercer Mayer | A boy and his dog spend a day trying to catch a frog outside. |
| *The Line* | Paula Bossio | A little girl discovers a line that takes on many different shapes. |
| *A Ball for Daisy* | Chris Raschka | Daisy the dog is heartbroken when her favorite toy breaks. |
| *Unspoken: A Story from the Underground Railroad* | Henry Cole | A young girl helps a runaway slave escape. |
| *The Lion and the Mouse* | Jerry Pinkney | A beautifully illustrated version of the fable about the lion and the mouse. |
| *Good Dog, Carl* | Alexandra Day | Carl, a Rottweiler, takes care of a baby while his mom is out of the house. |

Figure 2.6 Wordless Picture Books for Oral Language Development

and literacy development (Bodrova and Leong 2003). Participating in imaginative play fosters students' cognitive capacities, such as memory, the ability to think from multiple perspectives, abstract reasoning, and problem solving. Children who play with other children also practice social interaction in safe spaces, learning important life skills such as sharing, conflict resolution, and communication. Through play, children are able to negotiate unpleasant emotions, such as jealousy and frustration, by observing their peers. Unfortunately, research indicates that children are spending less and less time engaged in this type of play both at home and in school (Gray 2011). Thus, it is even more imperative to make a case for play's inclusion in your classroom day.

Without a doubt, dramatic play can be used to build children's oral language (Roskos and Christie 2001). As children play in social settings, they progress through types or levels of play. The beginnings of play are more solitary endeavors, such as self-play and parallel play. Self-play occurs when a child is engrossed with an activity alone; for example, a child sitting at a table completing a puzzle. Parallel play occurs when children are in close proximity, perhaps playing with some of the same objects, but not interacting as they move around the environment. Once children begin playing with one another in the same setting, taking on roles, interacting to act out scenarios and think through problems, they are then engaged in much richer kinds of play. This dramatic play is ripe for oral language development, for students are talking with one another in character and in new and different contexts.

To foster this deep level of play, you as the teacher have several important roles (Enz and Christie 1997). First, you are a preparer *for* play. Children cannot play deeply in new, unfamiliar settings. You need to prepare children for play ahead of time. Depending on the play scenario, you may find that field trips are an appropriate way of introducing new play themes. If children are exposed to a real zoo, then their play of the zoo is going to be much richer with details they actually observed. For example, after going to a real zoo, children may begin to play new roles, such as cashiers for concession stands, maintenance workers who clean animal enclosures, staff members who host talks about the animals, and veterinarians who attend to sick animals. Sometimes field trips are not always possible. When you cannot go to the location, you may try instead inviting a guest speaker into the classroom to discuss his or her work with children. On one occasion, my students' faces lit up in amazement when a zookeeper came in with an owl perched on her shoulder.

Another possibility for preparing children for play is reading both narrative and informational texts to children about the play setting. In one of our classrooms, we prepared children for playing in a police station during a community helpers theme by reading a variety of children's books, including *Officer Buckle and Gloria* (Rathmann 1995), *I Want to Be a Police Officer* (Liebman 2000), *Police Officers on Patrol* (Hamilton 2009), *A Day at the Police Station* (Scarry 2004), and *Keeping You Safe* (Owen 2003). Lastly, you can prepare children for play through planned classroom discussions. Talking with students about what they already know about the topic from personal experiences and sharing your own insights can go a long way toward introducing students to different ways to play in a new setting.

Your second role is as a preparer *of* play. To help children play, certain things need to be in place or at least planned for ahead of time. First and foremost, children need a place to play. Traditionally, the location of play in the preschool classroom has been a distinct dramatic play center. This center may have for furniture a miniature refrigerator, kitchen sink, and oven. Many kindergarten classrooms no longer have this set of furniture in a distinct play center because it takes up too much room in the classroom. Whether your classroom has this furniture or not, it is important to physically set the location for play. A large cardboard box can be turned into a space ship, a boat, or a bus. We once worked with a teacher who used recycled milk containers to construct an igloo and then covered the igloo with brown paper to turn it into a cave for the next unit of study. Other inventive teachers have created entire ocean scenes by hanging streamers, fabric, and children's sea creature artwork from the classroom ceiling.

Children also need things to play with in the center. You may have toys that are appropriate for certain themes, such as community helper costumes, toy telephones and cash registers, or doctor's kits. However, many of these things can also be made using recycled materials, children's artwork, and craft-store supplies. We have found that crafty parents are great allies in volunteering their time and creativity to producing these play props. As you accumulate props over the years, consider organizing them in labeled containers for each theme so that it is easy to pull out your supplies when you are ready to study that unit again.

You may be thinking right now that this classroom transformation sounds like a lot of work. It is. However, do not feel like you have to go all out for every theme you cover in the year. Pace yourself. We think it is a much better idea to space out three or four total transformation play centers throughout the academic year, mixing in other themes in between that require fewer props so that you do not burn out in the preparation stages.

Finally, you also need to play the role of coplayer (Enz and Christie 1997). Since our instructional goal in this chapter is to boost children's oral language, having a model of oral language in the play is a good thing. While children certainly provide models of oral language for one another, you as the teacher bring much more knowledge, experience, and language connected to the play context. You are a valuable resource for moving the play in appropriate directions that will spark children's use of language in meaningful ways. Being a good coplayer does not mean sitting on the sidelines and giving children directions for how to play. Instead, it requires you to get into the play by taking on an imaginary role and interacting from that perspective with children who are playing other

## Classroom Vignette: Old MacDonald's Farm

Ms. Emma is in her second year of teaching preschool at a publicly funded early childhood education center. She has a bright, energetic personality and is enthusiastic about learning. Emma uses a thematic approach to develop units of study with her students, engaging them in conversations about what they are interested in learning and then designing integrated units around a topic. This month she and her students are exploring farms. To prepare for play, Emma took her students on a field trip to a working dairy farm. She has read several narrative books on farm life, including *Mrs. Wishy-Washy's Farm* (Cowley 2003), *Pete the Cat: Old MacDonald Had a Farm* (Dean 2014), and *Farm* (Cooper 2010), and informational texts, including *Farm Animals* (Dickmann 2010), *Farming* (Gibbons 1990), and *Chicks and Chickens* (Gibbons 2005). In addition, the class has had several discussions on farming, different types of farms, and jobs on a farm.

During the farming unit, Ms. Emma's class decides to turn the dramatic play center into a farm (see Figure 2.7). They work together to paint a large cardboard box red and attach a white silo made out of a cardboard tube wrapped in foam. In the art center, students create animals, crops, and tractors. Ms. Emma adds bushel baskets with plastic and cloth corn, tomatoes, potatoes, carrots, and wheat. She includes a sensory table with soil, rakes, gloves, and seeds. For costumes, Emma includes a trunk with plaid shirts, jean overalls, straw hats, and work gloves. She includes stuffed farm animals, such as horses, pigs, cows, and ducks. There are troughs for students to feed the animals and there is a vegetable stand for students to sell organic vegetables, fruits, and homemade pies. To encourage students' taking specific roles during play, Emma includes name badges for farmers, gardeners, farmers' family members, market cashiers, customers, and even a large-animal veterinarian.

Figure 2.7 Farm Scene in Dramatic Play

## Classroom Vignette: Old MacDonald's Farm (continued)

Ms. Emma tries to play with different students in the dramatic play center at least once each day during center time. She knows that by coplaying with her students she can model oral language. Let's listen in as she plays with a group of three students.

Ms. Emma first observes the children who are playing in dramatic play. One boy is wearing the farmer name tag, another girl is pretending to be the market cashier, and a little boy is gardening in the soil. Ms. Emma goes over to the name badges and selects one for a customer. She grabs a purse and hat from the costume trunk and walks over to the farmer's market. Addressing the market cashier, Ms. Emma asks, "Howdy, how are you today? These pies look delicious! Are they homemade?"

The cashier responds, "Yes, they are homemade."

Ms. Emma replies, "Oh good! I love homemade apple pies! How much are they?"

The cashier thinks for a minute before saying, "They cost $1.00."

Ms. Emma squeals, "Oh wow! That is a bargain. I will take two homemade apple pies. I am going to look in my purse to see how much money I have. Oh, look, I have a $5.00 bill. Do you have change?" The little girl nods her head. They exchange money.

The little girl puts the two pies in a bag and hands them to Ms. Emma. "Here you go," she says. "Thanks for coming."

Ms. Emma thanks the little girl and walks over to the farmer. "Hello, you must be the farmer of this great farm. What kinds of animals do you have on your farm?"

The little boy smiles and says, "I have horses, pigs, ducks, cows, and rabbits."

Ms. Emma asks, "Can you show me where you keep them?"

The little boy grins. "Of course, in the barn. Come with me." He leads Ms. Emma to the barn and shows her the stuffed animals and cardboard animals in the stalls. He declares, "It is time to feed them now."

"Can I help?" Ms. Emma asks. "I have always loved farm animals."

"Sure, take this." He hands Ms. Emma a small handful of hay and a bucket of apples. "Give this to the horses."

"OK, I will feed the horses this hay and some apples for their breakfast. They don't bite, do they?"

"They might, make sure you hold your hand down flat." The boy mimics what the farmer taught the children during the class field trip to the farm.

After feeding the horses, Ms. Emma thanks the farmer for letting her feed his animals, and she waves good-bye to the girl running the market stand. As she exits the dramatic play area, she gives her customer costume to another little girl who is going to play in the center. Ms. Emma pauses to observe the oral language interactions occurring between the cashier and her new customer. She records an anecdotal record of the conversation between the two girls to add to their portfolio and moves to a new center to work with other students.

roles in the play environment. It is a slippery slope from coplayer to play manager. We do not recommend that you take over and begin directing exactly what happens in the play. Instead, as a coplayer, you should take the children's lead as to where the play goes while inserting appropriate events or details to spark language and discussion when you see an opportunity. The classroom vignette on pages 24–25 gives you a glimpse of what this level of coplay might look and sound like in the preschool classroom.

If you teach first- and second-grade students, you may be thinking at this point that dramatic play is not appropriate in your classroom. We agree that it may not be appropriate or even practical to develop such complex play centers; however, we do see an important role for play in the elementary classroom in order to foster students' oral language. Play for older students may take the form of dramatic retellings of books you have read in the classroom, or dramatic reenactments of what life was like during the colonial times during a social studies unit, or even a dramatization of the life cycle of the pumpkin in a science unit. Even older children love acting things out to help aid their understanding; I have college students who sometimes act out complex theories or role-play classroom scenarios in order to envision what could happen. We think you will find that children become engaged in the learning process during play and they also use oral language in new ways when their imaginations are at work.

# Author's Chair

Author's chair presents an opportunity for students to share their writing or their thoughts on their writing with the class (Fletcher and Portalupi 2001). We like this as an instructional method for developing oral language as well because it gives students something very concrete and personal to talk about. In order to gain more confidence with speaking in public and with oral language in general, students need meaningful opportunities to practice. When author's chair is a built-in part of the writing routine in your classroom, it becomes meaningful to students as an authentic context for speaking.

To facilitate author's chair in your classroom, we recommend designating some physical space or object to indicate who the author is who is sharing. This may be an actual chair in the classroom. Some teachers have room for a comfortable rocking chair, a jazzy stool, or a chair that is larger than a normal student chair where the author sits to share his or her writing (see Figure 2.8). However, the author's chair object does not have to be a chair. You could have a special hat or crown that the author who is sharing wears. We have been in one classroom where there is an author's wand in the shape of a very large pencil! No matter what the object (or space) is, one of the ground rules for author's chair is that the members of the audience listen to whoever is sitting on or holding the object or in the special place.

It is a good idea to discuss ground rules for author's chair with students at the beginning of the year. Students are often quick to come up with appropriate rules for their own behavior, such as actively listening and showing respect, not making rude or offensive statements about someone's writing, offering praise and critical feedback to the writer when asked, and not discussing someone else's writing outside of the author's chair time. You may find it a good idea to record the class rules for author's chair and review them with students at regular intervals.

Author's chair offers both the writer and the audience members opportunities to talk about writing. The student author during author's chair should volunteer. If a student is forced to participate, then he or she may become embarrassed, upset, or resentful. Writing is a very personal process, and we believe in protecting a student's choice to share or not share. When a student does volunteer for author's chair, he or she should be given the floor for a certain amount of time to share by reading a selection of the writing sample or talking about where he or she is in the writing process. Once the student has had time to share, he or she should open the

Figure 2.8 A Second Grader Shares His Writing in the Author's Chair

floor to the audience for discussion, also for a set amount of time. We think that it is a good idea for the writer to set the agenda for the discussion. He or she may be seeking feedback to improve a part of the writing sample, or may want input on the brainstorming process of prewriting or revising before final publication. The writer will get the most out of the experience if he or she can focus the discussion on what is most pressing in his or her mind about the writing. For younger students, this process will require quite a bit of modeling and scaffolding by the teacher; however, once the author's chair routine is up and running, it can greatly support both writing and oral language in the classroom.

# Creative Expression

Whether you are in an early childhood or elementary classroom, creative experiences can provide great opportunities for developing children's oral language. Following we describe methods for connecting oral language practice with visual art, music, and games.

### Visual Art

Just as author's chair can create an opportunity for students to talk about their writing, asking students to talk about their artwork is also a meaningful oral language experience. You can ask children to discuss both the content and the process of their artwork with fellow students. In terms of content, students can describe the subject of their piece and use of lines, shapes, forms, space, and colors. In terms of process, students can describe the artistic medium they used and their decision making as they were creating. If you have introduced the works of famous artists, students can compare and contrast their work. The ability to express a critical response to a work of visual art provides students with practice in oral language and art appreciation at the same time.

### Music

Young children love to sing and dance to music. Learning the words of new songs and singing along to music also develops oral language. There are many songs and fingerplays appropriate for early childhood and elementary classrooms. Some of our favorites include "Over in the Meadow," "Joshua Giraffe," "Baby Beluga," "Fruit Salad," "Down by the Bay," and "Marching Around the Alphabet." We recommend choosing songs that children will find enjoyable because they are fun, silly, and catchy. You can also find songs that connect to your theme or unit of study. When you introduce a new song to your class, we highly recommend writing the lyrics on chart paper or the board so that children can see the words as they sing. Even in preschool classrooms where the majority of students may not be able to read yet, the printed lyrics help develop children's concept of word and understanding that print carries meaning. Shared singing experiences help create classroom community, provide enjoyment, and enable children to practice oral language and literacy skills.

### Games

Consider providing age-appropriate games for children to play with one another during center time, small groups, or indoor recess periods. Games that require small groups of children to play are ideal for engaging them in conversation. As children play, they will naturally talk with one another as the game requires. There are many commercially available games that encourage discussion. Figure 2.9 provides a list of some of our favorite games for getting children talking.

## Technology Integration

There are several technologies that can be used in the classroom and at home to help model oral language or offer opportunities for students to practice oral language. Presentation software can help students organize information and record their narration to accompany

| Game | Description | How It Targets Oral Language |
|---|---|---|
| **Pictionary** | Partners take turns drawing a picture and guessing what the target word is. | The partner guessing the drawing uses various vocabulary and description words to try to guess the correct answer. |
| **Go Fish** | Players try to match pairs of colors or numbers by asking one another if they have a match to share. | Children work on taking turns, asking appropriate questions, and responding politely. |
| **Charades for Kids** | Partners take turns acting out a concept and guessing what the concept is. | The partner guessing the action uses various vocabulary and description words to try to guess the correct answer. |
| **Hedbanz** | Players each get a headband with a card on it and take turns guessing the person, place, or thing on their headband. | The players take turns asking appropriate questions and responding appropriately to descriptive questions. |
| **Rory's Story Cubes** | Players roll cubes with pictures on them and then develop stories incorporating the images. | Children can work individually or in groups to develop an oral story using images from the cubes. The players can add as much description and detail to their story as desired. |
| **Apples to Apples Junior** | Players use word cards to make the best comparisons between adjectives and nouns. The players take turns being the judge of the best comparison for each round. | Children match descriptive words with appropriate nouns and make their case for the best comparisons. |

Figure 2.9 Games That Target Oral Language

their visual images or text. Sharing classroom presentations provides students with practice in presentation skills and gives them an authentic context for oral language.

One technology-enhanced presentation format is the podcast. There are many podcasts that are appropriate for children to listen to as models of oral language. Topics range from readings of classic children's books to scientific topics geared toward kids' interests, such as space exploration and 3D printing. However, podcasting can also be a great format for children's own presentations. Several free apps are available to help children create their own podcasts to share with fellow students.

Figure 2.10 summarizes some technology that can provide students with practice in oral language and communication.

| Website or App | Description |
|---|---|
| Photo Story (Microsoft software) | A software program that enables students to record narration to go with selected photographs and images for oral reports and projects |
| Animoto (web-based program) | A program that allows students to create short, narrated animations by recording their voice, selecting music, and uploading photographs or images |
| Prezi (web-based program) | A program that allows students to create dynamic presentations by uploading images and videos, adding text, and recording narration |
| Wild Animal Chronicles (podcast) | A free podcasts produced by National Geographic on wild animals from all over the world |
| Audacity (web-based program) | A free program that enables students to record and edit their voices to create their own podcast |
| Children's Fun Storytime (podcast) | A free podcast of recorded read-alouds of classic children's stories. |
| Storynory (podcast) | A free podcast of children's stories read by actors |
| Fun Kids Digital Radio (podcast) | A free podcast on a variety of topics for kids from animals to Star Wars to chemistry |
| Stuff You Should Know (podcast) | A free podcast covering nonfiction topics about how things work |

Figure 2.10 Websites and Apps That Target Oral Language Development

# Connecting with Families

We know that the amount and quality of oral language spoken in the home varies by family and is shaped by family context, cultural values, and available time. It is worthwhile to make suggestions for activities families can do at home to help support the oral language development of their child. The following activities are time efficient and require few materials; however, they engage children and families in conversation.

### Show-and-Tell

Show-and-tell is an obvious choice for developing oral language because the *tell* part requires students to talk about a special item they bring to school. An important aspect of preparing for show-and-tell is not only choosing the item to show but also practicing what to say about it. When setting up the structure for show-and-tell in your classroom, encourage families to practice first at home. This rehearsal enables parents to offer suggestions and encouragement, and the children benefit from another layer of practice with public speaking.

Show-and-tell has been used in classrooms for a long time. Socially, it enables classmates to learn about one another and foster friendships around shared interests. In terms of oral language, it provides students with something personal to talk about. It is always easier to talk about something you know than something you do not know, and the easiest thing to talk about is yourself. Therefore, show-and-tell provides a very safe and comfortable starting point for children to practice oral speaking in front of their peers.

However, without parameters or structure, show-and-tell can quickly devolve into a time waster. If it takes too long, especially in the younger grades, preschool children will quickly grow impatient and possibly even disruptive. Good show-and-tell structures include a defined time for the sharer to share and for the audience to ask relevant questions. When students are expected to ask questions of the sharer, they tend to pay better attention and gain practice forming appropriate questions. It is also a good idea to have a set routine or rotation for sharers. Whether you follow a daily routine in which the same children go on a certain day of the week or a weekly routine in which one child presents each week, make sure everyone in the class gets a turn.

### Mystery Readers

My son's school uses a program called Mystery Readers. At the beginning of the school year, the teachers invite parents to sign up for certain days during the year when they can come into the class to read. The date and identity of a Mystery Reader is kept hidden from the students so that when it happens it is a special treat. When a Mystery Reader comes into the class, he or she shares a little bit about himself or herself with the class. This introduction provides a model of oral language to students, exposes them to different role models, and gives them an opportunity to practice being a good audience—actively listening and forming questions.

### Ask Me Prompt

Sometimes asking "What did you do in school today?" gets a vague response. Or sometimes we as parents forget to ask. That's why it can be very helpful for both kids and parents to provide a physical clue for something specific to ask about. A clue can take the shape of a paper bracelet, a sticker on a T-shirt, or a note in the assignment pad. No matter what the physical format, the clue should be a simple prompt, such as "Ask me about the class visitor today," or "Ask me about the trip to the planetarium." Simply by putting the ask me idea in writing for parents, you have laid the groundwork for a conversation.

### Explain How

No matter what children have been assigned for homework, a great closure to the activity can be for a child to explain to a parent how he or she did it. For example, if a math assignment is to complete a workbook page, then the first step is for the child to complete the page. However, the second step is for the child to then explain how he or she did it to his parent or caregiver. This second step not only helps the child to begin to self-check responses but also serves as an opportunity for communicating ideas through speech. This strategy can be used with math, science, social studies, language arts, and special homework.

### Read and Discuss

Nightly reading can also provide students and their parents with something to discuss. Whether you work with younger students who need their parents to read to them or older elementary students who can read to their parents, books offer good topics for conversation. Consider creating a classroom mechanism for sharing books with children who may not have access to many books at home, such as a classroom library check-out system. Also, you may suggest a time frame, such as twenty minutes for reading and then five minutes for discussion. Parents may appreciate a list of sample questions to ask when discussing books with their child. Remember that not all parents know that simply reading together for a short time every night can go a long way toward developing their child's language and literacy skills; therefore, offering encouragement is one of your most important roles as their child's teacher.

# Assessment

Several standardized assessments exist for evaluating young children's oral language development. Two widely used formal measures include the Test of Oral Language Development (TOLD; available from Pro-Ed at www.proedinc.com) and the Teacher Rating of Oral Language and Literacy (TROLL; Dickinson, McCabe, and Sprague 2001). These assessments are good choices when you have concerns that a student may be behind his or her peers and can be used to document concerns before approaching parents. However, to track oral language for most of your students, we recommend an informal assessment process of anecdotal records.

The beauty of the anecdotal record for recording oral language is that it is authentic, flexible, and informative. Listening to students as they talk and interact with one another during play, in centers, or during partner projects is authentic because it is not asking them to participate in artificial language tasks. When they are talking with peers, they are using talk for real purposes. As a result of not being aware that their speech is part of an assessment, they are not shy, nervous, or stressed. This form of assessment is flexible, because it is up to you when to record a particular conversation and can be done over time. The most striking benefit of the anecdotal record is the amount of information it can reveal about the student's progress.

To take an anecdotal record, we recommend recording a student's oral language verbatim for a three- to five-minute period (see Figure 2.11). If you have access to an audio recorder, it is always more accurate to record and then type a transcript. To analyze the transcript, think back to the components of oral language discussed earlier—phonology, semantics, syntax, and pragmatics. Read and reread the student's transcript, coding examples of each of the four language components. We recommend using color coding to help organize your analysis; for example, marking semantics examples in blue and syntax examples in red. Once you have completed the transcript, total the number of miscues for each of the four components. If you take an oral language sample for each student every two to three months, by the end of the year you should see progress in each of the four areas of language as the student develops.

---

Date: 9/22/15

Students: Owen M. and Reid A.

Place of Observation: Block Area

Observed Conversation:

Owen: "Let's build a football stadium that is really high like a skyscraper."

Reid: "Yes, let's do that. I want to build the Broncos stadium. Then the football players can runned through the field."

Owen: "I'll be the visiting team. Can I be the Eagles?"

**Teacher Comments:**

Owen used the vocabulary word *skyscraper* correctly.

Reid confused the past tense of the verb *run*.

---

Figure 2.11 Sample Anecdotal Record

## Summary

A solid foundation in oral language goes a long way to supporting children's short- and long-term reading development. There are many developmentally appropriate, hands-on activities you can engage your students in to foster oral language growth in the classroom and at home. Certainly the primary instructional method is modeling language throughout the day. It takes conscious thought to remember to think aloud as you go about the normal business of the classroom, but the oral language you model in the process greatly influences children's semantics, syntax, phonology, and pragmatics.

Whether it is setting up an appealing dramatic play in your preschool classroom or encouraging second graders to share during show-and-tell, instructional methods for oral language all involve creating opportunities for children to talk to you and to one another in authentic contexts. A classroom that targets oral language growth is one that is a fun, engaging, happy place to be, so happy talking!

# Chapter 3

## Fostering Word Knowledge

We took my son to a Harvest Festival when he was three years old. It was October, so we encountered the typical decorations—pumpkins, scarecrows, black cats, and witches. We took a hayride out to a pumpkin patch and explored a corn maze. On the way back to the car my son announced, "I'm drinky, let's get some apple spider." My husband and I looked at each other in confusion for a moment as we tried to process his request. Then we got it. He was thirsty and wanted a drink of apple cider!

Children experiment with words all the time as they acquire new language. Sometimes the result of the experimentation is babble, sometimes it's pairing new words together in unconventional ways like "apple spider," and sometimes it's getting the meaning and the vocabulary just right. To parents and caregivers watching children experiment with language, the process is often amazing and endearing.

## The Beginning of Language

Children's language development begins at birth and is a natural process. Infants are fascinated from the beginning with sounds and quickly learn to use them to express different needs and desires. Toddlers continue to explore oral language and begin to use high-utility words in their environments. Because of its relationship to survival, the word *no* is an important first word for young children to understand; as a result, it is not uncommon to witness a toddler trying out the word *no* in various contexts. I still chuckle when I think of my toddler crossing his arms, stamping his foot, and stating "no" emphatically. He knew the power that word carried!

Toddlers rapidly add to their word knowledge during periodic vocabulary growth spurts, adding new words almost overnight, to the amazement of their caregivers. Typically, children understand words before they can accurately express them in multiple meaningful contexts. Receptive vocabulary refers to the words children hear and comprehend when spoken even though they may not be yet able to use them orally themselves. Think of the toddler who clearly understands when her mom asks her to "put the toy on the table." In order for the child to follow these directions, she must have an understanding of both the objects and the actions in the sentence. Expressive vocabulary refers to words the child not only understands but can successfully use in speech. When the toddler turns to her mom and says, "No, I won't," she is using her expressive vocabulary knowledge to communicate her ideas. As toddlers become preschoolers, their vocabulary knowledge grows rapidly. Preschoolers experiment with new combinations of words in various social situations and practice using words that are connected by topics or places of interest to them. Have you ever met a four-year-old who knows all the dinosaur names? It's astounding how a spark of personal interest can lead to a vocabulary explosion!

## The Vocabulary Gap

You may be wondering, if vocabulary acquisition is such a natural process, why should I be concerned with it as a teacher? This is a good question. Vocabulary acquisition is a natural process that is fueled by children's exposure to words in their environment. Children can only experiment with the words they have heard in their native language through exposure from fluently speaking models in their lives. Young children play with the words that they hear in their home and school environments. However, the quantity and quality of words children are exposed to in the home are unequal and highly connected to socioeconomic status (Hart and Risley 1995; Labbo, Love, and Ryan 2007), resulting in a vocabulary knowledge gap among children entering school (Biemiller 2001; Neuman 2006).

Early literacy research findings are abundantly clear: a vocabulary gap begins early and only widens over time. More alarming is that once that gap has been established, the differences in vocabulary knowledge remain constant. Children who come to school with the strongest vocabularies have had rich language experiences at home, lap-time reading sessions, bedtime stories, and a wide array of experiences outside the home to develop their vocabulary and world knowledge, while children with the weakest vocabularies have not been as engaged as frequently or deeply with books or conversations at home. Within your class of students, chances are high that you will have great diversity among students' vocabulary exposure and knowledge.

The differences in children's vocabulary knowledge becomes extremely dramatic when they begin formal reading instruction in elementary school. A strong foundation in oral language and vocabulary supports children's development as beginning readers (Snow, Burns, and Griffin 1998) and journey into becoming more sophisticated comprehenders of text (Cunningham and Stanovich 1997). Conversely, children lacking rich vocabulary knowledge tend to struggle with the reading process (MacDonald and Figueredo 2010). Children's vocabulary knowledge plays a significant role in reading success since it directly impacts their expressive language and reasoning, their relative ease of reading increasingly sophisticated text through grade levels, and, ultimately, their overall reading comprehension (Stanovich 1986). Over time, this vocabulary gap transforms into a knowledge gap affecting comprehension, motivation, behavior, and cognition (Biemiller and Slonim 2001). Because of these early differences, it's crucial that we intervene right away. While we may not be able to close the gap completely, early and intensive oral language and vocabulary instruction can work toward narrowing the gap. We can help children build vocabulary and increase their chance of success both inside and outside school.

## How Do Children Learn New Words?

Vocabulary instruction works best when it is integrated, repeated, and meaningful. Children learn new vocabulary best when instruction integrates new word learning with their prior knowledge. It makes sense that if children can connect a new word to an old word, then they have a reason to hold on to the new word. For example, if children already know the word *pretty*, then introducing the new word *beautiful* is a natural fit. In addition, children need multiple repetitions when learning and thinking about the new word. One exposure in one storybook read-aloud is not enough to place a new word in a young child's vocabulary; instead, children need repeated readings that allow them to hear, see, and internalize the same words. Planned instruction and review activities across a variety of contexts, such as read-alouds, center work, whole-group discussions, and hands-on activities, teach kids to know words well enough to use and apply them accurately in multiple ways. Finally, vocabulary instruction must be meaningful to children. Children will find words useful when they have multiple opportunities to use them in conversation, in reading different books, and in their own writing. Finding ways to extend word learning beyond the storybook context is an important step and involves both repetition and meaningful use.

Figure 3.1 provides a preview of the instructional methods described in this chapter for fostering children's word learning. In the sections that follow, we will explain each instructional method so that you can begin implementing the strategies in your own classroom.

| Instructional Method | Format | Characteristics | Strengths |
|---|---|---|---|
| **Word Walk Read-Aloud** | Whole Group or Small Groups | • Embedded within read-aloud<br>• Uses two-day sequence of before, during, and after reading procedures | • Can be used with fiction and nonfiction texts<br>• Focuses on same target words for two days to build repetition and exposure |
| **Word Wall** | Whole-Group or Centers | Teachers post vocabulary-word picture cards for display. | • Enables teacher and student to review learned words<br>• Visual reminder of words covered |
| **Play-Based Learning** | Small Groups or Centers | • Children play in various contexts (block area, dramatic play, sensory table, outdoors, etc.)<br>• Teachers support word learning through inclusion of props and coplay and by encouraging role play. | • Children exposed to or use words in authentic contexts<br>• Children practice expressive vocabulary in safe environment |
| **Conversations** | Whole Group or Small Groups | • Teachers can plan intentional conversations around words connected by theme, topic, or book.<br>• Teachers can capitalize on spontaneous "teachable moments" surrounding words. | • Informal methods for engaging children in authentic discussion<br>• Capitalizes on student interest and engagement at the moment |
| **The Language Experience Approach** | Whole Group | • Teachers encourage discussion of a common experience involving target vocabulary words.<br>• Teachers record in writing what students say to post in the classroom. | • Good informal assessment of student understanding<br>• Helps students make connections between vocabulary words and personal experiences<br>• Connects vocabulary and writing instruction |
| **Creative Expression—Art and Drama Experiences** | Small Groups or Centers | • Students use multiple forms of creative expression to illustrate their understanding of new words, including visual art, music, movement, dramatic art, etc. | • Good for hands-on, experiential learning<br>• Good for reviewing words introduced during read-alouds<br>• High student engagement |
| **Games** | Small Groups or Centers | • Teachers purchase or develop games designed to review several target words.<br>• Games can take on many formats, such as Bingo, Memory, Concentration, Matching, Pictionary, Dice Roll, or Beach Ball Toss. | • Good for hands-on, experiential learning<br>• Good for reviewing words introduced during read-alouds<br>• High student engagement |
| **Technology Integration** | Small Groups or Centers | Various websites and apps designed to target vocabulary knowledge | • Good review activity<br>• High student engagement<br>• Potential to foster twenty-first-century technology skills |
| **Connecting with Families** | Multiple Formats | • Parents reinforce word learning at home. | • Fosters home-school connection<br>• Boosts word learning outside of classroom context |

Figure 3.1 Preview of Instructional Methods in This Chapter

# Tried-and-True Read-Aloud

One component of the early childhood classroom day that we can turn to our advantage in increasing vocabulary is shared storybook reading (Aram 2006; Beck and McKeown 2007; Collins 2010). Our spoken language is no rival for the vocabulary found in high-quality children's literature. A good children's book is positively brimming with wonderful words that children would not likely encounter in their daily lives. Further, research suggests that storybook readings that include teacher-child interactions and rich discussion around these wonderful words lead to an even greater degree of vocabulary knowledge (Layne 2015; Walsh and Blewitt 2006).

## What Words Do I Teach?

Many teachers are overwhelmed by the open-ended task of choosing vocabulary words. There is no developmental list that indicates what words should be known at what age and grade level. Lists such as those in Fry's *1,000 Instant Words* (2004) can help beginning readers to recognize words by sight. However, no such list exists for vocabulary words that children should know for meaning. Often, commercially available reading curriculums suggest vocabulary to be taught in conjunction with a unit of study or a story in a reading anthology. But curriculum authors do not know your particular students' strengths and needs as well as you do. We suggest using a more nuanced approach when selecting words for vocabulary instruction.

It is helpful to use a tiered framework in word selection. We find this method helpful as a starting point when trying to figure out exactly which words would be the most useful in our vocabulary instruction. According to Beck and McKeown (2007), words can be classified in terms of three tiers. Tier 1 words are basic words frequently found in oral language and need not be taught directly; for example, *of*, *sun*, and *happy*. Tier 2 words occur more frequently in written text. Typically, they have easier tier 1 synonyms; for instance, *enormous* versus *big*. An important characteristic of tier 2 words is that they can be used across multiple contexts. For example, *furious*, *enormous*, and *delightful* are tier 2 words. Tier 3 words are limited to one domain of use and are highly specific; for example, *photosynthesis* and *peninsula*. Beck and McKeown (2007) recommend focusing instructional time on tier 2 words, since these are of high-utility to readers and comprehenders of written text. See Figure 3.2 for a description of Beck and McKeown's tiered words.

## How Many Words Should I Teach?

Two trains of thought emerge when developing an approach to vocabulary instruction with young children: breadth or depth. Simply put, a teacher can give students many words to

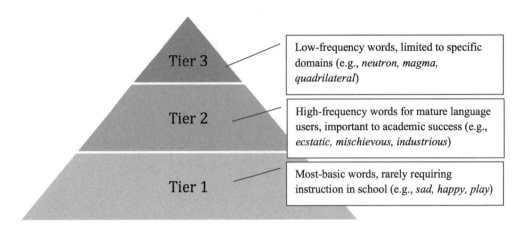

**Figure 3.2** Tier Word Categories
Based on Beck, McKeown, and Kucan (2002)

learn a little bit about or a few words to learn a lot about. We lean toward the latter. We want young children to truly learn the words we are teaching, even if that means limiting the total number of words covered in an academic year. For that reason, we suggest targeting one word for instruction as you and your students become accustomed to classroom routines. Then, gradually, as you adjust to the new procedures, you can ramp up to include targeted instruction of two or three words per storybook. We have found that presenting more words than three per reading tends to lose young children; the cognitive demands become simply too intense.

## How Do I Define New Words?

Research indicates the need to define new vocabulary words in child-friendly terms (Johnson and Yeates 2006; Justice 2002; Wasik and Bond 2001), which translates into defining unknown words with known, tier 1 words. It is not always easy to compose a child-friendly definition of a rich vocabulary word. We admit we have created several ineffective definitions along the way. In one classroom, we were trying to define the word *hand* for children who were learning English as a second language. We felt it was important for them to understand the word in order to comprehend the book *The Kissing Hand* (Penn 1993). How would you define the word *hand* in child-friendly terms? We started out with "a hand is a part of your body at the end of your arm with a palm and five digits." Looking back, it was silly of us not to use the word *fingers,* but we learned from our mistakes and quickly revised our definition to be more child-friendly. To work, a definition must succinctly define a word in simple terms that children already know and can understand. For example, a child-friendly definition of the word *patient* is "waiting without getting upset." Since there is no magic child-friendly definition fairy, we recommend going through several revisions using children as your critics before establishing one firm definition. The children in our preschool classroom quickly indicated to us that our first definition of the word *hand* was not going to work! Figure 3.3 includes some examples of wonderful words and our child-friendly definitions.

| Wonderful Word | Child-Friendly Definition |
|----------------|---------------------------|
| Enormous | something that is very big |
| Excited | to be really happy about something |
| Fortunate | to be lucky |
| Curious | wanting to find out about something or someone |
| Scrumptious | something that is tasty or yummy |

Figure 3.3  Wonderful Words with Child-Friendly Definitions

To help cement children's understanding, research suggests showing them a picture vocabulary card or, whenever possible, a concrete prop to help explain the word and its definition (Wasik and Bond 2001; Wasik, Bond, and Hindman 2006). See Figure 3.4 (and the appendix) for an example of a vocabulary picture card we have used to define and discuss the word *patient* before and after a read-aloud. When defining the word *patient*, we show a picture of a child waiting to get on the school bus. In addition to defining words so that young children can understand them, research indicates the importance of asking children during the read-aloud experience to point to, label, or discuss the words in the context of the storybook (Senechal 1997; Walsh and Blewitt 2006; Wasik, Bond, and Hindman 2006). So, during the read-aloud, you can ask children to point to an illustration in the book in which the character is being patient and a discussion could follow.

## What Books Should I Read?

An important task in planning your read-aloud is book selection. What books are ripe for targeting vocabulary development? Some books are better than others for teaching new words. We prefer books that have engaging illustrations, relatable characters, strong plots, and, of course, good words! A quick read-through of a children's fiction or nonfiction selection will indicate whether the book contains words ideal for instruction. Words chosen

**patient**

**Waiting for something or someone without getting upset.**

Figure 3.4 Vocabulary Picture Card for Before and After Reading

for explicit teaching should be interesting and useful to children, and you should be able to define the words in child-friendly terms. Fiction selections will typically contain tier 2 words that are more sophisticated synonyms for words children may already know, which provides a nice hook to their prior knowledge. Nonfiction selections, on the other hand, will typically contain tier 3 words specifically related to the topic of the text, and, therefore, these words may be related to one another conceptually. The relationships among words in nonfiction texts also provide a nice connection from which to begin instruction; for example, previewing tier 3 words on ecosystems can help build background knowledge before launching into more in-depth instruction on characteristics of ecosystems.

Throughout the year, we organize units of study around a specific author, as in an author study of Kevin Henkes; around a content area, as in the case of social studies or science investigations; or around a theme or topic, as in Going to School or Emotions. Once we decide on an overarching unit, we scan our classroom libraries to find high-quality children's literature selections that will fit. In the past few years, we have pushed ourselves to be much more deliberate about including both fiction and nonfiction within every unit of study. Figure 3.5 shows some sample text sets we created around several different themes.

## Word Walk Read-Aloud

Now that we've looked at the planning pieces of a read-aloud, such as choosing books and defining words, it is time to look at the read-aloud itself. We use a specific read-aloud sequence developed to target vocabulary instruction called *word walk* (Blamey

| Text Set Theme | Fiction Selections | Nonfiction Selections | Sample Vocabulary |
|---|---|---|---|
| **Going to School** | *Chrysanthemum* by Kevin Henkes | *Do I have to Go to School?* by Pat Thomas | Appreciate<br>Dreadful<br>Miserably<br>Precious<br>Envious<br>Principal<br>Grade level<br>Classroom<br>Specials |
| | *The Kissing Hand* by Audrey Penn | *Deron Goes to Nursery School* by Ifeoma Onyefulu | |
| | *David Goes to School* by David Shannon | *School Bus* by Donald Crews | |
| **Families** | *Julius: The Baby of the World* by Kevin Henkes | *Who's in a Family?* by Robert Skutch | Sibling<br>Relative<br>Traditions<br>Culture<br>Antagonize<br>Dependent<br>Patience<br>Rivalry<br>Protect |
| | *The Relatives Came* by Cynthia Rylant | *Families in Many Cultures* by Heather Adamson | |
| | *Llama Llama Mad at Mama* by Anna Dewdney | *Who's in My Family?* by Robie Harris | |
| **Emotions** | *Wemberly Worried* by Kevin Henkes | *Lots of Feelings* by Shelley Rotner | Terrible<br>Horrible<br>Scrunched<br>Invisible<br>Feelings<br>Anxiety<br>Smithereens<br>Rage<br>Furious<br>Frustrated<br>Content |
| | *When Sophie Gets Angry— Really, Really Angry* by Molly Bang | *Understanding Myself* by Mary Lamia | |
| | *Alexander and the Terrible, Horrible, No Good, Very Bad Day* by Judith Viorst | *Feelings* by Aliki | |
| **Planting** | *Planting a Rainbow* by Lois Ehlert | *From Seed to Plant* by Gail Gibbons | Seed<br>Sprout<br>Trowel<br>Bulb<br>Vine<br>Pollination<br>Dormant<br>Stem |
| | *The Tiny Seed* by Eric Carle | *One Bean* by Anne Rockwell | |
| | *How many Seeds in a Pumpkin?* by Margaret McNamara | *How a Seed Grows* by Helene Jordan | |

**Figure 3.5 A Sample of Children's Books for Targeting Vocabulary Instruction**

and Beauchat 2011). Word walk is a repeated reading sequence in which the same book and target vocabulary words are used for two days in a row. This procedure includes the repetition that young children need in order to truly learn new words.

## *Day One: Before Reading*

On day one of the word walk sequence, there are four steps to follow before reading the storybook aloud to children (see Figure 3.6 and the appendix). First, introduce the target word by showing the word written on a card with an accompanying picture, prop, or acting activity (see Figure 3.7 and the appendix). This step is brief, no more than one minute, but essential for targeting the word for instruction. Having the typed word on a separate card with the child-friendly definition not only helps with instruction, but also serves as a reminder for future review. We have had teachers quite successfully add the picture vocabulary cards to their word walls in order to help children identify the words and use them in their own writing. The visual picture or tactile prop helps make the abstract word under discussion much more concrete for young children. For example, if targeting the word *scrumptious* in the terrific children's book *The Wolf's Chicken Stew* by Keiko Kasza (1996), you would hold up a picture vocabulary card of something scrumptious; our example in Figure 3.7 is a picture of a scrumptious chocolate cake. You would say something like, "Today we are going to talk about the word *scrumptious*. I have a picture of a piece of chocolate cake because I like to eat chocolate cake; it is scrumptious."

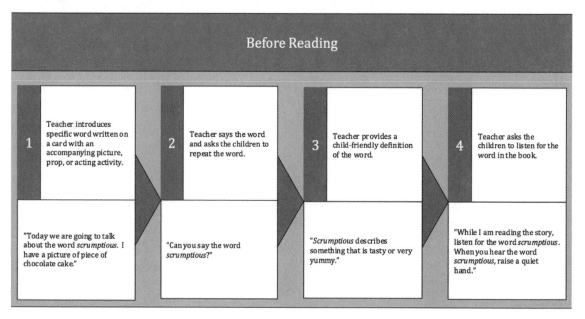

Figure 3.6  Day One: Before Reading

Figure 3.7  Vocabulary Picture Card

The second step in the introduction is to say the word and ask children to say the word. This step leaves a phonological imprint of the word in the children's minds. It is important that children say the word aloud several times throughout the entire lesson. You might quickly ask, "Can you say the word *scrumptious?*" Next, provide a child-friendly definition of the target vocabulary word. The definition should be brief and utilize words with which children are already familiar. For example, you may say, "Scrumptious describes something that is tasty or very yummy." Lastly, you can encourage your students to listen for the word in the book. This is important for engaging children in the listening process. We like to ask children to give us a quiet, physical cue when they have heard the word in the book. This serves as an informal assessment, but also as a fun challenge to be the first one to hear the target vocabulary word. This might sound like, "While I am reading the story, listen for the word *scrumptious*. When you hear the word *scrumptious*, rub your hand on your belly like you are hungry for a scrumptious snack." The physical cue can be as simple as raising a quiet hand, placing a finger on an ear, or giving a thumbs-up.

## Day One: During Reading

During reading, you can conduct your normal read-aloud routine, modeling literacy targets and engaging children in discussion around the text. To target vocabulary instruction, pause briefly while reading when the word is encountered in the book and check to see if your children are indicating they heard the word as well (see Figure 3.8 and the appendix). You may say, "I just heard the word *scrumptious*, and I noticed that many of you are rubbing your bellies because you heard the word in the story too!" Also during reading, you can quickly provide the child-friendly definition of the word. This may sound like, "*Scrumptious*, remember, *scrumptious* describes something that is tasty or very yummy."

Explicit vocabulary instruction during reading consists of those two steps; you then continue to read the remainder of the story as you normally would.

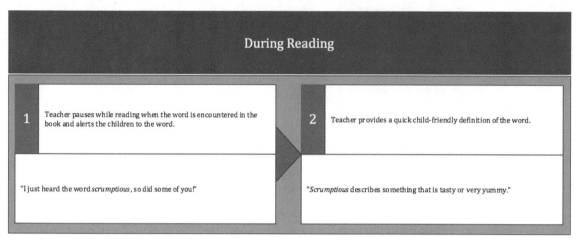

Figure 3.8 Day One: During Reading

## Day One: After Reading

The bulk of word walk instruction occurs after reading the storybook since students have just been exposed to one use of the word in the context of the story. The after-reading sequence includes six steps (see Figure 3.9 and the appendix). First, you reintroduce the word and vocabulary picture card or prop used in the introduction before reading. You repeat this step to reorient students to vocabulary learning. For example, you may say, "Remember, today we are talking about the word *scrumptious*. The chocolate cake in this picture looks *scrumptious* to eat." Second, you can invite the children to say the word again: "Can you say the word *scrumptious*?" Third, you provide the same child-friendly definition used before and during reading: "Remember, *scrumptious* describes something that is tasty or very yummy."

Next, to ground the discussion of how the word is used in the context of the story, you should go back into the book, turning the pages in front of the children to find where the word is used in the story. You can say, "Let's go back into the book to see where the word *scrumptious* is used. Oh, here it is. The wolf made a stack of 100 *scrumptious* pancakes. Those pancakes look really yummy." Once children have discussed how the word is used in the book, you move discussion of the word outside the context of the text to other meaningful contexts. For example, you can provide two or three other things that can be scrumptious to eat. You may explain, "Other things can be *scrumptious to eat too. I think Thanksgiving dinner is scrumptious.* In the summer time, I think chocolate ice cream is *scrumptious* to eat." Lastly, you want to reinforce the lesson by asking the children one

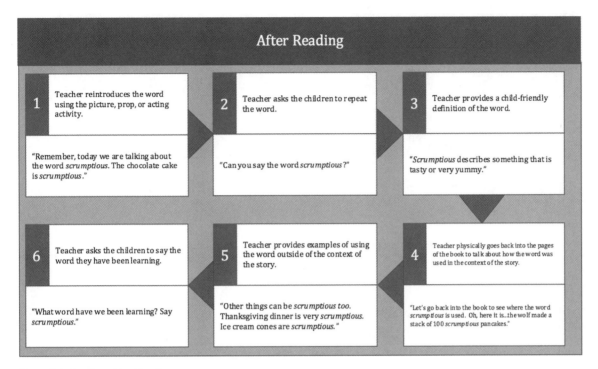

**Figure 3.9** Day One: After Reading

last time to say the word they have been learning: "What word have we been learning? Say *scrumptious!*"

## Day Two: Before Reading

The second day of the word walk sequence releases more responsibility to the children, asking them to be more active participants than on the first day (see Figure 3.10 and the appendix). You will see built-in repetition between procedures in day one and day two. This purposeful repetition supports the word learning of young children. By engaging them in learning the same word or words within the same storybook reading over two days, Word Walk provides enough repetition for children to process and digest unfamiliar words. Once children have a firm model of how to use the new word both in the storybook and in other contexts on day one, you can invite them to provide their own discussion and examples on the second day of instruction.

Before reading on the second day, introduce the target word or words using the same picture vocabulary card or prop you used on the first day. If you are targeting the word *scrumptious* in *The Wolf's Chicken Stew* on day two you would say, "Remember, we learned about the word *scrumptious* yesterday. In our picture, the chocolate cake looks *scrumptious.*" Next, ask your children to say the word: "Can you say the word *scrumptious*?" Finally, invite your children to comment on the word from what they remember from their

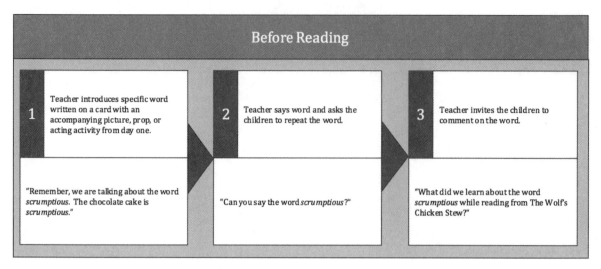

Figure 3.10 Day Two: Before Reading

discussion and reading the previous day. You may ask, "What did we learn about the word *scrumptious* while reading *The Wolf's Chicken Stew*?"

## Day Two: During Reading

The during-reading piece on day two of word walk consists of three steps (see Figure 3.11 and the appendix). First, pause while reading when the word is encountered in the text. Many times students remember the physical cue from the first day of reading and may indicate that they have heard the word by rubbing their stomachs like in day one. Call attention to the word: "I just heard the word *scrumptious*, and I can see that some of you heard the word too." Next, provide the same child-friendly definition: "*Scrumptious* describes something that is tasty or very yummy." Finally, ask the children to discuss or comment on how the word is used in the context of the story immediately while reading: "How is the word *scrumptious* used in our book?" This step is different from day one. Since students have already been exposed to the storybook on day one, they have the previous experience to draw from in order to discuss how the word is used in the story. This level of scaffolding sets young children up to be more successful than asking them to comprehend how the word is used in the story after only one reading.

## Day Two: After Reading

Just as in the first day of the sequence, the majority of the time spent on vocabulary instruction occurs after reading on day two (see Figure 3.12 and the appendix). The first three steps are consistent with day one. First, reintroduce the target word or words using the vocabulary picture card or prop. Remind your students, "Remember, today we are

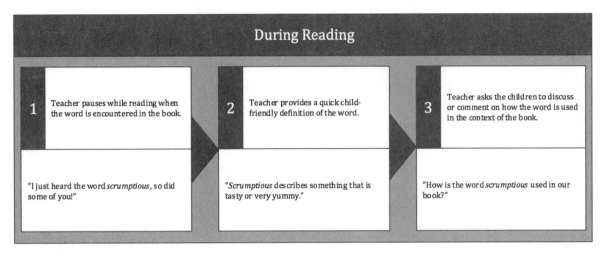

Figure 3.11 Day Two: During Reading

talking about the word *scrumptious*. This chocolate cake looks *scrumptious*." Next, ask the children to repeat the word: "Can you say *scrumptious*?" Third, provide the child-friendly definition: "*Scrumptious* describes something that is tasty or very yummy."

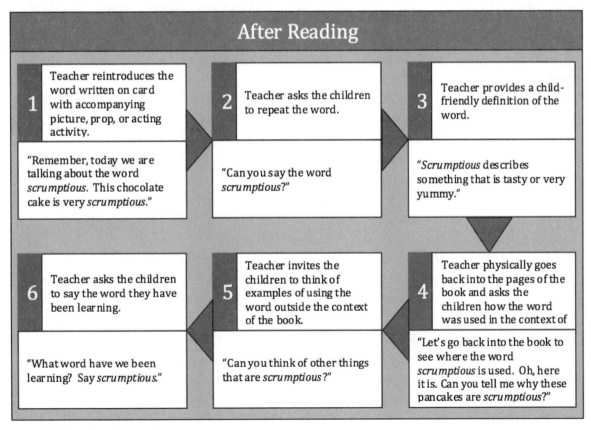

Figure 3.12 Day Two: After Reading

The fourth and fifth steps after reading on day two are different than day one. In the fourth step, go back into the book where the word is used and ask the children to explain how it is used in the context of the story. Rather than telling the children by thinking aloud how the word is used in the text, this time ask the children to take the lead in the discussion. "Let's go back into the book to see where the word *scrumptious* is used. Oh, here it is. Can you tell me why these pancakes are *scrumptious*?" Once you have discussed how the word is used in the context of the story, ask the children to think of examples of using the word outside the context of the book. On day one, you provided examples outside the book; however, on day two the children are asked to extend the word into a new context: "Can you think of other things that are *scrumptious*?" This step can tell you a lot about individual children's understanding of the target word. If children can think of a new context for using the word correctly, then it is a strong indicator that children truly understand the word. Finally, ask the children to say the word they have been learning one last time, "What word have we been learning? Say *scrumptious*."

## Classroom Vignette: Using Word Walk with *Llama Llama Red Pajama*

Now that we have reviewed the steps in the word walk instructional sequence, let's listen in as a preschool teacher implements the method with her students. Ms. McCue is a lively teacher working with eighteen children in a federally funded early childhood education center. Her students are four years old, receive reduced lunch, and are culturally diverse. Ms. McCue has utilized the word walk method since the beginning of the year to target her students' word learning. This is the first day Ms. McCue has read the storybook *Llama Llama Red Pajama* by Anna Dewdney (2005).

Ms. McCue settles herself on the rug with her students. "Good morning girls and boys! Today we are going to read one of my favorite storybooks—*Llama Llama Red Pajama* by Anna Dewdney. We read a different Llama Llama book a few weeks ago. Do you remember when we read about baby llama being mad at his mama? Today we are going to read about baby llama getting ready to go to bed. What kinds of things do you do at night that help you get ready to go to sleep?"

After calling on several students to share their connections to the story, Ms. McCue moves the conversation to the new vocabulary word under consideration. "Children, today as we read the story we are going to talk about a new word—*patient*. I have a vocabulary picture card of the word *patient*. In the picture, the little boy is waiting *patiently* for the bus to come. Can you say *patient*? *Patient* means to wait for something or someone without getting upset. While I am reading today, please listen carefully for the word *patient*. When you hear the word *patient*, please put a quiet finger on your nose. I am going to be watching to see who has heard the word *patient* in the book. Ok, let's start reading."

Ms. McCue begins reading the book as she normally does during the morning read-aloud. She reviews concepts of print, such as the roles of the author and illustrator, and builds comprehension by modeling how to make predictions while reading. Ms. McCue and her students have been working on the comprehension strategy of predicting, and she slowly moves from modeling her own predictions to asking her students to make predictions at pivotal moments in the story. When she gets to the page in the story where the word *patient* occurs, Ms. McCue pauses and states, "Aha! I just heard the word *patient*, and so did many of you. I see you have put a quiet finger on your nose because you heard the word *patient*, which means to wait for something or someone without getting upset." After commenting on the vocabulary word, Ms. McCue continues to read until the end of the storybook.

After reading, Ms. McCue asks her students if they enjoyed the book and to explain their reasons for either liking or disliking the story. Ms. McCue reviews the comprehension strategy of predicting and discusses why good readers make predictions while they are reading. Next, Ms. McCue returns to her vocabulary instruction: "Remember, today while reading we are talking about the word *patient*. On my picture vocabulary card I have the word *patient* and a picture of a child waiting *patiently* for the bus to come. I know many of you have to wait *patiently* in the morning for the bus to come to take you to school. Can you say *patient*? Excellent! *Patient* means to wait for something or someone without getting upset. Let's go back into the story to see how the word *patient* is used."

Flipping back to the page in the book where llama is not being patient, Ms. McCue shows the colorful illustration to the students. "Here it is. Llama is not being *patient* here when he starts to jump and shout and cry for his mama to come to his bedroom. You know, sometimes I have to be *patient* for things too. Sometimes when I get stuck in traffic, I have to be *patient* and wait for the cars in front of me to move. I also have to be *patient* when I want to open my birthday presents at a party. What word have we been learning about today? Say *patient*. Good! We will think about the word *patient* again tomorrow. When you go home tonight, try to think of times when you have to be *patient*."

Ms. McCue concludes her read-aloud and targeted vocabulary instruction. When she reflects on her instruction, she is pleased with the implementation of the day one word walk steps; she used each of the steps of the instructional procedure and witnessed the engagement of her students in talking and thinking about new words. She plans to review the word *patient* the very next day by rereading *Llama Llama Red Pajama* and inviting her students to comment on what they remember about the word from the previous day and on their own ideas for using the word outside the context of this particular story. There are many opportunities for children to identify situations in their own lives when they needed to be patient or to connect the word to characters being patient in other stories that they have read together that year. Ms. McCue is excited to listen for her students using the word in her classroom when appropriate.

# Word Wall

We know that a second method for engaging children in word learning is making conscious decisions about the print in your classroom environment. Think about the walls in your classroom right now. Are there posters, photographs, signs, student work? Just as young toddlers begin to notice print from seeing signs and billboards outside of the car window, young children tune in to print in the classroom. By including vocabulary words in the print of your classroom, you are creating a word-rich environment.

Creating word or picture cards for new words provides children with a visual reminder of the target vocabulary words they are learning (Wasik and Bond 2001). Making cards that include both the word and a supporting picture can make an abstract discussion of a word much more concrete for young learners. The next step is to make these materials visible and accessible to the children in the classroom. The most common method is to create a word wall.

Teachers often discover that an effective word wall does more than merely display words; it also engages children in conversations surrounding the words. I was reading a book to a group of preschoolers once when they stopped me to point out that the word *gasp* was on the word wall from a book we had read earlier in the year. This sparked an impromptu conversation about how they remembered the word being used in the other book compared to how the word was being used in the book we were currently reading. The children were excited to have made this word discovery on their own.

To encourage peer conversation about words, consider ways to make your word wall more interactive. For example, one teacher with whom we work used a cartoon picture during an instruction to illustrate the word *looking*. The teacher found that the cartoon picture was easily dismissed or forgotten by her students. To connect the word *looking* to her specific group of students, the teacher took a picture of a child looking through a telescope on the playground to attach to the word card. When attached to the word wall, this new, enhanced word card energized her students.

Occasionally, a word selected for instruction has high utility in the classroom environment. For those words, teachers may elect to display word cards in the appropriate classroom setting. For example, in one classroom, the word *alone* hangs just outside the bathroom door. As the teacher in this classroom worked with her children on the difference between public and private spaces, she capitalized on the word *alone* to help designate the bathroom as a private space where it is not only appropriate but also expected for children to be alone.

In addition to a word wall, you can create classroom books of words simply by putting the word cards used during read-alouds together in folders or binders. When placed in the classroom library, the wordbook often becomes popular with students. For example, one teacher we work with reported that the vocabulary wordbook was the most read book in her library for several months.

# Play-Based Learning

Some of the best word learning opportunities can come at the sand and water table in a preschool classroom, where children experiment with objects sinking and floating. Children with an intentional teacher can be exposed to wonderful words such as *sink, float, experiment, hypothesis, graph, estimate, prediction, conclusion, weight, measurement,* and *buoyancy.* Similarly, play opportunities for teaching new words can be found in a dramatic play corner, a block center, a classroom library, or at an art table. When teachers are conscious about inserting new words into hands-on activities, children benefit by connecting vocabulary to their experiences.

To facilitate word learning through play, consider a few tips. First, consciously select target words for instruction that meet your overall learning goals for the students and fit authentically into the play area. Children are very aware when teachers try to force a word into play; we want the word to fit seamlessly. Try to weave the new word into play without being didactic about it. For example, if you are playing in the block area with some children who are building a room at the top of a house, you can insert the word *attic* by asking a simple question such as, "Oh, that is a great room at the top of the house, is that the family's attic for storage?" Typically children will absorb a new word introduced in this manner right into their play.

Second, take on a role in the play yourself. Rather than being a teacher of words from a position of authority, be a coplayer (Enz and Christie 1997). Children will respond much better if you are also playing a role in the scenario. We love to jump into the dramatic play corner as a disgruntled customer at a hair salon or a concerned pet owner. When we are playing a role, the vocabulary we use is authentic to the scenario and meaningful to the context of the play. It often helps children's play to become more sophisticated if you discuss with them the importance of defining the role that they are playing in the dramatic scenario. We like to facilitate this role selection by providing headbands, necklaces, or hats to help children indicate to themselves and one another the role that they are playing.

Finally, consider the play environment carefully. A primary role for teachers in play is to make careful decisions about what kinds of props to add or take away in order to continuously support children's learning (see Figure 3.13). If the same toys and props are available for play from the first day of the unit until the last, there is no moment of discovery. Instead, carefully select items that connect to new and interesting words for children to learn and insert them into the play when children are ready for a change in their play. This moment of discovery is key for reenergizing play scenarios and targeting vocabulary development.

Figure 3.13 Preschooler Playing the Role of Grocer in Dramatic Play

# Conversations

Children's vocabulary knowledge is tightly interwoven with their oral language development. The two skills develop hand in hand as children listen to and communicate with more advanced language users. Conversations, particularly those surrounding targeted vocabulary words, can provide the multiple exposures to new words that children need in order to own the words in their vocabulary stores (Beck and McKeown 2007). Conversations bring attention to words, resulting in increased word consciousness.

There are two types of conversations surrounding words—planned and spontaneous. Some teachers plan sustained conversations around words that interest their children and are connected to their theme or unit of study. For example, one kindergarten teacher we know planned a unit on farming. He knew he had several storybooks related to the theme of farming and that a common set of vocabulary words would be important for children to know in order to understand the unit. He planned for several conversations during his weekly routine. For an initial conversation, he constructed a web of background knowledge and ideas children had about farming (see Figure 3.14). By recording the web on poster paper during his conversation with students, he not only targeted vocabulary instruction but also modeled writing and ended up creating a visual to add to the classroom walls.

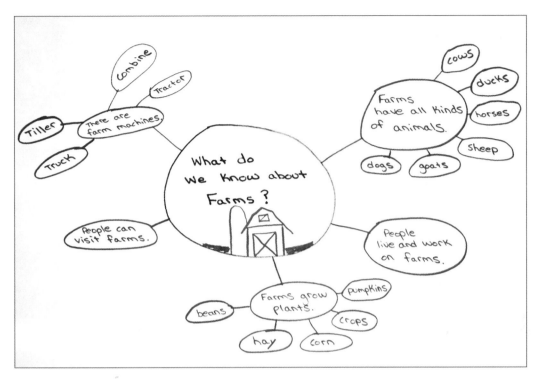

Figure 3.14 Kindergarten Conversation Web

Planned conversations around books and themes are essential to developing children's vocabulary knowledge; however, equally important are the unplanned, spontaneous teachable moments surrounding targeted vocabulary words. For example, when riding on the bus to a field trip, you can have a conversation with the children sitting near you about the *enormous* buildings you are passing on the city streets. Or, imagine *gasping* with children at their appearances in the bathroom mirror after a busy day. In order to have these spontaneous moments, it is crucial to recall the vocabulary words taught throughout the year. Having a visible word wall is a valuable aid to jog children's memories.

# The Language Experience Approach

Vocabulary instruction should be personal. An effective and evidence-based strategy to make it personal is called the Language Experience Approach or LEA (Stauffer 1970). This is a technique in which teachers elicit and record children's responses surrounding a question, topic, or class event. For example, you may decide to capture children's responses to an LEA topic titled "Our Class Trip to the Apple Orchard" by recording children's memories from the field trip on a poster board.

What makes this approach so personal is that the children come up with the idea and use their own words. Children are able to see their own thoughts and ideas translated to the

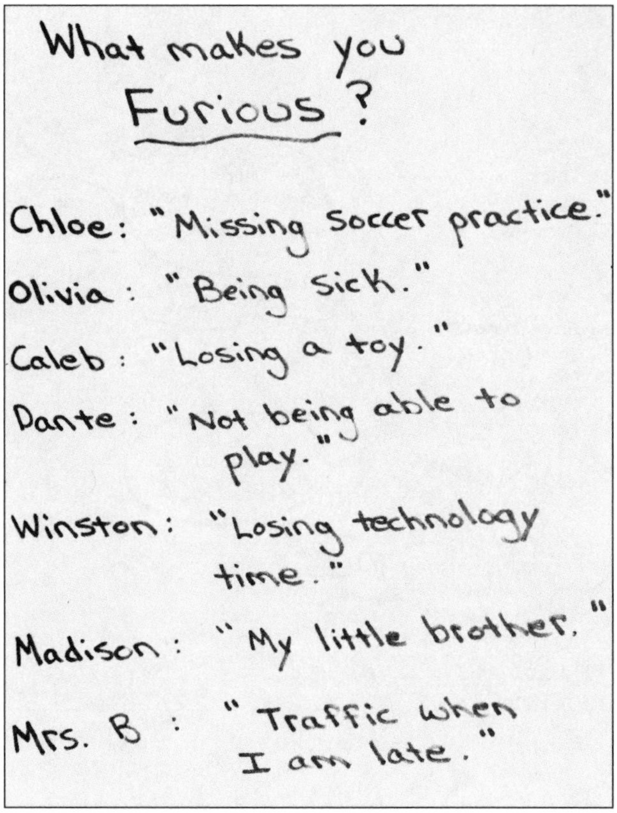

Figure 3.15 Language Experience Approach with Vocabulary Word

printed word. It's a proud and exciting event in children's emerging literacy development. This same idea can be translated into a vocabulary extension activity when you pose questions like, "Can you tell me about something that's *enormous*?" or, as in Figure 3.15, "What makes you *furious*?" This instructional approach is explicit, effective, meaningful, and helps to promote long-lasting vocabulary development.

## Creative Expression—Art and Drama Experiences

Integrating creative arts into early childhood and primary education enhances the personal connections children make with new words they are learning. Children love expressing their knowledge with paint, musical instruments, or movement. It's fun!

If a child hears a new vocabulary word, internalizes that word, and uses it through creative expression appropriately, then you have a good indication that the child now possesses some understanding of the word. For example, several teachers we work with encourage children to visualize words and depict what the word means to them through visual or dramatic art. In one classroom, children's drawings of the word *captivity* included pictures of animals at the zoo and dogs at the rescue center (see Figure 3.16); in another

**Figure 3.16** A Preschooler Illustrating the Word *Captivity*

classroom, students used modeling clay to create three-dimensional representations of the words they were discovering. No matter the creative medium, integrating vocabulary into the creative process is popular with students.

Children also love the dramatic arts. Acting or physically demonstrating a personal understanding of a word is considered to be a mnemonic device—that is, something that helps you remember a key concept or idea. Do you remember the sentence "Please Excuse My Dear Aunt Sally," used to remember the order in which to conduct mathematical operations? This idea also holds true for children learning a vocabulary word. When children see or hear that word, wherever they are, they will remember acting it out, which will immediately cue the meaning of the word and they will be able to relate it to the current context.

## Games

In addition to participating in hands-on creative art activities, children also love to learn words by playing games. There are some great commercially available games that target vocabulary; Figure 3.17 describes some of our favorites. Playing these games at a vocabulary center or during indoor recess can boost children's word learning. One teacher we worked with capitalized on her children's love of play by creating some original games around new vocabulary words. The beauty of the games was that they combined fun with practice using the new vocabulary words in appropriate contexts, and, unlike the commercial games, these vocabulary games included the specific target vocabulary words that the class was focused on learning. For example, the teacher created one game in which children were asked to use clues in a photograph to guess which *grin* belonged to which friend in the class. These games were easy to make and engaged children immensely because they involved pictures of themselves. The teacher utilized the games as one option for children to participate in during freeplay and center time in the classroom.

| Game | Description | How It Develops Vocabulary |
|---|---|---|
| Bananagrams | A multiplayer game with letter tiles in a banana-shaped bag. There are several variations of play; in the most common one, players create a personal-word crossword grid. The object is to use all the letter tiles as a group. | Children work to spell real words and must peer-check for accuracy. |
| Guess Who? | A two-player game in which children secretly select a person and their partner poses descriptive questions to figure out who it is | Children use expressive vocabulary to describe physical attributes in order to guess the correct person. |
| Scattergories | A multiplayer game in which a category is chosen and players must brainstorm as many words as they can to fit the category | Children use their prior knowledge to come up with related vocabulary words. |
| Scrabble Junior | A multiplayer game in which children create real words with letter tiles connected in a crossword grid | Children work to spell real words and must peer-check for accuracy in spelling and meaning. |
| Word Pirates | A multiplayer, pirate-themed game in which children use letter dice to build paths and bridges toward the treasure chest | Children must spell real words correctly and peer-check for accuracy. |

Figure 3.17  Commercially Available Games That Target Vocabulary

# Technology Integration

Let's face it: kids love technology. Using websites and apps to target and reinforce word learning can be extremely engaging for children. If you have computers or iPads in your classroom, they can be used to target vocabulary development. As with any technology, there is a range of quality in terms of available programs for children. New websites and apps are being developed as we write these words. We could not possibly address all the potential websites and apps that are currently available. However, we provide a few of our current favorites in Figure 3.18. While we will always prefer discussing new words in the context of a great book, we acknowledge here the incredible draw technology has for many students and parents.

| Website or App | Description |
|---|---|
| The Opposites (App) | • In this game, children race to match words with opposite meanings before the screen fills with unmatched words.<br>• Great way to reinforce word learning |
| Funbrain (Website) | • www.funbrain.com<br>• Wide selection of games targeting multiple content areas, including reading and vocabulary<br>• Also offers books and comics to read online |
| Between the Lions (Website) | • www.pbskids.org/lions<br>• Games and stories based on television show address vocabulary and other literacy skills |
| Starfall (Website and App) | • www.starfall.com<br>• Interactive stories and games designed to develop children's literacy skills<br>• Appropriate for children from preschool through second grade |
| Words with Friends (App) | • http://wordswithfriends.en.softonic.com/webapps<br>• Yes, this is the extremely addictive, adult Scrabblelike game.<br>• Parents playing a game with their children can easily develop word consciousness and spelling at the same time. |
| Raz-Kids (Website and App) | • www.razkids.com<br>• Includes interactive e-books that children can read or be read to, vocabulary and comprehension questions for practice and informal assessment |
| What's the Word (App) | • Players see four pictures and must find the word that connects all four pictures together.<br>• The pictures are increasingly difficult, offering greater levels of challenge. |

Figure 3.18  Popular Technology for Targeting Vocabulary

# Connecting with Families

There are many meaningful ways to extend vocabulary learning from your classroom into children's homes. In the following section, we provide several examples of quick, easy, and fun vocabulary activities that link families and children with opportunities to read, write, speak, and listen for wonderful words at home.

## Communicate with Families

We certainly cannot stress this enough. Parents and families are far more likely to be actively involved in their children's academic lives if teachers and educators create consistent and supportive communication systems. A good idea is to provide families with the words you are targeting during that week. This can be a simple list of the words or individual word cards given each week. Explain to parents that you have been working on these words in class and encourage them to talk about these words at home. This simple communication system will lay the foundation for the activities described here.

## Use the Word in My World

Vocabulary is more likely to be retained when children can make meaningful and personal connections to the words. Encourage families and children to find ways to connect the vocabulary words to experiences in their world. For example, if the target word is *scrumptious* and children learned that *scrumptious* means tasty or yummy, children can be asked to write down or draw pictures of food items that they ate that week that were *scrumptious*. This same procedure can apply to words you send home. Think of the many possibilities for words like *enormous, mysterious, voracious,* and *tantalizing*! Children may also be given the opportunity to "share the word in their world" with fellow classmates every week. Due to the meaningful opportunities provided by families and school, these words have a far greater chance to live in children's permanent vocabulary.

## Ask Silly Questions

Another interesting way for families and children to interact with words you send home is to play Ask Silly Questions! These are questions that take the target word and place it in a silly scenario in the form of a question. Parents and children can take turns asking each other the questions and engage in meaningful conversations surrounding the words. Send home some silly questions and it's guaranteed to support meaningful conversations, rich oral language, and critical thinking.

Some silly questions may include:

- Is an elephant *tiny*? Why? Is an ant *tiny*? Why?
- Would you *grin* if your Mom made you your favorite dessert? Why? Would you *grin* if it started raining when you were about to go play outside? Why?
- If you are on a crowded bus are you *alone*? Why? Are you *alone* in our classroom today? Why?
- Is a giraffe *enormous*? Is a mouse *enormous*? Why?
- Is your friend sitting next to you today *invisible*? Why?
- Would you still be thirsty if you drank from a glass that was *empty*? Would you like

to open a birthday present that was *empty*? Why?

- Would you be *excited* to open presents at your birthday party? Why? Would you be *excited* to clean your messy room?
- Does a *farmer* take care of lions and zebras? Why? Would you find a *farmer* in a barn? Why?
- Would you be *furious* if you saw a rainbow outside your window? Why?

## Develop a Book Buddies System

Book buddies is a system in which you send home book buddies bags once a week for families and children to complete together. The book buddies bag contains a book and various activities to extend the learning opportunities from the selection. One of these extension opportunities could include a discussion about some wonderful words in the story. Provide a list of two or three words from the story with quick, child-friendly definitions for each. After the parent and child have read the story, encourage the parent to go back into the story and have a discussion of what the words means in the context of the story. You can also ask the parent to expand on that discussion and provide the child with one or two ways of using the word. For a challenge, the parent can ask the child to provide his or her own example or experience with that words or words.

## Find Interesting Words

In most elementary classrooms, children are required to read at home for a set period of time, and parents and children typically complete some sort of reading log to document this at-home reading time. One activity that children can be asked to complete during this time is to find interesting words in their reading. These are words that children choose on their own that they find interesting for whatever reason. Children may be given a "My Interesting Words" bookmark where they write down several words while reading. It may also require them to provide the meaning of the word in context, their own definition of the word, or why they thought this word was interesting. This stimulates a vocabulary phenomenon called *word consciousness,* whereby they are intrinsically interested in words when they read them, hear them, or see them in their environment. They have a natural curiosity about words and what they mean as they move through their daily lives. Since most words we learn are learned incidentally, this is a wonderful means by which children can add words to their personal vocabulary stores.

# Vocabulary Assessment

There is no set list of vocabulary words that children must master at each age or grade level. That list just does not exist. So assessing vocabulary is very different than assessing other literacy skills. When we think of vocabulary assessments, we may often think about standardized testing. Though standardized testing measures do have a vocabulary component, these are blunt instruments that only assess general vocabulary knowledge. Vocabulary itself is far too vast and limitless to accurately assess and link to an individual's specific word knowledge. One way that you can capture students' word understanding is to assess individual words that were explicitly taught in class. This can be done in a whole group, small groups, and individually.

## Assess Through Every Pupil Response (EPR)

You will get an informal and accurate indication of word learning by engaging a whole group or small groups of students in Every Pupil Response (EPR) activities (Hopkins 1979). EPR activities may include:

- Provide the definition of the word and have the children call out the word in unison.
- Provide the definition and have the children hold up a picture that matches the word in unison.
- Provide a scenario with the word in use and have the children call out the word in unison.
- Ask silly questions and have each child turn and talk with a buddy to answer the question. The teacher should monitor the conversations.
- Provide the word, one at a time, ask the children to provide a real-world example of each word, and have each child turn and talk with a buddy to develop the scenario. The teacher should monitor the conversations.

## Assess Through Curriculum-Based Measures

You may also be interested in assessment that delves into individual students' levels of word knowledge. One way to accurately assess an individual's word knowledge of explicitly taught words is a curriculum-based measure (CBM) or curriculum-based assessment (CBA). These are short assessment measures based on specific content taught in class. CBM results often serve as progress monitoring measures so that teachers can chart children's progress over the course of the year or term and make any needed changes in grouping and instruction. In this case, a vocabulary CBM would directly assess the specific words taught over the course of a week, two weeks, or a month. It may not include every word taught but rather a sample of the words, and can provide teachers with an insight into each student's vocabulary development. It is important when developing a CBM that the types of questions or activities asked of the student reflect the types of activities they would have previously completed during whole-group or small-group instruction. In Figure 3.19, we provide sample CBM questions and activities for six target vocabulary words.

---

**Target Words to Be Assessed Through a CBM:**

*spontaneous, admonish, malice, profound, scrumptious, voracious*

---

**Match the word to the comment:**

"That was such an amazing speech."

"Clean up your room. It's a mess."

"The volcano erupted with no warning."

"When are we stopping to eat? I'm starving!"

"He was teasing the boy and all of the children started to make fun of him too."

"That was the best Thanksgiving dinner yet!"

---

**Describe the relationships between two target words:**

Describe a time when someone might do something that is *malicious* because they were *voracious.*

Why might someone be *admonished* if they said something that was *profound*?

What is something that you might do *spontaneously* after you ate something that was *scrumptious*?

---

Choose two of your wonderful words and draw a cartoon to explain their meaning. Write a sentence under your cartoon that explains and uses both of your vocabulary words.

---

Figure 3.19 Sample CBM Questions and Activities

# Summary

Vocabulary knowledge is a pivotal piece in a child's foundation for reading and writing success. Much is known from research about the instructional methods you can use to boost children's vocabulary development. Without a doubt, the cornerstone of vocabulary instruction is the read-aloud. When teachers select high-quality children's fiction and nonfiction texts and integrate explicit vocabulary instruction with a specifically chosen set of words based on children's needs and interests, children become excited about learning new words. And research is clear that explicit vocabulary instructional procedures are effective; not only are children engaged in word learning, but they also increase their vocabulary knowledge.

However, we also know that read-alouds alone are not sufficient. We can only truly hope to narrow the vocabulary gap if we are developing word consciousness in children. When we engage children in talking about and using new words in a variety of extension activities during the classroom day and when we invite parents to become our partners in word consideration, children can make even greater vocabulary gains. Utilizing home–

school connections and a carefully crafted assessment plan to track progress over time in meaningful ways can help you strategically plan the kinds of words to teach and review with students throughout the school year.

Vocabulary instruction can be both enjoyable and rewarding. A classroom community that is excited about word learning shares a unified quest—it is always on the lookout for new words. Students cheer each other on when they share word discoveries inside and outside the classroom. They track progress of the words they have learned and the number of times they have encountered them during reading and in the real world. They encourage each other to use rare words that are also more sophisticated vocabulary words. Their enthusiasm about words is contagious to other classrooms, other teachers, and parents. Once a group of students has caught the fever for word learning, it is hard to quell the enthusiasm. And that enthusiasm fuels the fire for word learning across a lifetime.

# Chapter 4

# Learning the Alphabetic Code and Phonological Awareness

Have you ever noticed that the first letter of the alphabet children usually learn is the first letter in their own name? Alexandra will learn *A*, and Owen knows *O*. Typically children learn the first letter in their name and "own" it as a matter of pride. They quickly see it in the environment and become excited. Michael exclaims, "Look, Mom, my letter *M*!" in front of a McDonald's restaurant. Indeed, this became a problem in my classroom once when I had two children whose names began with the letter *J*. As the children were finding a seat on the letter rug, Jack sat on *J* before Julie. Julie turned to Jack indignantly and explained, "*J* is *my* letter." The tears were genuine as Julie thought she had to change her name after three years of owning it!

Once children understand that letters carry meaning, they become naturally curious about them. As literate adults, we must remember that to children the alphabet is an unfamiliar code that must be deciphered. Part of unlocking the code is knowing the sounds that the letters and combinations of letters produce. The letters and their sounds can be quite easy for some children and very challenging for others. With exposure and repetition during instruction, children can acquire alphabet knowledge and phonological awareness.

## What Do Children Need to Know About the Alphabet?

Knowing the letters of the alphabet is an essential building block for eventual reading. Children need to know three things about the letters—what they are, how to write them, and what sounds they make. First, children need to be able to identify each of the twenty-six letters of the alphabet. Singing the letters of the alphabet is a good start but not sufficient. Children need to be able to point to a letter on a page and identify it by name. Next, children need to know how to write each letter. Beginning instruction may include forming letters with dough or blocks, but eventually children will transfer what they know to writing each letter with a pencil. Finally, children need to associate each letter with the sound or sounds it makes. This is called letter-sound correspondence and is an important skill when readers start to sound out words. The ideas for alphabet instruction in this chapter include ways to teach the alphabet in a variety of classroom contexts, including small-group and play-based, and integrating creative expression formats.

## What Do Children Need to Know About Phonological Awareness?

Phonological awareness is the understanding of the sound structure in our language. In English, we have four levels of sound that children need to be able to hear. The easiest is the word level. When children know that sentences are made up of words and that compound words are made up of two smaller words, they have word awareness. The second level is a little bit harder because it asks children to listen for a smaller part of a word—the syllables. Children have syllable awareness when they can count the number of syllables in multisyllabic words. The third level is onset and rime awareness, or the ability to hear when words rhyme. The fourth level of sound, and the most difficult, is identifying the individual sounds in words, or phoneme awareness. Children with a strong foundation in phonological awareness are poised to become independent readers (Adams 1990).

Sometimes phonological awareness and alphabet instruction get a bad reputation for being dull—deservedly, when they are reduced to endless worksheets. We've all seen the worksheets where children circle pictures that begin with, end with, or rhyme with the target sound. After the third or fourth time of doing this type of activity, even the most well-behaved student gets bored! The good news is that phonological awareness and alphabet instruction can be fun and engaging. When selecting activities for this chapter, we chose those that successfully taught the skills and that our students enjoyed doing. Figure 4.1 provides an overview of the methods discussed in this chapter for developing children's alphabetic and phonological awareness.

| Instructional Method | Format | Characteristics | Strengths |
|---|---|---|---|
| A Literacy-Rich Environment | Classroom Organization | Teachers include alphabet posters and strips, environmental print, children's writing, teacher dictation, and rhyming posters throughout the classroom. | If letters and print are all around them, children will become curious and draw inspiration from the environment. |
| Explicit Instruction | Small Groups | • Teachers differentiate small-group instruction for the needs of learners.<br>• Allows time for review of concepts that particular students might still need<br>• Typically lasts between fifteen and twenty minutes | • Targeted instruction to meet the needs of the learners<br>• Small groups allow for more individual attention from the teacher.<br>• Particularly helpful for struggling students |
| Play-Based Learning | Small Groups, Partners, Individuals | • Children play in various contexts (block area, dramatic play, sensory table, outdoors, etc.).<br>• Teachers support alphabet learning through inclusion of props and coplay. | Likely high student engagement |
| Games | Small Groups, Partners, Individuals | Children play teacher-created or commercially available games designed to provide additional practice with alphabet identification and phonological awareness. | Likely high student engagement |
| Creative Expression— Art and Music Experiences | Small Groups, Centers, Partners | • Children can use various visual art mediums to represent letters of the alphabet.<br>• Children can sing songs that practice letters of the alphabet and phonological awareness. | Likely high student engagement |
| Read-Aloud | Whole Group, Small Groups | • Teacher reads aloud an alphabet book and engages children in finding and identifying letters of the alphabet.<br>• Teacher reads aloud a rhyming book or poem and engages children in completing rhyming activities. | • Enables teacher to model alphabet and phonological awareness skills to whole class<br>• High-quality alphabet and rhyming books connect to multiple themes and units of study. |
| Technology Integration | Small Groups, Centers | Various websites and apps designed to target alphabet and phonological awareness | • Good review activity<br>• High student engagement<br>• Potential to foster twenty-first-century technology skills |
| Connecting with Families | Multiple | Parents reinforce alphabet and phonological awareness learning at home. | • Fosters home-school connection<br>• Boosts alphabet and phonological awareness learning outside of classroom context |

Figure 4.1 Preview of Instructional Methods in This Chapter

# A Literacy-Rich Environment

Think about the print that surrounds you in your everyday life. We are bombarded with advertisements, sales, logos, traffic signs, retail signs, and more on a daily basis. Drawing inspiration from this, consider the environmental print in your classroom carefully. We have been in some classrooms that have too much print—overlapping posters, charts that are so old they are yellowing, bulletin boards sagging from too much weight. But we have also seen the opposite: classrooms with almost no print at all. Too much print becomes overwhelming, but a void of print is not good either. Instead, you want a balance.

Your classroom needs some print to serve as the second teacher in the classroom. To facilitate alphabet learning, you absolutely must have at least one alphabet visible in the classroom. In preschool settings, you want to make sure that the alphabet is at eye level with the children so they can see and reference it easily. In elementary school classrooms, teachers typically will have an alphabet strip or word wall posted in the classroom in addition to individual alphabet strips on students' desks to help them with their reading and writing. In preschool and kindergarten classrooms where phonological awareness is a central instructional focus, environmental print can include nursery rhymes, rhyming poems, alliterative poems, rhyming song lyrics, and the words of rhyming fingerplays.

Once you have the environmental print in your classroom, make sure to use it. The print does no good at all if it is just left on the walls to be forgotten. Instead, try to incorporate the print into one of your classroom routines, such as morning meeting, transition to snack, or read-aloud time. Reading a poem and talking about the rhyming words takes less than five minutes and targets phonological awareness. Similarly, singing the alphabet song takes less than two minutes and becomes a much stronger instructional activity when you or the children are pointing to each letter on an alphabet strip as you sing.

A literacy-rich classroom also needs high-quality children's literature for children to read and explore. An important concept when learning letters of the alphabet is that the letters have meaning and are used to communicate. Children who are surrounded by books and see letters used in them internalize the message that letters carry meaning. Preschool and early elementary classrooms should have classroom libraries with all kinds of books for children to enjoy. Books should include a variety of reading levels and genres. A good classroom library should contain narrative texts with beautiful illustrations and interesting characters and stories from many different authors. The classroom library should also contain informational texts on many different topics of interest to children. Figure 4.2 outlines the contents of our ideal classroom library for young children.

| Type of Text | Genre | Authors |
|---|---|---|
| **Narrative Text** | Fantasy | Eric Carle<br>Sandra Boynton<br>Chris Van Allsburg<br>Bill Martin Jr.<br>Margaret Wise Brown<br>Maurice Sendak<br>Anna Dewdney<br>Jane Yolen<br>Doreen Cronin<br>Lois Ehlert<br>Denise Fleming<br>Margaret and H. A. Rey |
| | Realistic Fiction | Mo Willems<br>Cynthia Rylant<br>Eve Bunting<br>Mem Fox<br>David Shannon<br>Patricia Polacco |
| | Wordless Books | David Wiesner<br>Suzy Lee |
| | Historical Fiction | Allen Say<br>Karen Hesse<br>Ellen Levine |
| | Traditional Literature | James Marshall<br>Jan Brett<br>Tomie dePaola<br>Paul O. Zelinsky<br>Jon Scieszka |
| | Mysteries | Mark Teague<br>David A. Kelly |
| **Informational Text** | Biography and Autobiography | Russell Freedman<br>Pam Munoz Ryan<br>Doreen Rappaport<br>David Adler |
| | Informational | Byron Barton<br>Gail Gibbons<br>Steve Jenkins<br>Seymour Simon<br>Jim Murphy<br>Anne Rockwell |
| **Poetry and Verse** | | Shel Silverstein<br>Jack Prelutsky |

Figure 4.2  Our Ideal Classroom Library

# Explicit Instruction

Typically, preschool and kindergarten students enter school with vastly different skill sets in alphabet knowledge and phonological awareness. In the same classroom, you can have children who know all the letters of the alphabet, children who have been exposed to some of the letters, and children who do not know any of the letters. The same developmental continuum is true for phonological awareness. Because of this diversity in individual knowledge, the ideal context for teaching and reviewing alphabet and phonological awareness skills is the small-group setting. The small-group setting allows you the opportunity to group students based on their prior knowledge so that you can then plan instruction for the needs of each group. For example, at the beginning of the year, you give students an alphabet identification assessment and discover that you can easily create three distinct small groups: (1) Group A needs explicit instruction in each letter of the alphabet, (2) Group B needs systematic review of several of the more obscure letters, and (3) Group C is ready to move beyond alphabet letter identification to letter-sound correspondence activities.

In terms of planning for each small group, there are two effective, research-based methods: (1) sorting and (2) segmenting and blending. Sorting is an educational method that is based on what we know about how the brain learns through categorizing information. The brain's natural tendency to categorize and sort becomes clear when you think about an activity such as opening a box of buttons. What do you naturally start thinking? Most of us start sorting by size, color, texture, and other defining characteristics in order to bring some organization to what appears to be the chaos of mixed buttons. Sorting is a versatile instructional method and can be used across content areas; you can sort in science (land animals versus sea animals), math (triangles versus squares), social studies (democracy versus dictatorship), and language arts (fiction versus nonfiction, uppercase versus lowercase) (Bear et al. 2011).

When describing sorting to target students' literacy growth, Bear et al. (2011) outline a very useful sorting sequence. First, model the sort so that children know exactly what is expected of them. When beginning a sort on the difference between pictures that start with the /m/ sound and pictures that begin with the /s/ sound, I always go through once just identifying the pictures for students. Then I go through each picture a second time to emphasize the beginning sound, the onset, and place the pictures of words that begin with the same sound together for students to see the sort. Second, scaffold the sort by having children work with a partner before releasing all the responsibility and having each individual child sort. After I have modeled the complete sort of pictures, I give a set of all the picture cards to each pair of students and ask them to work with their partner to repeat the same sort I just modeled for them. A key to making a partner sort successful is to remind students to say the name of the picture out loud as they are sorting. I always ask them to check their work after they are done as additional practice in making the sounds. Third, always have enough materials so that children can be sorting at the same time rather than waiting for a turn with the sorting manipulatives. Once I have had partners work together to sort, the last step is to give each child in my small group a set of picture cards to sort independently. This provides yet another round of practice and also allows me to quickly assess who has gotten it and who still needs work on this skill.

We love sorting because it can be used to teach almost any literacy skill. You can change the materials children are sorting to make the activity fit the skill you are targeting. You can also adjust the difficulty by using pictures or written text depending on the grade level. When using pictures, make sure children know what the pictures are—sometimes it can be tricky to identify which part of a picture is the focus. Finally, make sure to review the completed sort with children and talk about why they sorted the way they did—this is key to the learning process (Bear et al. 2011). Figure 4.3 shows an example of a child's completed sort. Figure 4.4 provides a list of sorts for developing children's alphabet knowledge and phonological awareness.

Figure 4.3 Rhyming Picture Sort

| Sort Type | Description | | Example |
|---|---|---|---|
| **Alphabet Sorts** | • Uppercase vs. lowercase<br>• Two-way letter sort<br>• Three-way letter sort<br>• Four-way letter sort<br>• Font sort | | • *A* vs. *a*<br>• *A* vs. *B*<br>• *A* vs. *B* vs. *C*<br>• *A* vs. *B* vs. *C* vs. *D*<br>• *A, **A**, 𝒜, A* vs. *B, **B**, ℬ, B* |
| **Phonological Awareness Sorts** | • Syllable sorts | • One-syllable vs. two-syllable words (or pictures) | • *cat, fun, girl* vs. *pancake, bobsled, flower* |
| | | • Two-syllable vs. three-syllable words (or pictures) | • *rainbow, chopstick, skateboard* vs. *bicycle, elephant, pineapple* |
| | • Rhyming sorts | • Two categories, words (or pictures) | • *cat, hat, bat* vs. *pan, can, ran* |
| | | • Three categories, words (or pictures) | • *log, dog, frog* vs. *sun, fun, run* vs. *pin, fin, skin* |
| | • Phoneme sorts | • Initial sound sorts, words (or pictures) | • *moon, man, map* vs. *nest, nose, nail* |
| | | • Final sound sorts, words (or pictures) | • *net, pot, hit* vs. *hip, stop, lip* |
| | | • Middle sounds sorts, words (or pictures) | • *not, pop, hog* vs. *pain, rake, case* |

**Figure 4.4 Sorts for Developing Alphabet Knowledge and Phonological Awareness**
Adapted from Bear et al. (2011)

Segmenting and blending are also powerful instructional methods for teaching phonological awareness (Walpole and McKenna 2007). Segmenting occurs when you break out each sound in a word. Blending happens when you push the individual sounds back together to make a word. Both segmenting and blending are key skills for children to have when they become beginning readers. When a teacher tells readers to "sound it out," she is essentially telling them to segment and blend. You can use segmenting and blending in small groups to help children hear the individual sounds in words (phoneme awareness). To help support children with this abstract process, we recommend using Elkonin boxes (Elkonin 1971) like the one shown in Figure 4.5. Elkonin boxes can be created on paper and laminated for reuse or drawn on dry erase boards during the lesson. Depending on the number of sounds in the words you are using, you will need two, three, four, or more boxes—one box for each sound—with an arrow underneath to help children blend from left to right. When using Elkonin boxes, you should always model the segmenting and blending first and then invite children to do it with you

**Figure 4.5** Using Elkonin Boxes for Full Phoneme Segmentation

in their own boxes. You can use manipulatives such as chips, coins, beans, or counting bears to push into each box as you say a sound. With older children, you can use alphabet tiles to show the correspondence between letter and sound. As you move each chip into a box, say the sound of the letter. Then use your finger to trace along the arrow from left to right as you say the whole word slowly.

## Classroom Vignette: Small-Group Sound Sort

Mr. Reid is a kindergarten teacher who has been working at an urban elementary school for fifteen years. He teaches two half-day programs, one in the morning from 9:00 to 12:00 and one in the afternoon from 12:30 to 3:30. During his three-hour block of time with students, Mr. Reid plans a morning meeting with a whole-group read-aloud. He also has daily centers; while children are working in them, Mr. Reid meets with each of his small groups for fifteen minutes. Let's listen in as Mr. Reid works with one of his small groups this morning.

Mr. Reid is seated in the middle of a horseshoe table with six children sitting across from him. "Good morning, everyone! Today we are going to begin by reviewing some of our letters from last time." Mr. Reid holds up a letter card and indicates that the group should read it together. After each letter, Mr. Reid repeats what the children say: "*A*, good. *G*, good. *M*, excellent. And *R*, fantastic. You really know these letters! Now, let's look at a new letter. The letter *L*." Mr. Reid holds up a card with the letter *L*. "The letter *L* looks like this and it makes the /l/ sound. Can you say that with me? Good, *L* says /l/ like in *letter* and *light* and *lemon*. I brought some pictures with me today of things that start with the /l/ sound. This is a lion. Can you say /l/ *lion*? This is a lamp. Can you say /l/ *lamp*? This is a lollipop. Can you say /l/ *lollipop*? And this is a llama, can you say /l/ *llama*?"

Mr. Reid continues, "Do you remember the letter *M* that we worked on yesterday? *M* makes the /m/ sound like *mouse* and *mountain*. Today we are going to sort some pictures that begin with the /l/ sound and pictures that begin with the /m/ sound." Mr. Reid models the sort with children first. "This is a picture of a mountain, /m/ *mountain*. I am going to put it here on the *left*. Here is a picture of a lion, /l/ *lion*. Does *lion* sound like *mountain*? No, so we are going to put it here in a new pile on the right. Here is a picture of a lollipop, /l/ *lollipop*. Does *lollipop* start with the same sound as /m/ *mountain* or /l/ *lion*? That's right—*lollipop* starts with the same /l/ sound as *lion*." Mr. Reid continues sorting in this way as children watch and help him make the letter sounds. Once the sort is complete, Mr. Reid asks children to work in partners to complete the same sort together as he watches and offers help as needed.

When Mr. Reid notices that the groups have finished their sort, he says, "Good, let's check our sorts. Mary, can you tell us what words you have that start with the /l/ sound? As Mary tells us the pictures she has that begin with the /l/ sound, check to see if that is what you and your partner have too. OK, Mary." Mary calls out each of her pictures that begin with the /l/ sound. Mr. Reid calls on another student to repeat this check with the pictures that begin with the /m/ sound. When a student makes a mistake, Mr. Reid pauses. "Oh, let's listen to that again. /m/ *map*, /m/ *map*, do you hear the /m/ sound at the beginning of that word like the /m/ sound in *mountain*? OK, good, so you moved that picture over to be with the other /m/ words."

Mr. Reid directs students to put their picture sorts away. Next, he gives each student a dry-erase board with Elkonin boxes written on them and an arrow underneath the set of three boxes. He also passes out three chips to each student. "OK, group. Let's segment and blend some words that begin with the /l/ sound that we have been working on. Watch me first. I am going to put my three chips under the boxes. Next I am going to segment the sounds I hear in the word *lip*. I am going to move the first chip up for the /l/, the second chip up for the /i/, and the third chip up for the /p/. Now I am going to blend the sounds back together, /l/ /i/ /p/, *lip*. Now, let's all try that one together. Get your chips and segment out the sounds, /l/ /i/ /p/, good. Now blend them together, *lip*." Mr. Reid continues this process of modeling and then watching students for several more three-sound words that begin with the /l/ sound.

As his fifteen minutes come to an end, Mr. Reid congratulates the group. "Good work today with the letter *L* and its /l/ sound. You worked hard to sort pictures that begin with the /l/ and /m/ sounds. You did a great job with segmenting and blending words that begin with the /l/ sound too. Tomorrow we will review the letter *L*."

Mr. Reid dismisses his first small group to go back to the centers and calls over his next group. While Mr. Reid will be sorting and segmenting and blending with all three groups, the content of the groups differs. The second group will be sorting rhyming words—words that rhyme with *bat* versus words that rhyme with *bag*. The third group will be doing a three-way sort—words that begin with /l/, /m/, and /b/. By using the same instructional methods, Mr. Reid is using what he knows about best practice. By changing what is sorted, Mr. Reid is adjusting the content to meet the needs of his students.

# Play-Based Learning

There are many centers in the preschool and kindergarten classroom that can develop students' alphabetic knowledge and phonological awareness. With a few key props or toys, you can transform a typical center in the classroom to integrate either skill. In the sections that follow we discuss ideas for making your centers work for you.

## *The Sensory Table*

We have worked with one teacher who was a master at using her sensory table to target not only tactile perception but also alphabet knowledge by adding interesting materials that children could not wait to explore. During a unit on fall, she added acorns, pinecones, gumballs, and leaves to her sensory table. The alphabet awareness came from the leaves, because by using inexpensive silk leaves from a craft store she was able to write a different letter on each one. As children picked up leaves, they recorded the letter of the alphabet on a clipboard. Later in the year, the same teacher had a bin of water on the sensory table and added magnetic foam fish with letters of the alphabet on the bottom of each. The children spent days using fishing poles to catch and record fish letters on a class graph, working on both fine motor skills and alphabet knowledge in the same playful activity. Figure 4.6 lists some common preschool themes and ideas for integrating alphabet knowledge within the sensory table. Figure 4.7 shows a preschooler fishing for letters at the sensory table.

## *Dramatic Play Center*

Certainly by adding environmental print to your dramatic play area you can expose children to the alphabet. For example, cereal boxes, baking packages, and soup cans with labels can add print to a grocery store; timetables, tickets, maps, and signs can add print to a train station; and magazines, waiting room signs, and office forms can add print to a veterinarian's office. You can also create dramatic play themes that are specifically related to letters, such as a classroom where the "teachers" can teach one another the letters, or a letter store that only sells things that start with the same letter sound (Silberg 2005). You can set a letter store up and have children decide what the letter of the day is in the store, or you can have children set up the store for other children. This can be a great way to target letter-sound knowledge.

## *Block Center*

The block center can also be used to target emergent literacy skills. Some stores sell wooden blocks in the shape of letters of the alphabet, but certainly children can construct letters with rectangular blocks, too. In order to facilitate this process, you may want to create letter templates to add to the block center so that children who need support can use the pattern to set the blocks on top off. There are some great alphabet books in which the main characters are building the alphabet—*Alphabet Under Construction* (Fleming 2002), *Albert's Alphabet* (Tryon 1994), *Engineering the ABCs* (Novak 2009), and *The Construction Alphabet Book* (Pallotta 2006)—and adding these books to the block area may also inspire your young builders.

| Thematic Unit | Props to Teach Alphabet |
|---|---|
| Transportation | Boats with letters in water<br>Cars and trucks with letters in water<br>Cars and trucks with letters in gravel<br>Cars and trucks with letters in sand<br>Cars and trucks with letters in shaving cream<br>Construction trucks and construction cones with letters on each cone |
| Seasonal | Fall leaves with letters<br>Acorns with letters in leaves or soil<br>Rocks with letters in soil or sand<br>Flower petals with letters in soil<br>Seashells with letters in water or sand<br>Mini-pumpkins with letters in water to explore sink vs. float |
| Animals | Magnetic fish with letters in water, magnetic fishing poles or nets<br>Rubber ducks with letters in water<br>Foam animals with letters in water<br>Plastic animals with names that start with different letter sounds |
| Being Healthy | Plastic eggs with letters written on each side in water or sand<br>Plastic teeth with toothbrushes with letters in shaving cream<br>Apples with letters written on them in water |

Figure 4.6  Using the Sensory Table to Build Alphabet Knowledge

## Listening Center

A listening center can be an ideal place for working on children's phonological awareness. Purchasing premade CDs or recording yourself reading children's rhyming books and nursery rhymes can give children material to listen to that targets phonological awareness.

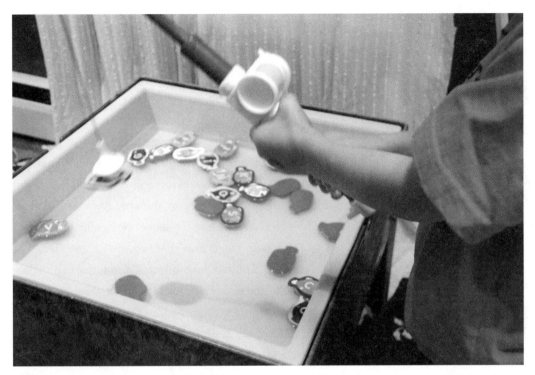

**Figure 4.7** A Preschool Student Fishes for Letters at the Sensory Table

# Games

There are many commercially available toys that you can purchase that target alphabet or phonological awareness. For the alphabet, consider purchasing alphabet puzzles, alphabet beanbags, alphabet wooden blocks, magnetic letters, letter tiles, and alphabet board games. For phonological awareness, consider purchasing compound word puzzles, rhyming baskets, rhyming memory games, and initial sound sorting games. However, there are also many games that you can easily make for children to play with. For example, the Bingo format works both for alphabet and rhyming words. Similarly, Memory, the game where you flip over two cards to see if you have a matching pair, also works for both letters of the alphabet and rhyming pictures or words. If you use the learning concept of sorting, you can create a game for any theme or unit of study in which children are sorting letters for alphabet awareness or sorting rhyming words or pictures that begin with the same beginning sounds for phonological awareness. For example, if you are working on a Johnny Appleseed unit, you can easily create a game where children are putting paper apples with letters written on them in alphabetic order. Or, if you are working on a transportation unit, children can sort paper train cars with pictures of rhyming words on them to practice phonological awareness. Figure 4.8 shows a student playing a teacher-constructed alphabet memory game.

# Creative Expression—Art and Music Experiences

**Figure 4.8** Alphabet Memory Game

Both visual art and music can be used to develop children's alphabet and phonological awareness. There is no limit to the visual art children can construct using letters for inspiration. Each letter of the alphabet can be painted, drawn, collaged, sculpted, or glued. Children can make the letters in scenes, in shapes of animals or objects that begin with the letter sound, or in an alphabet book. A fun class activity is to create a class alphabet book using letters and logos of things in magazines that begin with each letter of the alphabet. Children love hunting for letters that they know and the end alphabet book is a book that they can read.

For music, there are many songs that are fun to sing and also target literacy skills. There are multiple songs about the alphabet that can be played and sung in the classroom. Figure 4.9 includes some our favorites, many of which are available on iTunes. It is important to expose children to a variety of ABC songs so that they truly know the letters of the alphabet rather than having simply memorized the traditional song. Because of their tendency to rhyme, many preschool songs also develop children's ability to hear and recognize rhyming words. Figure 4.10 summarizes some of our favorite children's songs that are ideal for developing phonological awareness and can also be found on iTunes. Another use for the musical instruments in your classroom can be to help children hear the syllables in words. Distributing drums, triangles, cymbals, rhythm sticks, and shakers for children to use as they count out the number of syllables in multisyllabic words can create a wonderful syllable symphony!

# Read-Aloud

You can also use the read-aloud to target both alphabet and phonological awareness skills. When using a read-aloud to target alphabet knowledge, we recommend reading books that come in a Big Book format. Oversized books that fit on your reading easel have larger print, which makes it easier for children to see the letters of the alphabet. While ABC books are ideal, really any big book with letters can be used. To build explicit alphabet instruction into your normal read-aloud routine, consider adding one or two activities before, during, or after reading. There are many ways in which you can call children's attention to target letters; Figure 4.11 summarizes these activities.

| Artist | Song |
|---|---|
| Hap Palmer | "Marching Around the Alphabet" |
| Sesame Street | "Elmo's Alphabet Rap" |
| Sesame Street | "Big Bird's ABC-DEF-GHI" |
| They Might Be Giants | "Alphabet of Nations" |
| Ziggy Marley | "ABC" |
| Super WHY!, PBS | "ABC, Sing with Me" |
| Go Fish | "The ABCs" |
| The Wiggles | "ABC" |
| Barenaked Ladies | "Crazy ABCs" |

Figure 4.9 Our Favorite ABC Songs

| | |
|---|---|
| **Songs** | "The Name Game" |
| | "Down by the Bay" |
| | "Willoughby Wallaby Woo" |
| | "Five Little Monkeys Jumping on the Bed" |
| | "I'm a Little Teapot" |
| | "The Ants Go Marching" |
| **Fingerplays** | "Five Little Pumpkins Sitting on a Gate" |
| | "Here is a Beehive" |
| | "Itsy, Bitsy Spider" |
| | "I'm Bringing Home a Baby Bumblebee" |
| | "Open, Shut Them" |
| | "This Old Man" |

Figure 4.10 Our Favorite Rhyming Songs and Fingerplays by Multiple Authors

| Type of Alphabet Instruction | Example Activities |
|---|---|
| Letter Identification | • Children hunt for letters with a reading pointer or magic wand.<br>• Children hunt for letters with a fly swatter with a hole cut out.<br>• Children hunt for letters with a sample letter written on sticky note.<br>• Children hunt for letters with a puppet or class mascot. |
| Letter-Sound Correspondence | • Children repeat an alliterative title or a phrase in the book and identify the same beginning sounds.<br>• Children repeat an assonant phrase from the book and identify the same beginning vowel sounds.<br>• Children listen throughout the reading for the teacher to say the target sound at the beginning of a word and respond as a group when they have heard it.<br>• Children repeat the target letter sound after the teacher using words with the same beginning sound. |
| Letter Formation | • Children write letters in the air with the teacher modeling from the book.<br>• Children write letters with their finger on a partner's back.<br>• Children write letters on an individual dry erase board.<br>• Children write letters on poster paper, a whiteboard, or Smart Board. |

Figure 4.11 Alphabet Activities During Read-Alouds

Read-aloud alphabet activities differ depending on the type of alphabet instruction you are planning—letter identification, letter-sound correspondence, or letter formation. Letter identification activities encourage children to hunt through a book to find examples of a target letter or letters. This allows the child hunting for letters additional practice and the teacher an informal assessment to determine if the child knows the letter or needs additional review. Letter-sound correspondence activities engage children in understanding the sounds the letters make. These activities work best with the whole class and include alliteration, assonance, and listening for specific letter sounds. Finally, letter formation activities in a whole group focus on giving children opportunities to write a target letter or letters using the book's print as a model.

The read-aloud can also be used for whole-group instruction in phonological awareness. Children at the beginning levels of phonological awareness can benefit from pulling out compound words in a book to look at how the two smaller words fit together to make a larger word. They can also examine how multiple words fit together to make a sentence by looking at the writing and spacing on the page and clapping, snapping, or tapping each word in the sentence to help count them out. If you are developing syllable awareness, then you can lead children in clapping, snapping, or tapping out the number of syllables in words that appear in the book you read either during or after reading.

When teaching rhyming, children's rhyming books work well because they provide an authentic context for examining rhyming words. Children can listen for rhyming words as you read and then indicate to you when they have heard them, or you can read the first part of a rhyming phrase and leave the second part blank for children to fill in. For example, when reading *Green Eggs and Ham* (Seuss 1960), you may read, "Not in a box. Not with a fox. Not in a house. Not with a _____ ," pausing and allowing children to fill in "mouse!" Reading and leaving the second rhyming word out enables the text to act as a scaffold for children to generate rhyme. Another trick while reading a rhyming text is to read the beginning phrase correctly but fill in an incorrect word in the spot where a rhyming word should go to see if children catch you. For example, you may incorrectly read, "Not in a box. Not with a fox. Not in a house. Not with a taco." Children will very quickly realize that what they heard does not sound correct, and they will delight in correcting your mistake!

For children ready for more advanced phonological awareness, the read-aloud can focus on isolating the beginning sounds in words or segmenting and blending all the sounds in words. Sometimes children's books will include gems of alliteration or assonance that can draw children's attention. In other books, you can have a target sound for children to listen for at the beginning of words as you read. All-pupil responses such as quietly raising a hand or putting a finger on the nose when target sounds are heard work well and don't disrupt the overall flow of reading. A great activity for during or after reading is modeling and guiding children as they stretch the individual sounds in a word and then blend them together. For example, when encountering the word *house* while reading, you may pause and comment, "Let's stretch and blend this word together, /h/ /ou/ /s/, /h/ /ou/ /s/. Now let's say it fast, *house.*" You can also do this activity after reading with a list of interesting words from the book to allow children more practice with stretching and blending.

## What Books Should I Read?

When targeting alphabet knowledge, any book with letters can work to call children's attention to the alphabet, but ABC books are those organized around the alphabet. Typically, ABC books are sequential, beginning with the letter *A* and ending at *Z*; occasionally an ABC book will start with *Z* and go backward to *A*. A third kind of ABC book tells a story involving the letters as characters in the plot. You can find an ABC book on almost any topic or unit of study—from dinosaurs to construction vehicles to sports to dolphins. One of us even has an ABC book on tugboats in her classroom library.

Likewise, there are many children's books that, when read, can be used to target phonological awareness. You can pull out any book with interesting words and character names to clap, tap, or snap the number of syllables. There are thousands of children's books that rhyme. We have listed some of our favorite rhyming books in Figure 4.12. We have included both narrative and informational texts that rhyme to help add to the diversity of your classroom library. Occasionally you can also find children's books with alliteration, especially in the title, to help students focus on beginning sounds in words.

| Literacy Skill | Narrative Texts | Informational Texts |
|---|---|---|
| Alphabetic Code | *AlphaOops! The Day Z Went First* by Alethea Kontis | *Alphabet Trucks* by Samantha Vamos |
| | *Once Upon an Alphabet: Short Stories for All the Letters* by Oliver Jeffers | *Bugs A to Z* by Caroline Lawton |
| | *Alphabet Adventure* by Audrey Wood | *Alphabet of Space* by Laura Galvin |
| | *Z Is for Moose* by Kelly Bingham | *Amazon Alphabet* by Johnette Downing |
| | *LMNO Peas* by Keith Baker | *K Is for Kick: A Soccer Alphabet* by Brad Herzog |
| | *Q Is for Duck: An Alphabet Guessing Game* by Mary Elting and Michael Folsom | *T Is for Teachers: A School Alphabet* by Steven Layne |
| Phonological Awareness | *Llama Llama Red Pajama* by Anna Dewdney | *Pumpkin Circle: The Story of a Garden* by George Levenson |
| | *Rhyming Dust Bunnies* by Jan Thomas | *Waiting for Wings* by Lois Ehlert |
| | *Scranimals* by Jack Prelutsky | *Firefighters! Speeding! Spraying! Saving!* by Patricia Hubbell |
| | *Jake Bakes Cakes* by Gerald Hawksley | *In the Tall, Tall Grass* by Denise Fleming |
| | *Favorite Nursery Rhymes from Mother Goose* by Scott Gustafson | *Science Verse* by Jon Scieszka |
| | *Bear's New Friend* by Karma Wilson | *Building with Dad* by Carol Nevius |

Figure 4.12 A Sample of Children's Books for Targeting Alphabet Knowledge and Phonological Awareness

# Technology Integration

When planning for student work at the classroom computers or iPads, there are some phenomenal gamelike programs that build alphabet knowledge and phonological awareness. The Public Broadcasting Service (PBS) strives to create educational programming for young children, and the PBS Kids website is no exception. The website includes educational games featuring many beloved characters from popular television shows. Many of these games build school-readiness skills, including literacy. Some of our favorites for building alphabet knowledge and phonological awareness are included in Figure 4.13.

| Website or App | Description |
|---|---|
| **Balloon Letters** (App) | • This app teaches children a target letter and then provides multi-lettered balloons and asks children to "pop" as many of the target letters as possible in the time given.<br>• The fast-paced action involved with this game is sure to engage children. |
| **ABC Preschool** (App) | This app introduces each letter to children with a same-sounding picture example and provides balloons for children to "pop" with each letter in a certain amount of time. |
| **Starfall** (Website and App) | • Available at starfall.com<br>• The website and app include an alphabet wall with options to sing along to the entire alphabet song or to click on individual letters to see several screens devoted to the letter with animation, sound, and activities. |
| **AlphaTots Alphabet** (App) | The app provides an introduction to each letter of the alphabet and includes an action that begins with the same sound as the letter for children to do, such as "build, "dig," and "stack," in a game format. |
| **Rhyming Words** (App) | • Children are given real photographs to match based on rhyme. The levels start off easy with two pairs of rhyming pictures and increase in difficulty to six pairs.<br>• The real photographs of familiar objects are colorful and engaging. |
| **Alpha Pig's Alpha-Bricks** (Website) | • Available on PBSKids.org<br>• Children help Alpha Pig build his house before the Big Bad Wolf blows it down by choosing target letters of the alphabet when given three letters from which to choose. |
| **Letters to Big Bird** (Website) | • Available on PBSKids.org<br>• Children help Big Bird select pictures of objects that begin with the letter he receives in his mailbox.<br>• Helps develop lettersound correspondence |

Figure 4.13  Popular Technology for Targeting Alphabet Knowledge and Phonological Awareness

| Website or App | Description |
|---|---|
| **Bear's Skateboard Park** (Website) | • Available on PBSKids.org<br>• Children help Bear ride over specific letters with his skateboard in order to spell a target word. |

Figure 4.13 (continued) Popular Technology for Targeting Alphabet Knowledge and Phonological Awareness

# Connecting with Families

Because both alphabet knowledge and phonological awareness are skills that take time to develop, they work well when children practice them a little bit each day. This accumulated learning is ideal for engaging parents at home in practicing both skills with their children. The key to home-based practice is making the activities fun, engaging, and simple to complete. Seeking a balance between familiar routine and choice on a weekly basis is also important. Families appreciate when they can expect a certain type of activity each week but also enjoy having a choice in the kinds of activities they complete. Therefore, we encourage you to create a weekly homework routine in which children complete the same activities with a different letter of the alphabet on some days and on other days select an activity to complete from among a set of options. Here are several activities designed for home practice.

## Alphabet Mystery Bag

When my son was in kindergarten, his teacher assigned this great project. Each week, one of the students went home carrying a brown bag with a note attached. The note indicated to the family what the target alphabet letter was and that they should fill the bag with objects from their home that start with the target letter sound. Then the child brought the bag back to school and showcased each object while the other children in the class decided which letter of the alphabet connected each object. This project targeted letter-sound correspondence but also developed children's oral language skills as they introduced their objects to the class.

## Alphabet or Rhyming Walk

A simple activity for families to do together is to walk and talk about the things they see. Families can take walks to look for things that begin with a target letter, or they can walk and look for things that rhyme. To document these conversations, you can ask children to draw a picture and label one or two of the things they saw on their walk.

## Alphabet Costume Parade

If you have a target letter or letter sound each week, one creative activity can be to ask families to create a simple letter costume for children to wear on a designated day of the week. For example, for the letter *L*, a simple idea is to have parents work with their child to find pictures in magazines of things that begin with the letter *L* and attach them with tape or a safety pin to their child's shirt. Children love to see what everyone else is wearing to school on the letter day!

## Reading with a Purpose

Parents can apply the same activities that you use in the classroom during your read-alouds. When reading together after school or at bedtime, parents can ask their children to look for target letters, complete rhyming phrases, or clap out syllables. When communicated clearly to parents at a back-to-school night or in a carefully crafted letter, read-aloud activities can be easily incorporated into bedtime reading routines with high impact on children's learning. To facilitate this process, it may be useful to offer parents the option of checking out book backpacks from your classroom. These backpacks can include ABC books and rhyming picture books that families may not have in their homes.

## Alphabet or Rhyming Memory Game

Many teachers we know send home alphabet letter flash cards for additional practice at home. To get the same practice in identifying letters of the alphabet in a more gamelike format, consider sending home alphabet cards with instructions for how to play the game Memory. If parents instruct their children to say the name of each letter as they flip over their letter cards, then the child is getting practice identifying letters without the drill-like pressure of flash cards. The same game can also be played with rhyming picture cards to target children's phonological awareness at home. If sending home rhyming picture cards, it is a good idea to identify each of the pictures in a letter to parents so that the rhymes are matched correctly.

## Class Alphabet Book

To engage children in an alphabet review at home, you can assign each child a letter of the alphabet. Send home a piece of construction paper with a letter written at the top in upper- and lowercase. Ask parents to help their children draw or find pictures in magazines of objects that begin with their letter. When you assemble all the pages together, your class has created a class alphabet book that can be read in a read-aloud or explored in small groups in the classroom library.

# Assessing Alphabet Awareness and Phonological Awareness

Children who have strong alphabet awareness and phonological awareness possess critical foundational skills to become strong readers and spellers. There is considerable evidence that the primary difference between good and poor readers lies in the good reader's phonological processing ability (Smith, Simmons, and Kame'enui 1998; Snow, Burns, and Griffin 1998), and that children with weak letter-naming ability and phonemic awareness tend to struggle with decoding and spelling tasks. Children who lack the knowledge of the separate sounds that make up words will struggle with basic decoding and encoding tasks. Looking ahead into their reading careers, we also know that deficits in these skills will affect children's fluency, vocabulary, comprehension, and reading motivation.

The good news is that, if caught early, defects are easy to fix through targeted, systematic, and explicit instruction (Adams 1990). Therefore it is critical that teachers assess individual students' alphabet knowledge and phonemic awareness in kindergarten and first grade, and that informal assessments are made available to them as a means to differentiate instruction. Figures 4.14 and 4.15 list and describe several research-based assessments for alphabet and phonological awareness.

| Assessment | Purpose |
|---|---|
| **Alphabet Recitation and Tracking** | Children are asked to point to, or track, the letters of the alphabet while they sing or recite the alphabet song. Students should be provided with an alphabet strip and should be asked to touch and name each letter. Assessors should anecdotally record the observations and use as a means for differentiated instruction. |
| **Uppercase Letter Naming** | Children are to name, or identify, each of the letters of the alphabet. Students can be provided with an Uppercase Letter Naming assessment, a Lowercase Letter Naming assessment, or a combination of both Upper- and Lowercase Letter Naming assessments. The goal of alphabet awareness instruction is letter-naming fluency. Students should identify and name the letters with ease and no hesitation. |
| **Lowercase Letter Naming** | |
| **Lowercase and Uppercase Letter Naming** | |

Figure 4.14  Alphabet Awareness Assessments

| Assessment | Purpose |
|---|---|
| **Rhyme Awareness** | Children are asked to listen for the larger "sound chunk" at the end of words, so that they can hear how words are alike and different. Students can be asked if two words rhyme by answering yes or no or, in a more difficult task, be asked to produce a rhyming word. |
| **Onset and Rime Awareness** | Children are asked to blend, or put together, a segmented onset and rime (/c/ /at/ = cat), or, in a more difficult task, to segment, or separate, the onset and rime in a word (cat =/c/ /at/). Children with onset and rime awareness are able to chop off that beginning sound and say the rest of the word. |
| **Syllable Awareness** | Children are asked if they can hear syllables, or word parts, in words. Students are asked to tell how many word parts are in each of the words presented. For example, if given the word *table*, students should be able to tell you it has two word parts. |
| **Initial Sound Isolation**<br><br>**Final Sound Isolation**<br><br>**Medial Sound Isolation** | Children are asked to isolate individual sounds at either the initial, final, or medial position. Students are given a pair of words orally and asked if they can hear the same sound at the beginning, middle, or end of both words. For example, if given the words *mat* and *cat*, they would be asked if they hear the same sound in the beginning, middle, or end of the word. Students should say the middle, as both words have the short /a/ sound in the middle. |
| **Blending Phonemes** | Children are asked to blend the sounds, or phonemes, together in a segmented word. For example, if given the sounds /s/ /t/ /o/ /p/, they would be required to blend those phonemes together and respond with the word *stop*. |
| **Segmenting Phonemes** | Children are asked to segment a word into individual sounds, or phonemes, when presented with a word. For example, if given the word *stop*, they would be required to segment the phonemes by responding with /s/ /t/ /o/ /p/. |
| **Yopp-Singer Test of Phonemic Awareness (Yopp 1995)** | Children are asked to segment a word into individual sounds, or phonemes. This instrument assesses children's full phonemic awareness ability; namely, segmenting phonemes. Students are given a twenty-two-item test and feedback as they progress through each word. If they answer correctly, the assessor can say "that's right" or "correct," and if they respond incorrectly, they are corrected. No partial credit is given. Students must segment each individual phoneme for credit. For example, if given the word *keep*, students should respond with /k/ /ee/ /p/. |

Figure 4.15 Phonological Awareness Assessments

## Summary

Children with strong alphabet knowledge and phonological awareness are well equipped to become readers and writers. Since the letters of the alphabet and their sounds are the foundation for all future literacy, it is critical that we use effective, developmentally appropriate methods for engaging students in learning. A combination of explicit instruction and play-based learning, when occurring in a print-rich environment, can have lasting effects on children. Children learn the alphabet and the ability to manipulate sounds when the skills are introduced systematically and explicitly in large-group formats and then practiced using hands-on activities in small-group settings.

Given the importance of developing students' knowledge in alphabet and phonological awareness, ongoing assessment of students' learning is important in order to track students' progress toward mastery of the skills. Both informal and formal measures can be used successfully to determine each child's level of mastery in order to plan targeted review and extra support for specific students. The good news is that if we catch students who fall behind with alphabet knowledge or phonological awareness early, then we can plan instruction and review that will help catch them up to grade-level expectations quickly.

## Chapter 5

# Practicing Word Recognition and Fluency

A s teachers, we think there is nothing as exciting as seeing a child become a reader. For some children, the process is fairly quick and painless. For others, it is slow, laborious, and extremely frustrating. As a classroom teacher, you either have been or will be confronted with students from both extremes and every variation in between. Because the path of becoming a proficient reader is highly individual, it is a challenging task for teachers to plan instruction that meets everyone's unique needs. Thus, we strongly advocate for the use of differentiated reading instruction in your classroom—instruction in which you use assessment data to group students by ability, plan distinct instruction for each group according to need, and frequently monitor students' progress in order to regroup and plan future instruction (Walpole and McKenna 2007). Learning to read is one of the most important academic tasks during childhood; therefore, it is one of your most important jobs as a teacher of young children.

## How Do Children Learn to Read?

Learning to read is a complex process employing multiple skills that must fit together perfectly. Teaching reading has been compared to rocket science—and rightly so! The process involves recognizing words printed in text. In order to recognize words, children use several resources.

Some words children recognize automatically by sight—these are called sight words. Children's sight word vocabularies can include their names, words of interest to them, and high-frequency words that teachers have taught them. By looking at the frequency of words in written English, researchers have created lists of high-frequency words by grade level (Fry 2004). Curriculum developers frequently use the Fry sight word list to introduce sight words by appropriate grade level (see Figure 5.1). Many times, high-utility words are also words that are hard to decode using phonics concepts. Words like *was*, *are*, and *saw* are hard to sound out; therefore, if children know them by sight, then they do not need to struggle over trying to sound them out. The most important thing about sight words is automaticity; readers should recognize sight words in less than one second. As children become more proficient readers, their sight word vocabularies will continue to grow.

| The | At | There | some | my |
|---|---|---|---|---|
| Of | Be | Use | her | than |
| And | This | An | would | first |
| A | Have | each | make | water |
| To | From | which | like | been |
| In | Or | she | him | call |
| Is | One | Do | into | who |
| you | Had | how | time | oil |
| that | By | their | has | now |
| It | Word | If | look | find |
| He | But | will | two | long |
| was | Not | Up | more | down |
| for | What | other | write | day |
| On | All | about | go | did |
| are | Were | out | see | get |
| As | We | many | number | come |
| with | When | then | no | made |
| his | Your | them | way | may |
| they | Can | these | could | part |
| I | Said | So | people | over |

**Figure 5.1** List of First 100 Fry Sight Words
Adapted from Fry (2004)

Some words children do not recognize by sight. Since beginning readers have limited sight word vocabularies, they rely on decoding unfamiliar words in print. *Decoding* is the term for sounding out the individual phonemes in words. For example, when confronted with the word *cat* in print, a beginning reader may slowly read "/c/ /a/ /t/." The physical process of sounding out is made up of segmenting and blending, skills we discussed Chapter 4. Children first develop the ability to segment and blend sounds in words unrelated to print, which is why phonological awareness is a crucial foundational skill for learning to read.

Decoding the sounds in words also follows a developmental sequence. Children first begin to decode sound by sound. In order to do this, they must have a good understanding of the alphabetic principle—that each letter has a consistent sound. Children apply this understanding to sound out each letter in a word. As children gain more experience reading, they begin to recognize letter combinations (ch, th, sh, ph) and word families (-at, -og, -ip). Being able to recognize sounds in chunks enables beginning readers to spend less time decoding and ultimately to read faster. This process becomes even faster when children start to decode by syllable chunks, breaking multisyllabic words like *elephant* into more manageable pieces.

The speed with which readers read is one attribute of what is called fluency. Reading fluency involves not only the speed at which readers decode, but also the accuracy of that decoding and the ability to add expression to what has been read (Rasinski 2010)—using language easily and accurately. Expression is often key for understanding the context of the text and its meaning. Research indicates that oral reading fluency supports reading comprehension. It makes sense that readers struggling to decode every sound encountered in text have less cognitive energy to focus on actually understanding what they've read. The flip side is that if readers can quickly decode and recognize word meaning, then they have more cognitive capacity to focus on understanding. Researchers have developed fluency scales such as that developed by Hasbrouk and Tindal (2006), which measures words read correctly by minute (WCPM) and based on students' grade level (see Figure 5.2).

Once readers have sounded out a word, segmented the sounds, and then blended them back together again, word recognition is the next step. It is not enough just to sound out a word. If readers do not know what the word means, they will also struggle to comprehend the text. Thus, readers must draw on both vocabulary knowledge and comprehension ability to complete the entire reading process. In many ways, all the concepts we have addressed in the preceding chapters build toward this chapter. Successful readers know the letters of the alphabet and the corresponding sounds, have strong foundations in oral language and vocabulary knowledge, and know different comprehension strategies to use in order to understand what they are reading. Once children can wield these skills simultaneously and seamlessly, they can become fluent readers.

| Grade | Percentile | Fall WCPM | Winter WCPM | Spring WCPM |
|-------|-----------|-----------|-------------|-------------|
| 1 | 90 | | 81 | 111 |
| | 75 | | 47 | 82 |
| | 50 | | 23 | 53 |
| | 25 | | 12 | 28 |
| | 10 | | 6 | 15 |
| 2 | 90 | 106 | 125 | 142 |
| | 75 | 79 | 100 | 117 |
| | 50 | 51 | 72 | 89 |
| | 25 | 25 | 42 | 61 |
| | 10 | 11 | 18 | 31 |
| 3 | 90 | 128 | 146 | 162 |
| | 75 | 99 | 120 | 137 |
| | 50 | 71 | 92 | 107 |
| | 25 | 44 | 62 | 78 |
| | 10 | 21 | 36 | 48 |
| 4 | 90 | 145 | 166 | 180 |
| | 75 | 119 | 139 | 152 |
| | 50 | 94 | 112 | 123 |
| | 25 | 68 | 87 | 98 |
| | 10 | 45 | 61 | 72 |

Figure 5.2 Hasbrouck and Tindal's (2006) Oral Reading Fluency Norms by Grade Level

# What Does Instruction Look Like?

Figure 5.3 provides a preview of instructional methods described in this chapter for fostering children's word recognition and reading fluency. In the sections that follow, each instructional method will be developed and explained so that you can begin implementing the strategies in your own classroom.

| Instructional Method | Format | Characteristics | Strengths |
|---|---|---|---|
| **Word Work** | Small Groups or Centers | Teacher works with a small group of students who have similar literacy needs to introduce and reinforce particular word recognition and fluency skills. | • Differentiated instruction is highly effective because it is based on student need.<br>• Maximizes teacher attention for each small group |
| **Reading Groups** | Small Groups | Teacher works with small group of students who have similar reading needs to read and discuss the same narrative or informational selection. | Differentiated instruction is effective for meeting the students' needs and giving them practice reading texts at their level. |
| **Repeated Reading** | Small Groups or Individuals | Students work individually, with a partner, or with a teacher to read the same text multiple times in order to track and increase reading fluency. | Charting student progress in graph form is highly motivating for students to set goals and see improvement. |
| **Reader's Theater** | Whole Group or Small Group | Students work in small groups or as a class to rehearse by rereading scripts and perform the piece in front of an informal or formal audience. | Highly engaging and motivating as it provides an authentic context for rereading |
| **Centers Activities** | Small Group or Individuals | Students work together or individually at literacy centers to gain additional practice with target phonics skills, high-frequency words, or oral reading fluency. | • Students work at their own pace.<br>• Centers can be creative and engaging while providing needed opportunities for practice and review of skills introduced in small groups. |
| **Technology Integration** | Small Group or Centers | Various websites and apps designed to target word recognition | • Good review activity<br>• High student engagement<br>• Potential to foster twenty-first-century technology skills |
| **Connecting with Families** | Multiple | Parents reinforce word recognition in the home. | • Fosters home-school connection.<br>• Provides reading practice outside of classroom context. |

Figure 5.3 Preview of Instructional Methods in this Chapter

# Word Work

There are many commercial curricula available that advertise themselves as word work. We take a broad view of word work to include multiple formats—whole-group, small-group, or centers work—in which children are consciously examining the patterns in words. Word work is particularly effective as it fosters students' word recognition and spelling skills simultaneously (Bear et al. 2011). Word work has been adapted and applied in many different ways across elementary schools. In this section, we will describe how we see word work fitting in best with balanced reading instruction in which you are also developing students' phonological awareness, vocabulary, oral language, comprehension, and writing.

While it is certainly true that your language arts curriculum, whether it is a basal reading anthology or an isolated phonics package, will have lessons for introducing a phonics skill or concept to the whole class, we know that you have in your classroom students who are not yet ready for that particular phonics skill, students who are on level for it, and students who have already surpassed it. Therefore, differentiating your word recognition instruction for small groups of students who need the same skill just makes sense. The problem for commercial curriculum writers is that they do not know your students' strengths and needs. It really falls to you, as the expert on your students' literacy needs, to design the very best small-group instruction for your particular students. No one else knows your students like you do.

In order to plan for needs-based, small-group instruction, it is imperative that you begin with meaningful assessment data. Depending on the grade level at which you teach, you may begin assessing at a different skill level and then have the flexibility to go up or down depending on the student's performance. As a rule of thumb, we would begin with phonological awareness and letter-naming assessments in preschool; letter naming, phoneme segmentation, and sight-word recognition assessments in kindergarten; and phonics concepts, sight-word recognition, and oral reading fluency assessments in first through third grades. However, these are general starting points. We know that some students will be struggling readers, and the best way to assess their current knowledge is to move to a different skill test.

Armed with data of individual students' literacy skills, the next step is to group students based on need. Creating a chart to track all students' assessment scores on the same piece of paper can quickly show you visually which students are scoring similarly on assessments. When you first look at the data, it will be easy to see the patterns of low, middle, and high achievers in your class. On your second look at the data, you will notice those students who are falling somewhere in between. These students may score high in one area but not another. These are the students who are more difficult to group. The good news is that groups should not be bound for eternity; in other words, if you place a student in a group and realize you made the wrong decision, then you should by all means regroup that student the very next day. We are big proponents of grouping, reassessing, and then regrouping often as students make progress. In fact, if students are sticking in the same group over time, then that may be an indicator that you are not helping them to progress as they should.

Once you have your small groups organized, the next step is to plan instruction based on the groups' needs. Again, the content of this instruction varies greatly from group to group. Walpole and McKenna (2007) recommend selecting two areas of literacy for each group to target. For example, based on assessment data, you may see that one group could use support with phonological awareness and phonics and a different group could benefit from instruction in phonics and oral reading fluency. Once you have your areas to target, you are ready to plan for fifteen to twenty minutes of explicit, teacher-led, small-group instruction.

To target students' word recognition skills, we use the same instructional methods—(1) segmenting and blending and (2) sorting—as discussed in Chapter 4. These instructional methods can be used effectively to teach phonics concepts important for word recognition. When using segmenting and blending for phonological awareness, we say words orally and ask children to move chips, coins, or counters using Elkonin boxes. For word work, we ask children to segment and blend written words and to move alphabet letters when using Elkonin boxes. The use of written letters moves this instructional activity from phonological awareness into phonics development. During small-group instruction, it is important to show a written word card, say the word, and model segmenting the sounds and blending them back together as one word. We recommend using the gradual release of responsibility model, where you first model the process, then ask students to work together with you or with partners to practice the same process, and then finally ask students to work independently to segment and blend the same list of words.

Sorting is a powerful instructional method, for it enables students to explore the patterns in words and to make comparisons in order to group words based on similarities. The patterns students identify in words relate to the phonics concepts you have chosen to introduce to them. For example, if you are working on beginning blends with a small group of kindergartners, you may give them a list of words beginning with the "tr" blend, such as *train, tray, trip, tram, try,* and *trap,* and words beginning with the "br" blend, such as *brown, broke, break, brake, brick,* and *brush,* to sort. There are different kinds of sorts, including modeled sorts, where you as the teacher model the sort as students watch and help, and open sorts, where students work either in groups or independently to create their own groups based on characteristics they are seeing in the words (Bear et al. 2011). Sorts can be done using word cards for students to physically sort on their desks, word work journals or dry erase boards for students to write words in columns, or technology for students to sort words on an iPad, computer, or Smart Board screen. Whether you use a modeled or open sort in your instruction, it is important to build time into your small-group instruction for students to discuss with you why they sorted as they did and to verbalize the characteristics the words in each group have in common. This reflection of word features is at the heart of word work.

At this point you may be asking yourself, "Where do the words that I am segmenting and blending or sorting come from?" Again the answer lies in your assessment data. The types of words and the kinds of phonics skills you are targeting should come from your evaluation of which skills students still need based on assessment data. Figure 5.4 provides a developmental continuum of phonics concepts.

| | Phonics Concept | Examples |
|---|---|---|
| **Easier Skills** | Beginning Consonants | m, b, d, r, s |
| | Ending Consonants | t, d, m, r, s |
| | Beginning and Ending Consonant Blends | bl, pl, cl, tr, fr |
| | Digraphs | ch, th, ph, sh |
| | Short Vowels | a, e, i, o, u |
| | Long Vowels | a_e, i_e, ea, ee, ai |
| | Diphthongs | oi, oy, ow |
| **More Difficult Skills** | *R*-controlled Vowels | ar, ir, ur, er |

Figure 5.4  Phonics Skills Developmental Continuum

In addition to targeting phonics concepts, word recognition instruction also includes building students' high-frequency word vocabularies. Instruction focused on high-frequency words involves repetition. Depending on the grade level you teach, you may choose to target one or two words per small group with younger students or three to five words per small group with older students. Repetition may involve reading words in different formats—chanting, choral reading, echo reading, partner reading, whisper reading, even reading the words in different voices, such as a loud lion voice or a squeaky mouse voice. Flash cards work well to build in the necessary review and serve as an informal assessment for you as to which words students can truly recognize by sight. We also recommend adding high-frequency words to your classroom word wall or to individual word folders at students' desks for use during reading and writing projects.

# Reading Groups

Using part of your small-group time to work with students grouped by reading level is a worthwhile activity, for it targets students' individual reading needs. Not all readers in your classroom will be ready to read the same books. Thus, it makes sense to differentiate reading groups by ability. While there are many leveled reading programs available, including the well-known Guided Reading program (Fountas and Pinnell 2012), the structure can be used with class book sets from your own classroom library. The key to making reading groups work is having a variety of books on a range of topics and difficulty levels. Figure 5.5 summarizes the types of books needed for specific kinds of readers.

For emerging readers, particularly those in kindergarten, reading groups work well with short, decodable texts. Decodable texts are books that control for length, vocabulary, and phonics skills. For example, it is easy to tell that the text *The Fat Cat Sat on the Mat* (Karlin 1996) focuses on the -at word family, repeating many words using the same phonics concept. It is important to provide opportunities for students to practice reading words with the same target phonics concept introduced in students' word work instruction. Thus, a kindergarten teacher may have one small group working on the -at word family and reading *The Fat Cat Sat on the Mat*, and a different group working on the short vowel /e/ sound during word work and reading *Ten Men* (Maslen 1987). Instructional purposes for reading groups with emerging readers include practice reading phonics concepts in connected text and building confidence as readers. As the teacher leading the group, you can read the book together with students using a variety of reading formats—choral, echo, partner, and whisper—and call students' attention to words with phonics concepts they know.

As readers become more confident, possess a larger sight word vocabulary, and decode words more quickly, reading instruction switches to focus on building oral reading fluency. Teachers working with readers at this level need books that are longer, use more vocabulary words, and have a more advanced plot. There are several series that are ideal for beginning readers—the Elephant and Piggie books by Mo Willems are humorous and endearing, the Frog and Toad books by Arnold Lobel are classic tales of friendship, the Fly Guy books by Tedd Arnold are funny and relatable, and the Henry and Mudge books by Cynthia Rylant tell relatable stories using the endearing characters of a boy and his loyal dog. As the teacher working with beginning readers, you can practice reading in different formats, discuss new vocabulary words encountered in text, and develop comprehension.

| Type of Reader | Type of Book | Example Series |
|---|---|---|
| **Emerging** | Decodable Books | Bob Books by Bobby Maslen<br>*The Fat Cat Sat on the Mat* by Nurit Karlin<br>Reading A-Z Decodable Books, www.readinga-z.com<br>Starfall Learn to Read Books, www.starfall.com |
| **Building Fluency** | Beginning Readers | *Chicken Said, "Cluck!"* by Judyann Grant (My First I Can Read series)<br>Elephant and Piggie by Mo Willems<br>Fly Guy by Tedd Arnold<br>Frog and Toad by Arnold Lobel<br>Henry and Mudge by Cynthia Rylant<br>Mr. Putter and Tabby by Cynthia Rylant<br>Pete the Cat by James Dean |
| **Comprehending** | Chapter Books | A to Z Mysteries by Ron Roy<br>Ballpark Mysteries by David A. Kelly<br>Black Lagoon by Mike Thaler<br>Cam Jansen by David A. Adler<br>Captain Underpants by Dav Pilkey<br>Flat Stanley by Jeff Brown<br>Judy Moody by Megan McDonald<br>Magic Tree House by Mary Pope Osborne<br>Mercy Watson by Kate DiCamillo<br>Nate the Great by Marjorie Sharmat<br>The Time Warp Trio by Jon Scieszka<br>A Series of Unfortunate Events by Lemony Snicket<br>Stink by Megan McDonald |

**Figure 5.5** Children's Books Ideal for Reading Groups

Finally, readers who are at grade-level targets for oral reading fluency need instruction targeting vocabulary and comprehension (Walpole and McKenna 2007). You can allow these readers to choose from a wide variety of longer narrative and informational texts and more developed chapter books. There are many well-known authors who specialize in writing chapter books for this level of reader, including Beverly Cleary, Judy Blume, David Adler, and Mike Thaler. There are also many new series that are extremely popular with elementary children, including Judy Moody, Stink, Nate the Great, Magic Tree House, and Captain Underpants. As a teacher, it may be tempting to leave this group of students to read independently as you focus your attention on struggling readers; however, these independent readers benefit from instruction to build vocabulary and develop comprehension strategies. Since vocabulary and comprehension are unconstrained skills (Paris 2009), they have no end limit—children can continue to learn and develop them throughout their academic careers. Independent readers can benefit from instruction that pushes them to learn new and more advanced skills.

It can be tricky to manage reading groups of different reading abilities within the same classroom. Depending on the collaboration among your grade-level team, you may consider dividing and conquering with the other teachers. Grouping students across classrooms can be fun for students and allows each teacher to concentrate planning and instruction on one particular reading group. If collaborative grouping is not a possibility, consider the other adults in your classroom. Do you have help from other professionals or parent volunteers? In some classrooms, all reading groups occur simultaneously with different adult leaders. In other models, the teacher works with each reading group separately while other groups are exploring literacy centers, listening to books on audio recordings, or engaging in word work, writing, or independent reading (Boushey and Moser 2006; Diller 2007). Figure 5.6 shows a student self-selecting a book from the classroom library for independent reading.

We would like to include a quick word about student awareness of ability grouping. Let's face it, no matter how hard you try, even first graders are quickly aware of who the advanced readers in the class are and who are the slower readers. In our experience, this awareness can become a problem when students in one group see something that another group is doing and become envious. This can be easily avoided when you make sure that your lesson plans for each reading group are equally interesting, engaging, and challenging. For example, it is disheartening and simply unfair to only use laptops with one high reading group and never with a lower reading group. Instead, consider how you can use laptops for different tasks with different reading-ability groups. For example, one teacher we know used laptops with all her reading groups by selecting different websites with appropriate levels of reading for each group. As long as students are

**Figure 5.6** A Student Selects a Book from the Classroom Library

interested and motivated in their reading groups, they will not become envious of another group's experience.

# Repeated Reading

As the adage goes, practice makes perfect. This certainly holds true for reading. The more children practice reading, the better they will become at automatic word recognition, decoding multisyllabic words, and reading fluently with speed and expression. One instructional method for engaging children in the practice they need is repeated reading (Rasinski and Blachowicz 2012). Repeated reading can take on multiple forms in the classroom, but at its core is practice reading the same text several times.

Repeated reading in small groups can occur when you lead your small group using different reading formats—choral, echo, partner, and whisper. Choral reading offers the most support to the reader and occurs when everyone in the group reads the same text together. Echo reading releases a little responsibility over to the students. Echo reading occurs when you read the text first, pausing at appropriate spots to allow children to read back what you just read. Releasing still more responsibility to the readers, partner reading involves pairs of children reading to one another. Typically in partner reading, students will sit facing one another and one child will read one paragraph or one page of text while the partner listens and offers support, then the partners switch roles for the next paragraph or page of text. While students are partner reading, you as the teacher can provide support for difficult words and informally assess students' oral reading fluency. Finally, whisper reading releases the most responsibility to the students. Whisper reading occurs when students reread the same passage quietly to themselves. Rather than read completely silently, children whisper read so that you can hear that they are indeed on task and can provide support when needed. A tool that works well for whisper reading in small groups is a whisper phone, either purchased or made out of a curved piece of PVC pipe from a local hardware store. The whisper phone enables students to hear themselves read loud and clear without disturbing other readers around them.

Within a small-group setting, you can engage students in repeated reading by selecting a text and using the sequence of choral, echo, partner, and whisper reading. The text should be chosen carefully based on the phonics concept that the group is currently learning. For example, if one of your small groups is working on *r*-controlled vowels, then a good choice of text would be a decodable book that repeats words with the *r*-controlled vowel feature. This connects the word recognition instruction in your small group to the oral reading fluency-practice portion of your small group, reinforcing the word recognition lesson and providing practice in an authentic reading context.

Repeated reading can also refer to instances when a student works independently to read and reread a passage of text while self-timing for speed (see Figure 5.7). The students can chart progress over time to see if their reading speed improves. By keeping a visual bar graph of each reading time, the student can see how practice in repeatedly reading the same piece of text helps improve fluency. The practice of charting progress over time sends a powerful message to students and enables them to work toward a personal goal in reading.

# Reader's Theater

Reader's theater (Rasinski, Homan, and Biggs 2009) provides an authentic context for repeated reading because students reread in order to practice for a culminating performance. Unlike a theater production in which students memorize lines to speak, reader's theater involves students reading from a written script. Because students are reading and then rereading the same script, reader's theater offers students oral reading fluency practice.

In order to use reader's theater in the classroom, you will need a script. There are many scripts already crafted for use in the classroom available online and published

**Figure 5.7** A Student Reading Independently to Improve Fluency

in professional collections. Many of these scripts come from popular children's literature; however, there are also scripts for use across content areas. For example, we have seen reader's theater used with great success during a social studies unit to reinforce the content of the pilgrims' experience in the New World and at the same time providing meaningful reading practice. There are reader's theater scripts available on a wide range of social studies topics as well as science concepts. Of course, you can also use reader's theater as a connection to writing instruction when you engage students in writing their own scripts. We recommend beginning the process by adapting a familiar story such as a folktale or fairy tale before branching out and allowing students to creatively write completely from scratch.

When selecting scripts for reader's theater, consider your students' interests and the suitability for performance. You want to find a script that will interest students, since they will be rereading their roles several times prior to performance. We have found that elementary students particularly like scripts with humor, interesting characters, and lots of action. Also, consider the number of substantive speaking roles so that everyone in the class or in a small group will have an equal speaking role and, ultimately, more practice reading. You may also want to consider whether there are roles for students who need a little extra challenge and roles for students who need more manageable roles that will give them practice reading but not embarrass them in front of their peers.

Students will need class time to read their scripts both individually—to practice their roles—and in groups—to practice the flow of the roles together. The amount of class time depends on the length of the script and the type of performance. Frequently, an informal class performance at the front of the classroom is all you need. However, occasionally it is rewarding to make the performance more formal by inviting an audience of other grades in the school or even parents and other caregivers. Typically, students enjoy brainstorming ideas for costumes, small props, and sound effects for more formal performances; however, remember that the instructional purpose of a reader's theater is, first and foremost, to give students practice with oral reading.

## Centers Activities

Well-designed literacy centers (Diller 2003; Morrow and Gambrell 2011) can add valuable hours of word recognition and oral reading fluency practice. The best literacy centers are consistent, meaning you have the same centers each day so that students come to expect them as part of their routine. The best centers are also differentiated, meaning that not every group does the same thing at each center. For example, when one group arrives at the word work center, there should be a task for them targeting review of the phonics skills they are working on with you in teacher-led, small-group instruction; this task should be different for each ability group. In addition, literacy centers should include meaningful work—beyond busywork—and interesting work—practice that doesn't simply rely on worksheets. It is always a good idea to have several activities for each center so that if students finish one activity they can begin another one, using all of their center time productively and with less interruption to you.

There are multiple centers in which students can meaningfully practice word recognition and oral reading fluency skills. Figure 5.8 describes several important literacy centers. A word work center is the most obvious. In a word work center, students can engage in a variety of activities that directly target the phonics and high-frequency words taught in your teacher-led, small-group instruction. For example, in Figure 5.9 a second grader is practicing reading sight words by swatting the target bug with the fly swatter. Figure 5.10 summarizes several activities that can be used with a variety of phonics concepts to keep students engaged and practicing during a student-led center time.

| Center | Purpose |
|---|---|
| **Word Work** | Students work in small groups or independently to complete activities that practice the word recognition concepts (phonics or sight words) taught during small-group instruction. |
| **Listening** | Students listen to narrative and informational texts read on audio recordings in order to be exposed to models of fluent reading. |
| **Classroom Library/ Reading** | Students choose texts that they want to read either to a partner or independently. |
| **Technology** | Students play games on a Smart Board, laptop, desktop, or tablet designed to practice word recognition skills. |
| **Writing** | Students write in writing notebooks or journals, ultimately applying their understanding of word work in their own writing. |

**Figure 5.8** Literacy Centers for Word Recognition and Oral Reading Fluency

**Figure 5.9** A Second Grader Practicing Sight Words in a Learning Center

| Activity | Description |
|---|---|
| **Independent Sorts** | Students sort the same words sorted during teacher-led, small-group instruction. They can sort with a partner or independently. They can sort, sort and glue, or even write their sort. |
| **Word Work Notebooks** | Students keep word work notebooks to write sorts and reflect on what patterns they are seeing that help them sort as they do. The reflection is key to developing deeper student understanding. |
| **Word Hunts** | Students hunt through magazines or books to find the phonics concepts or high-frequency words they are studying. |
| **File Folder Board Games** | Teachers create file folder games with simple paths for students to follow as they roll dice and progress around the board. The words chosen for the board can involve any phonics concept or pattern needed for review. As students land on the piece, they can read the word aloud or discuss the pattern. |
| **Memory** | Students can play the Memory game with pairs of word cards that involve the phonics skills needed for review. For example, cards could include words with *r*-controlled vowels. As students flip over cards, they read the words and determine if they have found a match. |
| **Bingo** | Students play Bingo with Bingo boards containing words with targeted phonics concepts. One student can elect to be the caller, reading words for the other students to find on their boards. |
| **Build-a-Word Cubes** | Using paper cubes or purchased cubes featuring word families, students roll the cube and then generate a list of as many words as they can think of that contain that word ending. Students can record words on dry erase boards or paper. |
| **Flip Books or Word Wheels** | Students create flip books or word wheels containing word beginnings that can be applied to the same word ending or word endings that can be applied to the same word beginning. |
| **Go Fish** | Students play the Go Fish card game with cards that contain words using targeted phonics concepts. |
| **Pocket Chart or Smart Board Interactives** | Students use picture or word cards to sort words introduced in teacher-led, small group instruction. Students can complete the same sort using an interactive Smart Board. |

Figure 5.10  Word Work Center Activities

If you have access to listening equipment, such as headphones and CD players, a listening center can be a great place for students to listen to models of fluent reading. A well-stocked listening center will have both narrative and informational book recordings as well as written copies so students can follow along as they listen. One alternative to purchasing books on tape or CD is to create your own by recording yourself reading. This can also be a task for a parent volunteer or a project for an upper-level elementary class in your school building.

A classroom library or reading center can give students necessary practice reading connected text. It is important to set aside some time of your classroom day for students to be able to choose their own texts. Self-selection goes a long way toward motivating students and instilling a joy of reading. Whether you teach a preschool classroom in which students can choose books and look at the pictures or an elementary classroom in which students can read texts, a classroom library full of books is crucial. At a reading center, students should be aware of behavior expectations. Creating reading center guidelines, going over them, posting them where they are easily visible, and reviewing them periodically will help ensure that all students are actively reading during their time there. To help students read productively during center time, many teachers create a system for organizing books so that children can quickly identify a text that is just right for them. One teacher we worked with spent a lot of time color-coding her library so that students in different ability groups knew which color book to choose. Another teacher we have observed uses baskets labeled for each group during centers time. Whichever method you decide, keep in mind that students like choice and variety (Diller 2003). In addition, you may want to consider creating an accountability task, such as writing in response to a book, for students to complete after reading. However, we believe that while accountability tasks are important, they should be used sparingly so as not to diminish students' motivation.

If you have technology in your classroom, a technology center can also offer many opportunities for students to practice phonics and word recognition skills. There are several programs and websites that offer literacy games or online decodable texts for students to read. We discuss some of these in the section that follows on technology. With a teacher account, you can access many of the most popular leveled-reader websites, which also offer student tracking so you can see the progress students make as they move up the leveled readers. If you have a Smart Board in your classroom, consider allowing students to practice their word sorts together at the Smart Board during centers time. This is an often overlooked but popular activity with students of all ages.

Finally, a writing center is also important for developing students' word recognition. Because reading and writing are closely connected, opportunities to practice writing mean practice with word recognition. As students are figuring out how to write a word, they are using the same processes of segmenting and blending used in decoding. While writing, students should be responsible for correctly spelling high-frequency words that have been taught to them. Periodically collecting and analyzing student writing samples is a valuable informal assessment of their progress in applying phonics concepts correctly.

## Classroom Vignette: Small-Group Word Work

Mrs. Hatcher has been teaching first grade for many years. She loves the enthusiasm her first graders bring to every new task, and she especially loves watching them learn to read. In order to meet the unique needs of each of her students, Mrs. Hatcher dedicates a large chunk of her language and literacy block to small-group instruction.

Over the years, Mrs. Hatcher has experimented with different management techniques to enable small-group instruction to run smoothly in her classroom. For example, she organizes desks into pods of four and assigns seats so that groups of students sit together, travel together through small group and centers, and have an assigned color—red, blue, green, or yellow. All the materials for each group are color-coded in the center so that the red group knows to collect materials from the red tub, the blue group from the blue tub, and so forth. A group leader is chosen each week as one of the classroom jobs, and during centers, the week's group leader wears a color-coded visor so that he or she is easily visible, both so Mrs. Hatcher can identify noisy or disruptive groups and so students leaving and reentering the classroom can quickly find their team.

An important part of managing centers and independent group work is to establish a routine early in the school year. For the first two weeks of the school year, Mrs. Hatcher had her students go through the motions of working in centers to adjust to expectations at each center. The class discussed rules for working in each center and role-played what would be examples of good and not-so-good behavior. Mrs. Hatcher created an accountability system for behavior, clearly defining how good behavior would be rewarded in her classroom and how not-so-good behavior would be recorded and result in varying levels of action. Mrs. Hatcher knows that putting the time in up front to establish routines is crucial for getting first graders to work efficiently and productively during centers time.

Let's sit in on Mrs. Hatcher's small-group and centers time today. In one corner of the classroom, the red group is quietly sitting on the rug in the classroom library. When centers began, the students quickly went to the library and looked through a red tub of books selected for them. Mary chose a Henry and Mudge beginning reader, and Susan is reading a book on dolphins. Also on the rug, Paul and Mulan are taking turns partner-reading a Frog and Toad chapter book. When the timer goes off, warning the groups they have two minutes remaining, the members of the red group record what they read in their reading logs and whether they liked it or not.

When the timer rings again, indicating that the first centers rotation is complete, the groups quietly stop what they are doing and put their hands on their heads. They look to Mrs. Hatcher for the signal

## Classroom Vignette: Small-Group Word Work (continued)

that it is time to move to a new location in the classroom. Mrs. Hatcher nods and says in a singsong voice, "Ladies and gentlemen, time to switch!" On her verbal cue, the groups move to their next spot without any loss of time. This time the red group is working with Mrs. Hatcher at the teacher's group table. For her small-group instruction with the red group, Mrs. Hatcher has planned a lesson to introduce a new phonics concept and practice oral reading fluency.

Mrs. Hatcher begins, "Good morning, red group! Today we are going to be talking about words that have an *r*-controlled vowel. Sometimes *r* can be very bossy, and bossy *r* likes to change the sound that the vowel makes. Let's look at the word *car*. What vowel do you see in this word?" Devon indicates that she sees the letter *A*. "That's right, an *a*. We know that an *a* usually makes the short /a/ sound or the long /a/ sound, but in this word the a does not make either of those sounds. In the word *car*, the *r* is right behind the *a* and that bossy *r* is changing the *a*'s sound. Do you hear the /r/ sound in the word *car*? Yes! Today we are going to be sorting words that have the short /a/ sound like in the word *cat*, words that have the long /a/ sound like in the word *game*, and words that have the *r*-controlled vowel sound like in the word *car*."

Mrs. Hatcher continues by modeling the sort for students using word cards and a small pocket chart. "I am going to put my headings at the top of the three columns. Now, here is the word *hat*. I hear the short /a/ sound like in the word *cat*, so I am going to put the word *hat* under the *cat* column. Here is the word *far*. /f/ /ar/. I hear the *r*-controlled vowel sound like in the word *car*, so I am going to put the word *far* in this column with *car*." Mrs. Hatcher models the entire sort, and then continues, "Now I am going to ask Mary and Mulan to work together to sort the words and Paul and Susan to work together to sort *this* group of words." As the students sort, Mulan says to Mary, "*Far* . . . that sounds like *car*, let's put it in this column." When Mary agrees, the students consider more words.

Once students have completed their sort, Mrs. Hatcher leads them in discussion. "Susan, can you read the words you have in the short *a* column while we all read along? Let's listen for the short /a/ sound in each of the words." Susan reads, "Cat, bat, rat, sat, hat, and mat." Mrs. Hatcher asks the group, "Did she have them all correct? Yes. What did all of those words have in common, Paul?" Paul explains, "All the words have the /a/ sound." Mrs. Hatcher continues, "That's right, they all have the short /a/ sound like in the word *hat*." After the students have checked their sorts and discussed what vowel sounds each column of words share, Mrs. Hatcher reminds students that they will be repeating the sort and gluing it in their word journals during their word work center time.

Next, Mrs. Hatcher quickly moves into the reading part of her small-group instruction. She passes out individual copies of a decodable text that repeats words with the *r*-controlled vowel pattern. She asks students to chorally read the book with her first. Then she asks students to go back through the book and highlight all the -ar words they see on each page. Once students have done this, they whisper read the book again as Mrs. Hatcher listens and offers support when students struggle.

**Classroom Vignette: Small-Group Word Work (continued)**

When the timer goes off, the red group moves next to the word work center where they independently re-sort the words they just sorted with Mrs. Hatcher. Once the sort is complete, they glue the sort into their word work journals and write a sentence underneath to explain why they sorted how they did. Since Paul and Susan finish early, they begin to play a Memory game using *r*-controlled vowels that Mrs. Hatcher placed in their red word work tub. When Mulan and Mary finish their sorts, they decide to play a file folder board game, rolling dice and landing on words that contain *r*-controlled vowels to read aloud.

When the timer goes off again, the red group travels to its final center of the day—the listening center. The members of the red group each place headphones over their ears and read along in their own copy of *Jumanji* (Van Allsburg 1981) as they listen to the story being read to them. The students are mesmerized as the exciting tale of fantasy unfolds. When the timer goes off for the final time, the students wait for Mrs. Hatcher's cue and then return the materials to their place before returning to their desks for the next part of the day.

During the course of her centers period, Mrs. Hatcher has met with all four groups. She has worked on different phonics skills with each group, while also allowing students to practice applying phonics concepts by repeatedly reading connected text in multiple formats. By traveling to each center, the groups have all repeated their sort at the word work center and played a game or two to reinforce the same phonics concepts. The groups have had time in the reading center to choose books that interest them and to practice their oral reading fluency, and they have enjoyed listening to a fluent model of an award-winning children's fantasy being read to them at the listening center. Each activity has furthered students' word recognition and oral reading-fluency development by targeting their level of need.

# Technology Integration

There are many websites and applications that offer students valuable practice with phonics concepts and high-frequency word recognition. Given the gamelike formats, students are likely to be highly engaged while reviewing concepts such as beginning blends, short vowel sounds, or sight words. These games can be played in the classroom during literacy centers or at home for additional practice. Online resources also offer a wide variety of free decodable texts for leveled reading groups and practice with oral reading fluency. Often, language arts curricula come with a limited collection of books for each leveled reading group; therefore, dependable resources with high-quality leveled readers can be an affordable way to supplement your decodable text library. Figure 5.11 provides a list of resources for building students' word recognition and oral reading fluency skills.

| Website or App | Description |
|---|---|
| **Blending Bowl**<br>(Website) | • Available on PBS.org<br>• Children choose blends and word families as football players to match up on the field in order to create words. |
| **The Problem with Chickens**<br>(Website) | • Available on PBS.org<br>• Children practice phoneme blending in this game to create words. |
| **Starfall**<br>(Website and App) | • Available on starfall.com<br>• Children can practice phonics concepts by watching animated videos and playing interactive games involving letter patterns and word families. |
| **Reading Bear**<br>(Website) | • Available on ReadingBear.com<br>• Children can practice phonics concepts by watching and listening to audio flash cards of segmenting and blending examples (www.readingbear.org). |
| **Construct a Word**<br>(Website) | • Available on ReadWriteThink.org<br>• Students combine beginning consonants and blends with word family endings to create words. |
| **Raz Kids**<br>(Website and App) | • Available on Raz-Kids.com<br>• Leveled e-readers for children to listen to, read and answer questions about, or record themselves reading<br>• Huge selection of fiction and nonfiction texts |
| **Montessori Crosswords**<br>(App) | • Children practice segmenting and blending letter tiles into sounds of words.<br>• Pictures and audio help support students' success with spelling words. |
| **Sight Word Learning Games**<br>(App) | • Children play interactive games as they review common high-frequency sight words.<br>• Game formats include Bingo, Memory, Flash Cards, and Word Machine. |

Figure 5.11 Popular Technology for Targeting Word Recognition and Fluency

# Connecting with Families

There are many ways in which word recognition and fluency skills taught in the classroom can be extended and reinforced at home. It is important to include words for word recognition activities that children have used in their small-group instruction in class. Giving children brand-new words that they are not familiar with may cause confusion. It is also important to remember that children need additional practice with phonics, sight word identification, and oral reading fluency. A blend of all three activities can create a balanced homework assignment each night, giving students adequate practice and reinforcement of school-based instruction. Here are several activities that are ideal for work at home.

## *Re-Sort*

Students need repetition sorting and re-sorting their words in order to internalize the spelling pattern targeted in the sort. Thus, it is always a good idea to send home the same sort students practiced in class as a homework task. This can be done once or more during the week. Managing words written on small pieces of paper can be tricky, even with plastic bags, as words tend to disappear. Thus, we recommend sending home a new sheet of words at the beginning of the week for students to cut, sort, write, and glue at home. Asking students to keep track of the same bag of words both in school and at home may be a trying activity for both the students and you! As part of the sorting activity, ask students to explain their sort and the thinking behind it to someone at home. Verbalizing the thinking for why they sorted as they did is a key component to building understanding of the underlying word patterns. Students can also extend the sort at home by adding new word examples they find while reading or talking with their caregivers.

## *Read to Me*

An important part of building oral reading fluency is practice reading. A key homework activity can be students reading aloud to someone at home each night. In order to implement this as an activity for your students, it is important to make books available for them to check out of your classroom or school library. Some students may not have access to books in the home, so you will need to ensure that all of them have the option of checking books out. If your school does not already do so, the free Reading Is Fundamental (RIF) program (www.rif.org) also provides students with free books multiple times a year.

Depending on the grade level you teach, you will want to communicate your reading expectations—the types of books and amounts of time—with parents. If you teach kindergarten, reading may include ten to fifteen minutes of a child reading a decodable text to a parent or a parent reading a picture book to a child. If you teach first or second grade, reading may include twenty minutes of a child reading a decodable, a beginning reader, or even a chapter book. As children become better readers, they will want to switch from reading aloud to reading silently. We recommend asking children to read aloud for at least part of the time so that parents can hear how they're reading. Parents will be able to judge their children's fluency and progress over time as the school year passes.

Another key ingredient of reading at home is a system for tracking the titles of books or chapters students read. A visual reminder will help you evaluate reading progress and will also help parents remember to read with their children. We have seen teachers ask students or parents to record books read at home in assignment books, on daily, weekly, or monthly reading logs, and in graph formats. Think carefully about how often you want to check student progress and formats that will be easy for parents to maintain.

Consistency is also important; parents will become used to a normal routine for tracking reading.

While researchers still explore the role of extrinsic and intrinsic reading motivation, our experience indicates that children still value periodic incentives for encouraging reading at home. Children love little notes from you congratulating them on their reading. You can easily print little certificates of encouragement every other month or so. Children also like little trinkets, such as bookmarks, stickers, and pencils, after reaching certain reading milestones, such as at the end of the month or after one hundred books read. One of my son's teachers offered a free homework pass to students once they had completed a month's reading log. Another teacher in the same school gave students a pass for a free snack in the cafeteria as a reward for good reading over the summer. We like Gambrell and Marinak's (2008) finding that a reward selected with care can foster reading motivation, especially when the reward is a new book.

## Word Work Homework Menu

To practice phonics concepts taught in class, students can choose from a nightly word work menu of activities using the words targeted in their teacher-led, small-group instruction. Providing a choice of activities helps with student motivation and engagement. The variety also prevents students from becoming indifferent or spending too much time repeating the same activities. You can be extremely creative with the word work activities you include on your menu; however, in order to be feasible, activities should not require too much preparation or elaborate, expensive supplies.

Figure 5.12 provides an example of a homework word work menu. Activities could include rainbow writing words in the colors of the rainbow, writing words in chalk, writing words in shaving cream, writing words in rice or flour, finding words in magazines, newspapers, or books, writing words with letter tiles, writing words with magnetic letters, typing words on the computer, writing words in alphabetic order, writing words in cursive, drawing a picture and hiding the words in the picture, using words in sentences, illustrating words by drawing pictures, or writing a short story including the words. Giving students many creative options from which to choose will excite them. Your directions should include the number of activities students are expected to complete in the course of the week and a way to show that they have been completed. For example, you may ask students to check the activities they do each night off the menu and have a parent initial the appropriate box before returning the menu at the end of the week.

| | | | |
|---|---|---|---|
| **DIRECTIONS: Each night please select one activity from the menu to complete using your Word Work words. Ask your caregiver to initial and date the box to indicate which activity you completed each night. Please return your menu on Friday of week.** | | | |
| Write your words once in red. Then trace over the words a second time in green and a third time in purple. | Put some rice or flour on a baking sheet. Write your words by moving your finger through the rice or flour. | Use letter tiles or magnetic letters to write your words on a table or refrigerator. | Write a poem or short story using as many of your words as you can appropriately. For an extra challenge, illustrate your poem or story. |
| Go outside and write your words in chalk on a sidewalk or driveway. | Draw a picture and hide your words in it. See if someone else can find your hidden words. | Ask a caregiver if you can use a computer to type your words. | Choose four words and write a sentence using each one. Make sure to underline your target word in its sentence. For an extra challenge, see if you can use two words appropriately in one sentence. |
| Put some shaving cream in a tray or on a piece of wax paper on the table. Write your words in the shaving cream. | Look through a magazine or newspaper. Circle any of your words you find with a pencil or crayon. | Write your words in alphabetical order from A–Z or backward from Z–A. | Ask a caregiver to download the Spelling City app (www.spellingcity.com) on an electronic device to play games with your words. |

Figure 5.12  Word Work Homework Menu

## Sight Word Flash Cards

Because students need to be able to recognize high-frequency words by sight, they need multiple opportunities to practice reading the words so that they will eventually become sight words. Practice at home can include sending home weekly flash cards for parents to practice with their children. It may be helpful to provide parents with suggestions for having their children read the word in different ways; for example, quietly or loudly. Children can also write sight words quickly on a chalkboard, dry erase board, or piece of paper. Homework could include writing the words with sidewalk chalk, in rice or shaving cream, or even spelling them out with magnetic letters on the refrigerator. We recommend sending home review sheets of all the sight words taught so that parents can systematically review them in order to minimize lost or forgotten words.

# Assessment

Assessment of students' phonics and word recognition is an extremely important indicator of overall reading success because word recognition is highly connected to reading comprehension. In the early grades, students who are successful with word recognition tasks—namely, decoding and encoding—are better comprehenders as young readers, since word recognition is the major task that they face in the reading process. As automatic word recognition increases, so does fluency, which then serves as a bridge to reading comprehension.

The opposite effect also holds true. Students who demonstrate weaknesses in decoding, encoding, and automaticity tend to be disfluent, struggling readers. They may read slowly and laboriously, skip words, or misread words. As a result, a chain reaction is set off that affects fluency and results in compromised comprehension. This fluency struggle will become even more of a concern as students enter the intermediate grades where they will be required to read texts, such as content-area textbooks, expository texts, and encyclopedias, which are not forgiving of word recognition deficits. Educators tend to see a sharp dropoff in reading achievement and motivation to read at this point, often termed the "fourth-grade slump" by concerned teachers and reading researchers, referring to the point when schools and the curriculum expect children to transition from learning to read to reading to learn. The expectation is that students have mastered automatic word recognition; are fluent readers; can quickly decode novel, polysyllabic words; and can infer meanings from vocabulary and context.

In effect, any prior weaknesses in phonics knowledge and word recognition in the primary grades will show up even more dramatically in fourth grade and beyond. The good news is that if caught early, the deficit is easy to fix through targeted, systematic, and explicit phonics instruction. Therefore, it is critical that teachers assess individual students' phonics and word recognition in the early grades and have a variety of informal assessments available to differentiate instruction. Figure 5.13 provides a list of research-based phonics and word recognition assessments and their respective purposes.

# Summary

Children's word recognition is an essential skill on the road to becoming a reader. A child who possesses strong phonological awareness, vocabulary, and knowledge of letter-sound correspondence can apply his or her abilities when confronted with decoding and interpreting text on a page. You can facilitate this process by introducing and expanding children's sight word vocabularies to make it easier for them to encounter nondecodable words in print. You can also help make their decoding more efficient with systematic phonics instruction, introducing letter combinations and word families and allowing time

| Assessment | Purpose |
|---|---|
| **Sound/Symbol Relationship Assessment** (www.readinga-z.com) | Used as an early phonics assessment; assesses a student's ability to associate a sound with a given symbol |
| **Informal Phonics Inventory** (McKenna and Stahl [2003]) | Used to informally assesses all phonics elements on a scope and sequence from easier to more difficult elements; allows teachers to target instruction to specific phonics elements; and provides a baseline for meeting students at their instructional level |
| **Nonsense Word Assessment** (www.readinga-z.com) | Used as a phonics assessment and often considered a pure assessment because it requires students to use knowledge of the alphabetic code rather than memorization to read words. Using nonsense words in phonics instruction and assessment can increase a student's ability to read words with accuracy and automaticity. |
| **High-Frequency Word Assessment** (www.readinga-z.com) | Used to assess a student's ability to recognize and read high-frequency words, more commonly known as sight words. Automaticity with high-frequency words is a critical indicator affecting fluency. |
| **Spelling Inventory** (Bear et al. [2011]) | Used to differentiate instruction based on a spelling developmental stage; contain lists of words that are chosen to represent a variety of spelling features at increasing levels of difficulty. The words in the inventory are designed to demonstrate students' knowledge of these key spelling features at different stages of development with the purpose of differentiated instruction. Students engage in differentiated word study activities, including word sorts and various self-selected word study games. |
| **Fluency Probes** | Used to assess students' prosody, accuracy, and rate; can provide teachers with a *general* picture of students' word attack and recognition. Students are given a grade-level passage, or probe, and are asked to read orally for one minute. The assessor tracks the errors: skipped words, mispronounced words, word substitutions, words read in the wrong order or repeated, or words that they cannot decode after three to five seconds. At the end of one minute, the student stops reading and the assessor counts up the words per minute, deducting errors to get a words correct per minute (WCPM), which is then compared to oral fluency norms (Hasbrouck and Tindal 2006). Students scoring below 20 percent of the norm by grade level require further diagnoses, including a phonics assessment, to document if decoding is the primary cause for the disfluency. |

Figure 5.13  Research-Based Phonics and Word Recognition Assessments

to practice them.. Finally, you can speed up the entire process by engaging children with oral reading fluency activities.

When planning your word recognition instruction, keep in mind that children need practice, practice, and more practice. The more opportunities children have to stretch their word recognition muscles, the stronger they will become as readers. Unfortunately, we know that struggling readers tend to stop reading because it is challenging and frustrating. Just think about a task that you find extremely difficult. Are you more or less likely to do it? Most of us are much more likely to shut down and avoid that task whenever possible. The same is true of beginning readers. Therefore, it is crucial that we use ongoing progress monitoring to assess their phonics and fluency. If we catch struggling readers at the beginning, we can reteach concepts early and help get them back on track for success.

We have shown in this chapter that word recognition instruction can and should be active, embedded in reading real books, and differentiated by children's needs. Word recognition instruction, especially phonics instruction, has the potential to devolve into monotonous worksheets and handouts. This drill-and-kill process has earned phonics a bad name, and rightfully so. However, that does not mean that we should eliminate all phonics instruction from our classrooms. Indeed, we advocate that children need a healthy balance of both isolated skills instruction and practice reading real texts. A blend of individual skills training and big-picture instruction gives children both the means and the joy of actually reading. After all, the goal of word recognition instruction is to produce healthy, happy, independent readers!

# Chapter 6

# Developing Comprehension

e used to work with a teacher, Ms. Sara, who was a master at teaching young children to comprehend text. She loved reading aloud to kindergarten children and sharing her favorite books and authors. Her enthusiasm and love of reading was truly contagious, and the children quickly accepted that the books she shared were treasures worth treating with awe.

Ms. Sara was particularly skilled at teaching children to use their prior knowledge to make predictions about what was going to happen next in the story. I observed one lesson in which Ms. Sara was reading *The Lima Bean Monster* (2001) by Dan Yaccarino. With joy, her students eagerly awaited the beginning of the story, quickly settling down on the carpet to listen. As soon as Ms. Sara sat in her chair, the children started rubbing their heads. Thinking this odd, I leaned over and asked a little boy what he was doing. He replied matter-of-factly, "Oh, we're warming up our noodles to activate our schemas."

## How Do Children Comprehend?

Young children begin to understand what is read to them long before they read themselves. Listening comprehension precedes and lays the groundwork for later reading comprehension. When children listen to a parent or teacher reading a book aloud, they are practicing the skills necessary for comprehending text they will later read independently. Adults help to foster these skills when they engage children in conversations about what they are thinking about while they read.

Comprehension is a complex process involving many factors (RAND Corporation 2002). Think about the process you go through when you read. First, you probably identify, even subconsciously, why you are reading the particular text you have chosen. Identifying the purpose of your reading helps you to decide the manner in which you will do it. For example, I approach reading an entertainment magazine about celebrities differently than I approach reading an article in a professional journal. I read entertainment magazines cursorily to keep my mind occupied while I am exercising. However, I read journal articles carefully and slowly, with highlighter in hand to take notes. The purposes that we have for reading shape how we approach it.

Closely related to purpose is motivation. How motivated a reader is to read a text affects his or her understanding. Have you ever had to read something that you really did not want to read? It's miserable and painstaking, and you are likely to retain very little of what you've read. In contrast, if there is a new book or article that you really want to read, reading it is a delight and you can retell a friend all the details. Unfortunately, internal motivation is by nature highly personal and hard for a parent or teacher to change.

Similarly, comprehension is affected by the reader's background knowledge on the topic. It makes sense that if you already know a lot about the subject, then you will understand what you are reading better and more quickly than someone for whom the topic is completely foreign. If I read an article in a reading research journal, I am fairly confident in my ability to understand it because of my prior knowledge in the area. The opposite is true if I read an article in one of my husband's biochemistry journals. Because I do not have any previous knowledge in the field, I struggle when confronted with vocabulary and concepts that are brand-new to me.

In addition, readers bring with them a collection of cognitive capacities and skills to aid comprehension: short-term and long-term memory capacity, logical reasoning, problem-solving ability, and abstract thinking. In language experiences, a reader's strengths in vocabulary, concepts of print, and word recognition support his or her understanding of text. Cognitive strategies specific to reading comprehension include making predictions about what will happen in a story, making connections within the text and outside of it, retelling the text to check for understanding, visualizing what is happening in the text, inferring what the author is implying but not saying directly, and summarizing the text. Readers not only need to know the comprehension strategies but also how to use them and when they are appropriate (Harvey and Goudvis 2007; Harvey and Pearson 2005).

Simply reading more will also support reading comprehension. Readers with experience reading a wide range of genres will know what to expect when reading mysteries versus how-to books versus historical fiction. Similarly, readers who have been exposed to text features and structures will be more adept at using the internal structure of text to support understanding. Readers who know story elements—such as character, setting, problem, and solution—are much more equipped to comprehend than those who do not.

Clearly, reading comprehension is a complex process. Figure 6.1 summarizes many of the factors that contribute to whether readers comprehend a text. With so many contributing factors affecting success, it is no wonder that beginning readers often struggle to understand what they read. Unfortunately, many find themselves in a difficult cycle: struggling to read when the very thing that will help—reading more—is the thing that they are struggling with in the first place.

| Reading Purpose | Readers who set a purpose for their reading will read in the way that will best achieve that purpose. If they want to be entertained, they will read for enjoyment. If they want to learn information to achieve a purpose, they will read with a more searching eye. |
|---|---|
| Motivation | Readers who want to read a text are much more eager and willing than readers who don't. Readers who are reluctant to read a particular text are more likely to rush through and employ fewer strategies for understanding. |
| Background Knowledge | Readers who have prior knowledge of a topic will be able to apply it to what they are reading about in order to compare and contrast the information with what they already knew about the topic. Readers who are learning about a topic for the very first time have less with which to connect. |
| Cognitive Capacities | Readers with significant attention spans, memory, and vocabulary knowledge can utilize these resources to focus on and understand what they are reading. Those who are constantly distracted or forgetful will need longer to process what they have read. |
| Strategy Knowledge | Readers with knowledge of the comprehension strategies—what they are and how and when to employ them—will be better able to use them to aid their own understanding of more difficult texts than readers who do not have knowledge of the strategies. |

Figure 6.1 Factors Affecting Students' Comprehension

# When Should Comprehension Instruction Begin?

Just like the question of the chicken or the egg, teachers often wonder what comes first, the reader or the comprehender. It used to be that teachers would wait to introduce comprehension strategies until children were readers themselves, but we now know that is too late (Harvey and Goudvis 2007). Early childhood educators can and should begin comprehension instruction even with the nonreaders in their classrooms.

Figure 6.2 provides a preview of instructional methods described in this chapter for fostering children's comprehension. In the sections that follow, each instructional method will be developed and explained so you can begin implementing the strategies in your own classroom.

| Instructional Method | Format | Characteristics | Strengths |
|---|---|---|---|
| Picture Walk | Whole Group, Small Groups, or Individuals | • Embedded within read-aloud<br>• Involves discussing the illustrations without actually reading the words of the story | • Serves as good introduction on day one of repeated reading sequence<br>• Serves as a good previewing strategy prior to reading<br>• Targets oral language and comprehension |
| Dialogic Reading | Whole Group, Small Groups, or Individuals | • Embedded within read-aloud<br>• Teacher reads a book aloud and interjects a variety of questions while reading. | • Works with fiction and nonfiction<br>• Targets oral language and comprehension |
| Read-Aloud with Explicit Strategy Instruction | Whole Group, Small Groups, or Individuals | • Embedded within read-aloud<br>• Teacher reads and models how to use various comprehension strategies by thinking aloud while reading. | • Works with fiction and nonfiction<br>• Directly teaches comprehension strategies, how to use them, and when to use them appropriately |
| Dramatic Storytelling | Whole Group, Small Groups, or Individuals | • Can occur during or after read-aloud<br>• Productions can be low-key or include props, costumes, or puppets.<br>• Children work together to retell a story. | • Works well with fiction<br>• Engages children in active, hands-on experience<br>• High motivation |
| Technology Integration | Small Groups or Centers | Various websites and apps designed to target reading comprehension | • Good review activity<br>• High student engagement<br>• Potential to foster twenty-first-century technology skills |
| Connecting with Families | Multiple | Parents reinforce reading comprehension at home. | • Fosters home-school connection<br>• Provides comprehension practice outside of classroom context |

Figure 6.2 Preview of Instructional Methods in This Chapter

# Picture Walk

A picture walk occurs when you preview the pages of a book without actually reading the words. In this way, a picture walk is a previewing strategy, much like the process you go through when you quickly skim an article before committing to reading it carefully. Since children are usually eager to see the colorful illustrations in picture books, taking a picture walk enables them to carefully digest and discuss what they are seeing in each picture. Then when you read the book the next time, since children have already seen the illustrations once, they will be more likely to pay attention to the meaning of the words. We mentioned using picture walks with wordless picture books as a strategy for developing students' oral language. We can also use the picture walk technique as a means of previewing a text prior to reading.

As the teacher, you can facilitate a picture walk by pausing, calling attention to certain details in the illustrations, and posing thoughts of your own. For example, if doing a picture walk of the wonderful book *Finding Winnie: The True Story of the World's Most Famous Bear* (2015) by Lindsay Mattick, you might call children's attention to the plot by talking about the changes in clothing and setting across the illustrations. You might say, "Does anyone notice what the main character is wearing now in the story? I see a military uniform. I think this is a clue about what is going to happen in the story." Once students get used to the procedure, they will more than likely jump in with observations and comments of their own.

If you plan to use a repeated reading sequence with books in your classroom, you may consider conducting a picture walk on the first day of reading. We've worked with several teachers who do this. The strategy helps to build prior knowledge and comprehension, and to boost children's oral language and vocabulary. When children see teachers using picture walks during read-alouds, they often mimic the process when looking at books in the classroom library or at their desks. When children understand that it is acceptable to look at the pictures in a book, suddenly they are more apt to "read" books that may be beyond their reading level by conducting a silent picture walk of their own. In this way, the picture walk technique builds readers' confidence.

# Dialogic Reading

Dialogic reading (Whitehurst 1992) is a read-aloud in which the teacher engages children in conversation around the text, thus facilitating a dialogue. Dialogic reading targets reading comprehension by involving a variety of questions ranging in difficulty. Good readers ask and answer questions as they read. By using dialogic reading in the classroom, teachers model what good readers do while reading. They also expose children to the different kinds of questions they will be asked to answer about texts and model how to answer them correctly.

There are many types of questions that target understanding. One particular method uses the acronym CROWD (Whitehurst 1992) to describe five types of questions (see Figure 6.3 and appendix). The *C* stands for completion questions. You can create a completion question by rereading a phrase or statement in a book and leaving off one word for a child to fill in. For example, if you were reading *Love, Splat* (2008) by Rob Scotton, you might ask children to complete this sentence: "Whenever Kitten saw Splat, she pulled his ears and poked his belly, tied his tail and called him _____." Students can remember what they heard and their understanding of rhyme to answer "smelly." Completion questions check to see if children were listening and can recall verbatim what word was used in the text. This kind of question is very basic and does not require higher-order thinking; however, the high level of scaffolding ensures that many students can be successful in answering it during reading.

| Acronym | Type of Question | Example |
|---------|------------------|---------|
| C | **C**ompletion Questions | "Whenever Kitten saw Splat, she pulled his ears and poked his belly, tied his tail and called him _____." |
| R | **R**ecall Questions | "Who gave a valentine first? Second? Last?" |
| O | **O**pen-Ended Questions | "Why do you think Splat gets tongue tied every time he sees Kitten?" |
| W | **W**h- Questions | "Where are Splat and Kitten?" |
| D | **D**istancing Questions | "Have you ever sent or received a valentine? What did it say?" |

Figure 6.3 Dialogic Reading Using CROWD Questions

The *R* stands for recall questions. You can create a recall question by asking children to remember something that happened in the story in order. This type of question works well with fiction or nonfiction when a sequence is described. For example, in *Love, Splat*, you might ask students to recall the order in which valentines were given: "Who gave a valentine first? Second? Last?" This type of question requires a certain amount of memory to answer correctly. The more items or events you ask children to recall, the more challenging the recall question becomes. You may want to ask younger children to recall two or three items, while older students should be able to remember more items in sequence.

The *O* represents open-ended questions. Open-ended questions have no right or wrong answer and usually require more than one-word responses from students. These questions are great for getting more oral language out of children. An example of an open-ended question might be, "Why do you think Splat gets tongue-tied every time he sees Kitten?" There are several ways children could answer this, including, "He likes her," "He loves her," "He gets nervous around her," "He gets anxious," "He doesn't know what to do around her." Because there are no incorrect answers, all students in the class can feel successful answering this type of question.

The *W* stands for Wh-questions, which begin with words such as *who*, *what*, *where*, and *when* (and *how*). The answers to these questions are usually closely tied to the text and have a correct response. For example, the question "Where are Splat and Kitten?" asks children to identify the setting of the story, and the text and illustrations offer clues to the answer: "on the playground." Typically, Wh- questions are similar to the types of questions that children will be asked on comprehension assessments.

Finally, the *D* represents distancing questions. Distancing questions ask children to think about something in the text that is like something that they have experienced in their own lives. In this way, children are getting distance from the text by answering the question with their own experiences. For example, you may ask, "Have you ever sent or received a valentine? What did it say?" Children responding to this type of question are making connections. By asking this type of question, you can guarantee that all children in your class can respond successfully.

Dialogic reading using a variety of CROWD question types is a powerful method for fostering children's comprehension. By asking multiple questions and offering a range of support, you develop different kinds of thinking in students and ensure that all children successfully answer at least some of the questions. Because questioning is one of the most common means of assessing reading comprehension, children will be asked to answer the same types of questions after independent reading. By using CROWD questions, you are laying the foundation for your students to answer the many after-reading questions with which they will be confronted with in elementary school and beyond.

# Read-Aloud with Explicit Strategy Instruction

When children become independent readers, they will need to know a variety of comprehension strategies and how and when to employ them. Even though your students may not be readers yet or may be beginning readers, it is not too early to model the comprehension strategies as you read aloud. By laying the foundation now, you will set students up to be better comprehenders later. The read-aloud offers you the perfect context for modeling and thinking aloud how to use each strategy before asking children to be able to do it independently. We have found that children who have had models before they read are better equipped to then apply the same strategies when they are reading on their own.

Modeling comprehension strategies involves thinking aloud as you read. This is not an easy thing to do if you are a proficient reader. You have to force yourself to slow the process of understanding down to step-by-step actions in order to teach it to someone else. Sometimes it feels a bit awkward to do; however, the return is worth it. The good news is that you do get better at thinking aloud the more you try it. In the sections that follow, we will give you some sample language to help you practice thinking aloud the most useful comprehension strategies. Figure 6.4 (also in the appendix) summarizes the kind of explicit teacher talk that is necessary when modeling how to use the reading comprehension strategies.

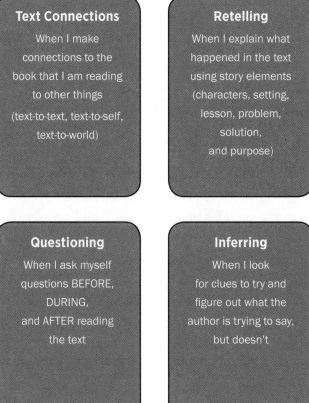

**Predicting**
When I guess what will happen next in the story using text clues

**Text Connections**
When I make connections to the book that I am reading to other things (text-to-text, text-to-self, text-to-world)

**Retelling**
When I explain what happened in the text using story elements (characters, setting, lesson, problem, solution, and purpose)

**Visualizing**
When I create a mental image in my mind using the details in the story to help me better understand

**Questioning**
When I ask myself questions BEFORE, DURING, and AFTER reading the text

**Inferring**
When I look for clues to try and figure out what the author is trying to say, but doesn't

Figure 6.4  Teacher Talk to Model the Comprehension Strategies

## *What Strategies Should I Teach?*

Research identifies the comprehension strategies that are the most beneficial for young readers (Harvey and Goudvis 2007). Figure 6.5 summarizes these strategies.

| Strategy | Description | How It Targets Comprehension | Sample Think-Aloud Speech |
|---|---|---|---|
| **Predicting** | The reader makes an educated guess, based on the text or the pictures, about what is going to happen next in the text. | The reader must process what is already known about the text and apply background knowledge in order to make an accurate guess about what might happen next. | "Because the author just told us that the little girl is really nervous about going to school and that she has run away before, I am going to predict that the little girl plans to run away before she has to go to school." |
| **Connecting** | The reader can make different kinds of connections:<br>(1) Text to Text—a connection between what in the text is like something in another book<br>(2) Text to Self—a connection between what is in the text and something in his own life<br>(3) Text to World—a connection between what is in the text and something happening in the real world | The reader must process what is learned in the text in order to make a connection between it and something from another book, from his or her own life, or from the real world. | "The little boy in this story always worries about what might happen. That reminds me of the character Wemberly from *Wemberly Worried* by Kevin Henkes. Remember when we read that story? Wemberly is always worried about bad things that may happen to her, just like the little boy in this story. I just made a text-to-text connection between two stories we have read with similar characters." |
| **Retelling** | The reader retells what he or she can remember about the text.<br>In fiction, the reader may retell the story elements, such as character, setting, problem, solution.<br>In nonfiction, the reader may retell the main idea and details about the topic. | In order to retell, the reader must have read and remembered what the text says about the story in fiction or the topic in nonfiction. | "Now that we just read the story, I want to check my understanding by retelling what I remember. This story is about a little bear that lives in a department store. One day a little girl named Lisa wants to buy him but he has lost a button. That night Corduroy goes on an adventure to find his button, but he does not find it. Instead, the next day Lisa comes back to buy him and sews a new button on him at home." |

Figure 6.5 Comprehension Strategies for Beginning Readers

| Strategy | Description | How It Targets Comprehension | Sample Think-Aloud Speech |
|---|---|---|---|
| Visualizing | The reader imagines what details from the text look like in his or her mind. | In order to visualize, the reader has to understand details and adjectives described in the text to paint a picture in his or her mind. | "The author just gave me some great details about the place that the train is passing. I am going to stop reading here, close my eyes, and imagine what the setting looks like. I see a snowy forest with a pack of grey wolves running beside the train. It is cold and dark and there are a lot of stars in the sky." |
| Questioning | The reader asks questions about the text while reading. | The reader must have an understanding of story elements in narrative text and text structure in informational text in order to ask appropriate questions. | "I just read that Officer Buckle does not want to do any more safety speeches. Why doesn't he want Gloria to do tricks behind him?" |
| Making Inferences | The reader reads between the lines to determine what the author means without directly stating it in the text. | Making inferences requires a sophisticated level of thinking, such that the reader can identify key ideas in the text and combine these clues with prior knowledge to determine meaning. | "Where does this story take place? The author has not told us, but I just read about the animals living outside in trees that are close together. This sounds like the setting of the story is a forest." |
| Monitoring, Clarifying, Fixing Up | The reader reflects on his or her understanding, clarifies unclear concepts or vocabulary, and rereads in order to understand something that was not understood the first time. | Monitoring understanding requires the ability to reflect on one's own understanding. Clarifying and fixing up require the reader to know resources and strategies to aid understanding. | "Wait, I thought Pluto was a planet, but the author just said Pluto is not a planet. I am going to go back and read that again." |

Figure 6.5 (continued) Comprehension Strategies for Beginning Readers

## Predicting

Predicting involves making informed guesses about what might happen next in the text. Some predictions are better than others. We want students to make good guesses based on their understanding of the information they just read. When using predictions for the first time with students, model how to make good ones based on clues from the illustrations or the text. Children will need several examples of you thinking aloud how to make a good prediction. For example, when looking at the cover of a book, you might say, "Friends, I think this book is going to be about animals on a farm. I am making a prediction, a guess about what I think this book is going to be about, because I see a cow, a duck, and a horse. I know these animals are usually found on a farm, so I think this book is going to be about the animals on a farm." Making the process of your thinking explicit will help support children as they begin to make their own predictions. We think it is very important to ask children to share their predictions, and also to ask them why they think something will happen. The reason behind the prediction makes the difference between a good prediction and a wild guess. Once you have shown children how to make predictions, be sure to also show them how to check to see if their predictions are true. If they do not come true, it is important to show children how to revise their predictions based on new information from the text or the illustrations. For example, "Wow, that was a great prediction, but now the author has told us that the character did this instead. With this new information, we can revise our prediction to make it more accurate." Some teachers we have worked with were concerned that children would be upset if their predictions did not come true. However, if you model making both good and not-so-good predictions, then children will understand that not all of them come true.

## Connecting

A second comprehension strategy is making connections. There are several different kinds of connections a reader can make to a text. A reader makes a text-to-text connection when something in the text reminds him or her of something in another text. For example, if you read *Mrs. Wishy-Washy's Farm* (2003) by Joy Cowley and *Click, Clack, Moo: Cows That Type* (2011) by Doreen Cronin, you can make a text-to-text connection because both books take place on a farm. When reading *Click, Clack, Moo* to your students, you may pause after learning about the setting and comment, "This book takes place on a Farmer Brown's farm. This setting reminds me of the farm we read about in a book last week, *Mrs. Wishy-Washy's Farm*. Do you remember her farm? Mrs. Wishy-Washy had a cow, a duck, and a horse just like Farmer Brown in this story. I just made a text-to-text connection because this story reminded me of another story."

A second type of connection is a text-to-self connection when something in the text reminds the reader of something in his or her life. We have found that books with characters who have strong emotions are great for making text-to-self connections since children are able to quickly connect to the feelings of the characters. For that reason, we love books by Kevin Henkes for modeling text-to-self connections. In *Chrysanthemum* (2008); *Wemberly Worried* (2010); *Owen* (1993); *Lily's Big Day* (1996); *Sheila Rae, the Brave* (1996); and *Julius, the Baby of the World* (1995) Henkes creates characters who experience strong emotions in situations that are very real to young children. It is hard not to have a text-to-self connection while reading one of Henkes' books! For example, if you are reading *Wemberly Worried* to your class, you may pause and discuss, "Friends, I know how Wemberly feels here. She is very worried about going to a new place that she has never been before. She is nervous that no one will like her and that she will not like being there.

I know how she feels because I felt the same way when I had to go away to college. I felt really scared to leave my parents and my friends to go away to a new place that I had never been before. I just made a text-to-self connection because I have felt the same way that Wemberly felt in the story."

A third type of connection is a text-to-world connection when the reader can think of a relationship between something in the book and something that has happened in the real world. There are many types of fiction and nonfiction texts to which children can make text-to-world connections; however, the ability to make this type of connection varies among students depending on background knowledge and experiences. A text-to-world connection may sound like, "We just read that a hurricane swept through the town in this story. That reminds me of the hurricane we had last August. Do you remember the big storm that we had with lots of rain and strong wind? That is like the storm that the characters in our book are having right now. I just made a text-to-world connection."

## Retelling

Retelling is a comprehension strategy that requires the reader to remember what he or she has read in the text. For narrative text, readers can retell the story elements—character, setting, problem, and solution. In informational text, readers can retell the main idea and details related to the topic. Retelling can be done orally or in writing, depending on the ability of the reader and the amount of support given by the teacher (Hansen 2004). You might ask young preschoolers to tell you what they remember as you record their ideas on chart paper. Or, you may ask elementary students to record their own retellings on a graphic organizer (Figure 6.6). No matter which format you are using for retelling, you will want to model how to retell well. Figure 6.7 (also in the appendix) provides an example of a retelling poem to help young students remember the important components of a good retelling. With young children, we begin lessons by introducing and discussing one story element at a time and slowly build up to include retellings that address all the elements at once. You can find endless graphic organizer variations for retelling online and in print.

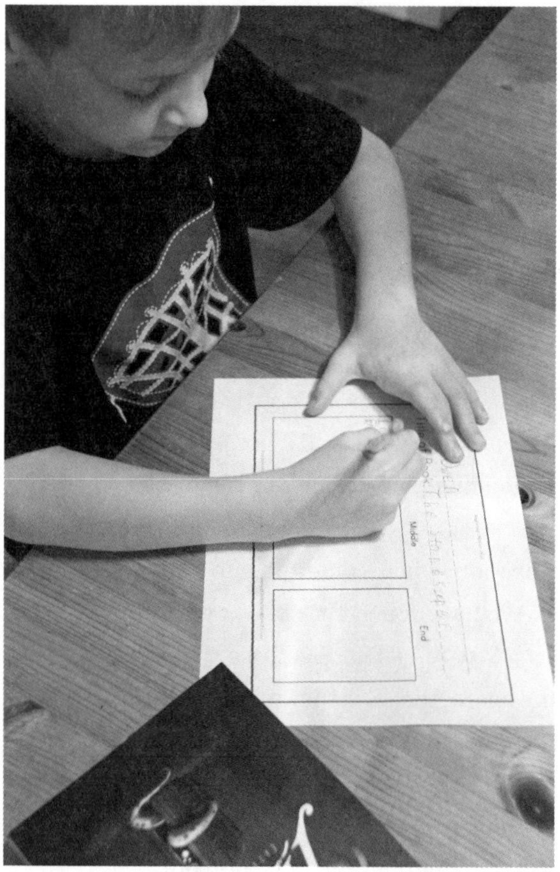

Figure 6.6 A Second Grader Completing a Retelling Graphic Organizer

When modeling retelling, it works well to have a book with a clear sequential order and strong story elements. For these reasons, we have found that retelling works really well with fairy tales and folktales. When reading *The Little Red Hen* (1985) by Paul Galdone, you can model retelling by explaining, "As I read I tried to remember in my mind what I was reading. Now I am going to retell what I read. To help do this, I am going to complete this story elements graphic organizer. The characters were hen, cat, dog, and mouse, so I am going to write their names in this box. The setting was a farm, so I am going to record the setting in this box. I am going to write the problem here: the hen wanted help growing and harvesting the wheat, but her friends would not help her. Last, I am going to write the solution here: the hen did all the work herself and did not share the bread with her friends. Now I have retold the important parts of the story."

Figure 6.7 Retelling Poem. Reprinted with permission from the author.

## Visualizing

Visualizing encourages readers to make a movie in their mind of what is happening in the text. Harvey and Goudvis (2007) describe visualizing as a form of inferring; in order to visualize what is happening in the text, the reader must be able to put pieces together and infer between the lines of what the author has told the reader. Authors who use thick description and rich adjectives in their writing make it easy for readers to visualize what is happening. Some of our favorite children's book authors for visualizing include Chris Van Allsburg, William Steig, Russell Freedman, Patricia Polacco, Roald Dahl, E. B. White, and Cynthia Rylant. When modeling visualizing for children, ask them to close their eyes and use the author's words to imagine what the setting or characters look like. For example, when reading *James and the Giant Peach* (1973) by Roald Dahl, explain, "Now I am going to pause while reading to close my eyes and visualize what I just read. The author told us that the peach is ripe and dripping with juice. It is sticky and fuzzy and soft. I am seeing a giant pink peach in my mind with James inside. If I run my hand on the side of the peach it is soft and tender and wet with sticky peach juice. When I imagine what the author is telling me, it helps me to understand the story."

## Questioning

Asking yourself questions while reading is a great method to check to see if you understand the text. In order to ask important questions about the text, readers need to know something about the type of text they are reading. If they are reading narrative text, they need to know that narrative structure includes elements such as characters, setting, problem, and solution. Then they can formulate important questions about the elements to aid their understanding. Formulating and answering questions such as, "Who is the story about? Where does this story take place? and How is the problem being solved?" will support reader understanding. In informational text, readers need to identify the underlying structure—sequential, cyclical, cause and effect, or compare and contrast—in order to ask questions about the main idea of the text and its supporting details. For example, readers may ask, "How are planets and dwarf planets alike and different?" if they have identified that the informational text structure is compare and contrast. In order to model asking questions, you will need to lay the foundation by teaching narrative and informational text structures. Once children have a firm grasp of story elements or text structures, you can model asking questions. For example, you may think aloud, "I am going to pause here while reading and ask a question to check to make sure I am understanding what I read. Do I know who this story is going to be about? Yes, I just read about a little girl named Trixie and her Knuffle Bunny, so I think the story is going to be about her."

## Making Inferences

A reader makes an inference when reading between the lines of the actual text to draw a conclusion about something that the text does not come out directly and state. To make a good inference, the reader needs to understand what the author says and does not say. Sometimes the reader also needs to rely on background knowledge in order to fill in the missing information. For example, if an author describes the setting as "hot during the day, cool at night, sandy, dusty, dry, and arid," the reader may infer that the setting is the desert even if the author never comes right out and says, "The family lives in the desert." In order to model making inferences, you will need to identify key places in narrative or informational texts where authors leave the reader room to fill in the gaps. In *Dr. De Soto* by William Steig (1982), the author tells us that Dr. De Soto refuses to treat animals dangerous to mice. This is a perfect place to pause while reading and explain, "We know that Dr. De Soto does not treat animals that are dangerous to mice, but the author does not tell us why. I can infer that the reason Dr. De Soto does not treat animals that are dangerous to mice is because he is a mouse and dangerous animals might eat him while he is working on their teeth. Even though the author does not tell me this directly, I know that animals like cats and foxes eat mice."

## Monitoring, Clarifying, and Fixing Up

Finally, good readers constantly monitor their own understanding while they read. The ability to monitor one's understanding requires a level of self-reflection that may be foreign to young readers. To model self-reflection, you will need to pretend that you do not understand something as you read in order to show children how to catch misunderstandings and use appropriate strategies to repair meaning. For example, you may pause while reading and explain, "Wait, I thought Dr. De Soto helped everyone, even large animals, but now he does not want to work on the fox. Let me go back and reread . . . Oh, here it says that he does not treat animals that are dangerous to mice; that must be why he will not work on a cat." Readers cannot fix up meaning unless they catch when they are not understanding. In addition, a reader cannot fix up if they do not have a broad repertoire of strategies and the knowledge of when, how, and why to use them to repair understanding. Thus, monitoring, clarifying, and fixing up are strategies that should come later in comprehension instruction.

Each of the strategies discussed here helps readers comprehend what they are reading by using different thought processes. Whether you are modeling predicting, connecting, retelling, or visualizing for your students, it will take more than one reading with different kinds of texts for children to be able to use the strategy independently. It is a good idea to concentrate on one strategy for a few weeks before introducing a new one. Similarly, it is also important to review past strategies so children do not forget them. Slowly, children will accumulate a backpack of strategies from which to choose when confronted with a new text. The skilled reader has a large repertoire of strategies and knows not only how to use each one but also when each strategy will be the most helpful for comprehension.

## *What Books Should I Read?*

Some books lend themselves to a particular read-aloud strategy better than others. Figure 6.8 gives an overview of some of our favorite books and authors for each strategy. When selecting books for making predictions, choose books that provide strong clues either in the text or illustrations. Books that include characters and situations with which children can easily relate are ideal for modeling making connections. For retelling, fiction selections should include strong example of the story elements for children to be able to identify. With nonfiction, books about cycles or processes lend themselves to retelling. Authors who use rich vocabulary, imagery, and descriptive details make it easy to visualize the scene. Mysteries and books that provide clues without explicitly stating the obvious are good for leading children to make inferences. Any texts can be used for questioning and monitoring, clarifying, and fixing up depending on the reader's understanding. More than likely your classroom library has several great books for modeling each of the strategies; it is worth the effort to reread them now with an eye for comprehension instruction.

| Comprehension Strategy | Narrative Selections | Informational Selections |
|---|---|---|
| Predicting | *A Wolf at the Door* by Nick Ward | *Just a Second* by Steve Jenkins |
| | *That Is Not a Good Idea* by Mo Willems | *The Earth Book* by Todd Parr |
| | *Suddenly!* (A Preston Pig Story) by Colin McNaughton | *Are You a Butterfly?* by Judy Allen |
| | *The Wolf's Chicken Stew* by Keiko Kasza | *A Drop of Blood* by Paul Showers |
| Connecting | *Owen* by Kevin Henkes | *Why Can't I Be Happy All the Time?* by Mary Atkinson |
| | *My Rotten Redheaded Older Brother* by Patricia Polacco | *Lightning* by Seymour Simon |
| | *No, David!* by David Shannon | *Some Things Are Scary* by Florence Heide |
| Retelling | *There Was an Old Lady Who Swallowed Some Books* by Lucille Colandro | *Farming* by Gail Gibbons |
| | *The Three Snow Bears* by Jan Brett | *From Wheat to Pasta* by Robert Egan |
| | *Giggle, Giggle, Quack* by Doreen Cronin | *How Do Apples Grow?* by Betsy Maestro |
| Visualizing | *Jumanji* by Chris Van Allsburg | *One Giant Leap* by Robert Burleigh |
| | *The Seashore Book* by Charlotte Zolotow | *Least Things: Poems about Small Natures* by Jane Yolen |
| | *The Legend of the Indian Paintbrush* by Tomie dePaola | *Growing Patterns* by Sarah Campbell |
| Questioning | Dependent on the reader | Dependent on the reader |

Figure 6.8  A Sample of Children's Books for Targeting Comprehension

| Comprehension Strategy | Narrative Selections | Informational Selections |
|---|---|---|
| Making Inferences | *Ballpark Mysteries #1: Fenway Foul-Up* by David Kelly | *Creature Features: Twenty-Five Animals Explain Why They Look the Way They Do* by Steve Jenkins |
| | A-Z Mysteries series by Ron Roy | *Our Solar System* by Seymour Simon |
| | Cam Jansen series by David Adler | *Roanoke: The Lost Colony—an Unsolved Mystery from History* by Jane Yolen and Heidi Stemple |
| Monitoring, Clarifying, Fixing Up | Dependent on the reader | Dependent on the reader |

Figure 6.8 (continued) A Sample of Children's Books for Targeting Comprehension

## Classroom Vignette: Modeling Comprehension

Let's listen as Mrs. Murphy uses the think-aloud method to model retelling to her second-grade class. Mrs. Murphy is experienced, having worked at several grade bands in her twenty-year tenure as an elementary school teacher. Second grade is one of her particular favorites because students are new readers and still navigating the ins and outs of comprehension. This year Mrs. Murphy has nineteen second graders in her room. During her reading block she conducts a whole-group read-aloud and also uses small guided reading groups to differentiate reading instruction. The focus of her whole-group read-aloud is to expose children to high-quality books, show her enthusiasm and love of reading, and model ways in which good readers understand what they read. Today she is reading a nonfiction selection entitled *From Seed to Pumpkin* by Wendy Pfeffer (2004).

"Boys and girls, today I am going to be reading you a great book called *From Seed to Pumpkin*. This book is nonfiction. You will remember that nonfiction means the book will be teaching us things that are true in the real world. This book is going to teach us about a life cycle—we will learn how a pumpkin grows. I want you to listen to the words carefully, because after we finish the book I am going to ask you to help me retell what we read. Experienced readers often are asked to retell things that they read to someone else, so we need to practice being able to retell."

Mrs. Murphy begins reading the book. The first several pages discuss what is happening to the seed after it is planted. At this point in her reading she pauses to think aloud. "What have we learned so far? The author has told us that pumpkin seeds are planted in the spring. They grow in the soil with roots growing down and stems sprouting up. The seeds need water and sunlight to grow." Mrs. Murphy continues to read about the next stages in the plant's life cycle. Once again she pauses and comments, "I have just read some new information about how the pumpkin plant grows. I am going to stop here and see if I can remember what I just read in order to keep it straight in my mind. The author just told us that the plant grows broad leaves and spreads out because it is a vine. Then flower buds appear with orange petals. The flowers attract bees, which pollinate the flowers. The petals whither and in their place grow hard fruits. I think I remembered the steps in the life cycle so far. Let's keep reading."

Mrs. Murphy reads to the end of the book this time. As she finishes reading, she explains, "Wow, there are a lot of steps in this life cycle. The author told us that the fruit grows larger and larger throughout the summer. Then in the fall, the pumpkins begin to turn orange as they ripen. When they are large and ripe, the pumpkins are picked off the vine and used for many different purposes. Some pumpkins are used for jack-o-lanterns, decorations, and even pumpkin pies. As the weather turns cool, the pumpkin vines whither up, but new pumpkin seeds can be planted again in the spring."

After reading, Mrs. Murphy continues to think aloud in order to model the retelling process. "So, as we read the book I practiced pausing while I read to retell the parts that I remembered reading. This is good practice to help me retell. Now that we are completely done reading, let's see if we can work together to retell the entire life cycle of the pumpkin. To help us retell what we read, let's write it down on the board. I am going to record the steps we retell in the form of a cycle, a circle that starts, goes around, and then begins again."

At this point, Mrs. Murphy draws a circle on the board. At the top of the circle she draws a rectangle and writes "Farmer plants a pumpkin seed" in the first rectangle. Then, she asks students for help. "Do you remember what happens next to the seed?" She calls on a student to help her retell the next part of the cycle, "Owen just told us that the next step is for the seed to get water and sunlight in order to grow roots and stems. I am going to write this in the next rectangle a little further along our circle. What happens next?"

Mrs. Murphy continues, "Good! Chloe just told us that the plant grows into a vine and buds flowers. Let's add that as the next step in our cycle." Mrs. Murphy continues working through each of the steps described in the book about the life cycle of the pumpkin, calling on students to retell what they remember and recording the steps in the diagram on the board. Once the cycle is complete, Mrs. Murphy concludes, "Wow! We remembered the entire life cycle of the pumpkin. You helped me retell what the nonfiction book told us about the pumpkin plant, and we were able to write it on the board together. Sometimes readers need to remember what they read and they do that by retelling just like we did today. Good work!"

Mrs. Murphy modeled the comprehension strategy of retelling by thinking aloud as she read. She broke the process of retelling down into manageable pieces of information, rehearsed them during reading, and then used a written graphic organizer to help her students retell after reading. She plans on modeling the retelling strategy several more times with her students and giving them opportunities to practice retelling using several different kinds of graphic organizers for support.

# Dramatic Storytelling

Many children love to act and role-play, so why not take advantage of this affinity for storytelling? Dramatic storytelling can take on many forms. Some teachers we know use a weekly repeated reading sequence and reserve the last day of their whole-group time for children to act out the story they have been reading together all week. Other teachers call students up during the reading to act out the action of the story as they are reading. Another possibility is to have a literacy center where students can have the option to act out familiar stories using costumes and props, puppets, or felt boards. No matter how you structure the dramatic storytelling, the end result is an engaging, hands-on approach for children to practice and explore their understanding of story elements, such as character and setting, and story structure, such as problem and solution.

# Technology Integration

When planning your comprehension instruction, do not overlook the possibility of integrating technology. With the right computer program or application, students can have added practice in comprehending text that either they read or is read to them electronically (see Figure 6.9). There are several programs that provide short fiction and nonfiction text passages with options for children to read independently or be read to. Most often, comprehension is evaluated by a series of multiple-choice questions after the passage. While these programs do not explicitly teach comprehension strategies, they do offer practice in applying the strategies and answering the types of questions that appear often on comprehension assessments. Especially for struggling or reluctant readers, technology can have a strong draw and provide needed motivation to engage students in practicing comprehension.

# Connecting with Families

Families are an excellent support system for developing critical thinkers. Educators certainly rely on parents and caregivers to support them in the instruction children are receiving in school. Parental support is key to growing children's personal and academic success. However, parents need the tools and guidance from teachers to make this a successful partnership. There are many ways to link families and teachers together to build children's comprehension skills, and we highlight three such strategies ideal for family-school activities here.

| Website or App | Description |
|---|---|
| **Raz Kids (Website and App)** | • Available on Raz-Kids.com<br>• Includes interactive ebooks that children can read or have read to them, vocabulary and comprehension questions for practice and informal assessment |
| **Storybook Reading (App)** | • Enables you to upload pages from your children's favorite storybook and record your own voice reading the text<br>• The voice recorder enables you to model comprehension strategies as you read! |
| **Kindoma Storytime (App)** | • Offers a large collection of ebooks that are read to the viewer<br>• Designed for two people on separate devices to be able to read and respond to the text at the same time |
| **NewsOMatic, Daily Reading for Kids (App)** | • Provides five news stories a day specifically tailored for children's reading levels<br>• Teaches current events and how to read nonfiction text |
| **Question Builder (App)** | Engages children in making inferences based on reading colorful e-text selections |

Figure 6.9  Popular Technology for Targeting Comprehension

## *Reading Logs*

One determining factor critical to children's comprehension is the time and amount spent reading. Teachers can use a reading log system to encourage children to read more and in a different way than they do at school. A wide range of reading logs can be used to vary the difficulty, time, and expectation of the home reading activity, but all logs should involve parent or caregiver participation. For example, a reading log for a kindergarten child may be called a "shared reading log" whereby reading with a family member can take many forms. The child might read a text that he or she has previously read in school to a parent; an older brother or sister could read a book or poem together with the child; or a parent can read a book or magazine article to the child. Reading on their own, together, or being read to ten minutes a night, every night, certainly adds up in comprehension miles! A reading log for a third grader should also reflect the cognitive demands of the third-grade literacy curriculum. Children may be asked to read thirty minutes per night from a chapter book and, in some cases, answer one inferential or open-ended comprehension question either orally or in writing. Parents can support the child in these attempts and initial the log. Teachers should provide a list of comprehension questions for parents to ask their children if this is an expectation of the reading log assignment. Again, the key is to increase the reading time and amount each day, develop critical thinkers, and give families clear directions and the tools to support this effort. We have provided some sample reading logs in Figure 6.10 (and in the appendix).

# Home Reading Record Log

Please help your child with this shared reading record.

Child's Name: _____    Parent's Signature: _____

| Date | Title of Book* Shared... | ✔ Read By Child | ✔ Read To Child | Comments... |
|------|--------------------------|-----------------|-----------------|-------------|
|      |                          |                 |                 |             |
|      |                          |                 |                 |             |
|      |                          |                 |                 |             |
|      |                          |                 |                 |             |
|      |                          |                 |                 |             |
|      |                          |                 |                 |             |

\* "Books" can be: books, magazines, news articles, recipes, menus, cereal boxes, etc. that are read together.

*Thank you for your support of your child's growth.*

Figure 6.10  Example Reading Logs

## Readers Are Thinkers! Cards

Aligning quite nicely with the reading log concept are a collection of questions we call Readers Are Thinkers! cards. Much time is spent in the classroom developing thoughtful, critical thinkers who can rationalize and cite evidence for their answers. These thoughtful answers are only crafted by providing thoughtful, open-ended questions. There are two main types of questions: thin and thick. Thin questions are literal and typically begin with *who, what, when, where,* or *how many.* Thick questions are open-ended and typically begin with *why, how,* or *what would you do if . . . ?* While asking thin questions from time to time is to be expected for quick comprehension checks, the majority of the questions asked should be inferential. These are the questions that require children to think and search and answer questions on their own.

# Reading Log

| | Book Title<br>Please have your child write the book title...it is good practice. | Parent's Initials<br>Read for 20 minutes and read each word on their word ring 1 time. |
|---|---|---|
| Monday | | ☐ Read for 20 min ——<br><br>☐ Practiced word ring —— |
| Tuesday | | ☐ Read for 20 min ——<br><br>☐ Practiced word ring —— |
| Wednesday | | ☐ Read for 20 min ——<br><br>☐ Practiced word ring —— |
| Thursday | | ☐ Read for 20 min ——<br><br>☐ Practiced word ring —— |

Dear Parents,
This reading log will go home with your child on Monday. Your child should keep it in their reading bag and I will collect it each Friday.

**Figure 6.10 (continued)** Example Reading Logs

Figure 6.11 shows a sample question from our Readers Are Thinkers! cards (also in the appendix). They provide parents with the critical comprehension questions to ask before, during, or after children have completed their reading time for the evening. These cards can be sent home with parents after a back-to-school event or parent conferences, and can include a letter explaining the purpose and expectations. The key is to communicate to parents that they are your partners in their children's education, that you value them, and that what they do at home makes a huge difference in their children's lives, both personally and academically.

# My Reading Log

S – Someone else read this book to me
H – I read it to someone with HELP
M – I read it to someone all by MYSELF

| | Title | S | H | M | How many stars does this book get? | Parent's Initials |
|---|---|---|---|---|---|---|
| 1. | | | | | ☆☆☆☆☆ | |
| 2. | | | | | ☆☆☆☆☆ | |
| 3. | | | | | ☆☆☆☆☆ | |
| 4. | | | | | ☆☆☆☆☆ | |
| 5. | | | | | ☆☆☆☆☆ | |
| 6. | | | | | ☆☆☆☆☆ | |
| 7. | | | | | ☆☆☆☆☆ | |
| 8. | | | | | ☆☆☆☆☆ | |
| 9. | | | | | ☆☆☆☆☆ | |
| 10. | | | | | ☆☆☆☆☆ | |
| 11. | | | | | ☆☆☆☆☆ | |
| 12. | | | | | ☆☆☆☆☆ | |
| 13. | | | | | ☆☆☆☆☆ | |
| 14. | | | | | ☆☆☆☆☆ | |
| 15. | | | | | ☆☆☆☆☆ | |

**Figure 6.10 (continued)** Example Reading Logs

## *Book Buddies*

We call this last family-school comprehension activity book buddies. Book buddies is essentially a take-home reading comprehension toolkit. Students are given a book buddies bag every Friday, and are asked to return with it the activities completed early the following week. Teachers keep a checklist of each of the book bags and rotate them throughout the year so students get a different one each week. Often, teachers introduce the book buddies activity at a back-to-school event at the beginning of the year so parents are aware of both the purpose and expectations of the program. Students (and parents) are always excited to receive their next book buddies bag! "What will the next book be? What fun activities am I going to do with this book? I can't wait to see!"

Figure 6.11 Example Readers Are Thinkers! Cards

Each book buddies bag contains a book, either fiction or nonfiction; a letter to parents providing a summary of the book; an overview of the activities in the bag; a list of before, during, and after reading comprehension questions for parents to ask; character puppets children can use to act out and retell the story; a story map or reader response journal; and a fun "craftivity" for parents and children to make together that links to the theme, events, or characters in the story (see Figure 6.12 and the appendix). Students then return the bags the next week and share something about the book and the craftivity they made at home.

**BOOK BUDDIES** | Week of 10/1 - 10/5

Dear Parents,

This week your Book Buddies selection is *Mrs. Wishy Washy's Farm*.  This is a fictional story with an engaging rhyming text.  You and your child are sure to love this story!

## DAY 1

This month, we are working on asking questions before, during, and after reading.  Good readers ask questions!  Please read the book aloud to your child and ask the following questions before you begin reading, while you are reading, and after you've finished the story:

**Before:**

1.  After reading title and looking at the cover: What do you think this story will be about?  Why?

2.  Have you ever visited a farm?  What kind of animals live on a farm?

**During:**

1.  Was your prediction correct?

2.  Why do the farm animals call her "Mrs. Wishy Washy?"

3.  Do you like to take a bath?

4.  Should the animals live in the city or on the farm?  Why?

**After:**

1.  What was your favorite part of the story?

2.  Can you tell me <u>3</u> things that happened in the story?

## DAY 2

Reread the story and ask questions!

We are also working on retelling a story in our own words and completing story maps.  Using the character sticks, prompt  your child to retell the story.  Be sure to provide help or to go back into the book to help them re-tell the story in the correct order.  After they've retold the story have him/her complete the "Beginning, Middle, and End" story map.  Provide assistance as needed.

Figure 6.12  Example Book Bag Contents for *Mrs. Wishy-Washy's Farm*

# Assessing Comprehension

As educators, we are interested in assessing and documenting individual students' levels of comprehension so that we can make informed instructional decisions. But how do we accomplish that, and what do we use to do it? Comprehension is so complex and multifaceted, can we really say at any one time whether a child has "good" comprehension? This central question, and many others about this aspect of reading, is what makes assessing reading comprehension controversial. The difficulty lies in the fact that children's comprehension is ever-evolving and growing and highly dependent on such factors as text difficulty, prior knowledge, vocabulary knowledge, genre, and interest in the reading topic. Other factors that influence comprehension are children's decoding skills, text fluency, and strategies for making meaning.

We take the approach that assessing children's comprehension is an ongoing process and should be documented at multiple points and through a variety of tasks, both orally and in writing. To accommodate this task, we provide a collection of evidence-based, informal comprehension assessment practices. These assessment techniques, summarized in Figure 6.13, allow teachers to isolate and target key areas of comprehension for day-to-day instructional purposes.

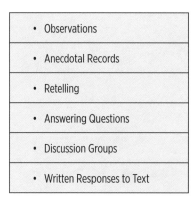

**Figure 6.13** Informal Comprehension Assessments

- Observations
- Anecdotal Records
- Retelling
- Answering Questions
- Discussion Groups
- Written Responses to Text

## *Observations and Anecdotal Records*

Much insight can be gained just by listening and tuning in to children as they participate in comprehension-related tasks throughout the day. For example, teachers can note how children are responding to questions during the daily interactive read-aloud. Are they participating? Can they provide thoughtful, well-elaborated answers, or are they struggling with responses or giving one or two word answers? Are they able to cite evidence from the text when answering comprehension questions? Taking the time to observe and write anecdotal notes serves as a powerful means of assessment and targeted instruction.

## Retelling

Retelling also serves as a powerful assessment practice because it taps into children's text comprehension; namely, the parts of a story, including setting, characters, problem, solution, and theme. Using a tool like a retelling checklist, teachers can identify specific strengths and weaknesses and make well-informed instructional decisions. See an example of a retelling checklist in Figure 6.14 (also in the appendix).

| **Retelling Checklist** | |
|---|---|

**Student's Name:** _____   **Date:** _____

**Title:** _____   **Author:** _____

| | | | | |
|---|---|---|---|---|
| Recalls main characters | ☐ | Makes comparisons/connections with other stories and own experiences | ☐ |
| Recalls supporting characters | ☐ | Retells fluently | ☐ |
| Summarizes main points | ☐ | Uses author's language in retelling (including vocabulary) | ☐ |
| Identifies setting | ☐ | Distinguishes between fact/fiction | ☐ |
| Identifies problem & resolution | ☐ | Distinguishes between fact/opinion | ☐ |
| States appropriate theme of story | ☐ | | |

**Comments:**

Figure 6.14  Retelling Checklist

## Answering Questions

The reading process requires students to engage with the text before, during, and after reading. A powerful way to check for understanding and assess if students are monitoring their comprehension is to ask specific questions before, during, and after reading. Children's response to these questions will indicate strengths or weaknesses in areas of comprehension and support instructional decisions. Figure 6.15 provides examples of before, during, and after reading comprehension questions.

| Before Reading | During Reading | After Reading |
|---|---|---|
| • Who is the author and illustrator of the book? | • Who are the main characters in the story? | • What lesson can you learn from this story? |
| • What is the title of the book? Why might the author have chosen this title? | • Where could the author have gotten the idea for this story? | • How was the problem solved? |
| • Have you read other books by this author? | • Which characters do you like the least? The most? Why? | • What connections can you make to your own life? |
| • Look at the pictures in your book. What can you tell about the illustrator? | • Choose two characters from the story. How are they alike? Different? | • What connections can you make to other books that you have read? |
| • What do you predict this story will be about? | • What is the setting of the story? | • What do you think will happen after the end of the story? |
| • Using the pictures as a guide, do you think this story is realistic? | • How would the story change if the setting was different? | • If you had been the main character, would you have acted the same or differently? |
| | • What was the problem in the story? How could you solve the problem? | • What was the best part of the story? |
| | • What caused the problem in the story? | • What was the theme or author's message? |

**Figure 6.15** Before, During, and After Questions

## *Discussion Groups*

Discussion groups offer students a unique opportunity to engage in creative, purposeful, and thoughtful conversations surrounding a common text. These groups are even more effective when students are assigned specific roles and responsibilities in which they each have the opportunity to lead the discussion, cite evidence, and share their points of view, while also learning from one another (Daniels 2002). Typically, teachers are facilitators rather than directors in literature discussion groups, so this offers an ideal time for teachers to observe and note students' strengths and weaknesses in relation to their exchanges. Asking discussion groups to complete an after-reading extension project is a means of authentic assessment for comprehension. Figure 6.16 provides a list of possible discussion-group extension activities.

| Book Talks |
|---|
| Students create a book talk, much like a movie preview, to present to other members of the class. The presentation can be oral or visual, or it can integrate technology. The book talk is both an assessment of the group's comprehension of the book and a mechanism for introducing other members of the class to a book they may want to read in the future. |
| **Dramatic Responses** |
| Students work together to act out a memorable scene or collection of scenes from the book. They can incorporate props, costumes, music, and dialogue. This also serves as both assessment and book preview for other readers. |
| **Written Responses** |
| There are endless possibilities! Students can write letters to a character or from a character's perspective, songs about the plot or the characters, book reviews, sports cards for characters, podcasts, talk shows featuring the characters, alternative endings, traditional essay prompts, or poetry inspired by the events or themes of the book. |
| **Visual Responses** |
| Some students may delight in the opportunity to express their understanding of a text through visual art projects, such as paintings, cartoons, sculptures, graphic design, game creation, dioramas, or mobiles. |
| **Culinary Responses** |
| One of my students baked and decorated a cake in response to a novel. Some books may lend themselves to creating meals in response to a character's personality, moods, or adventures, and it can be a lot of fun when the whole class gets to try a new treat! |

Figure 6.16 Discussion Group Extension Activities

## *Written Responses to Text*

Lastly, it may also be helpful to have a balance of oral and written informal comprehension assessment techniques in your teacher toolbox. There are a variety of creative and meaningful strategies that require students to write but also give them choice. Figure 6.17 offers some methods to capture students' ability to demonstrate written response to text.

- Reader response journals

- Short answer questions using an identified comprehension strategy

- Close reading activities

- Reader response prompts for fiction and nonfiction

- Using graphic organizers

- Writing research papers

- Designing a research brochure with nonfiction text features

- Creating a time line of events

- Writing a letter to a character in the story

- Writing a postcard to a character in the story

- Writing a poem about a theme of the story

- Writing diary entries that reflect the mood, tone, and voice of the character

- Developing interview questions for the author of the story

- Writing an alternate ending

- Writing the biography of one of the characters in the story

- Writing a content-specific ABC book

- Writing a song about a character or event in a story

**Figure 6.17** Written Response Activities

# Summary

In many ways, all the literacy instruction in oral language, alphabet, phonological awareness, and vocabulary lead to reading comprehension. As literacy educators in early childhood education, it is our goal to turn nonreaders into avid readers who understand and enjoy what they read. This is not an easy or obvious task. Reading comprehension is a complex process affected by many factors, including background knowledge, vocabulary, comprehension strategy knowledge, and motivation. One of the things that makes reading comprehension so complex is the relationship between the reader and the text. The reader-to-text relationship can be strengthened when there is a good match between text difficulty, subject matter, and quality on one side and the reader's strategy knowledge, interest, and engagement on the other side. Likewise, the relationship can be jeopardized when any one of the contributing factors is out of sync. Sometimes it feels like a miracle that children ever learn to read!

As the classroom teacher, you have an extremely important role to play in helping children become comprehenders of text. Certainly the read-aloud is the most important instructional strategy for modeling and thinking aloud how to use comprehension strategies such as predicting, connecting, and making inferences. Children need to understand what the strategy is, how to use it, and when to use it appropriately. They can only learn this by seeing you do it over and over again in your read-alouds. Children also need to learn about story elements—character, setting, problem, solution—and genre knowledge—narrative and informational text formats and structures. Children gain this knowledge when they are exposed to high-quality children's literature and informational text in the classroom and at home.

Assessing comprehension is an extremely tricky business. Many times it gets narrowly defined as asking questions after reading. However, this technique is problematic because it is easy to formulate bad questions and overuse has extremely negative effects on children's reading motivation and enjoyment. Thus, this chapter includes many alternatives that avoid asking children to answer multiple-choice questions after reading. While there is a place for that type of assessment, we caution you to be selective in your assessment choices. A portfolio that includes a variety of comprehension assessment types and purposes will give you a more complete picture of a child's reading comprehension.

Reading comprehension can be challenging to teach partly because of its highly individualized nature. Each child comes to each text with different strengths and weaknesses. That is the puzzle we find invigorating when we approach reading comprehension instruction. We know you are up for the challenge, for the benefits of creating strong readers will literally be life-changing for your students!

# Chapter 7

## Supporting Writing

**W**hen my son was two he grabbed a pencil and a clipboard during play and toddled over to the door. He motioned for me to come over to him, he babbled an incoherent statement, made a mark on his paper, and pushed me out the door. It took me a few minutes to understand what he was playing. He was mimicking what he had seen his daycare providers do every day when they move the class to the door and mark each child's name as they go onto the playground. By observing the world around them, young children come to understand writing and its various purposes. For my two-year-old, one of the purposes of writing was clearly to take attendance!

## How Do Children Learn to Write?

Learning to write is a complex process that develops alongside learning to read. Young children begin by observing the writing tasks they perceive being performed in their environment by adults or older children (Schickedanz and Casbergue 2009). Their first opportunities with writing utensils usually occur when they are given crayons and encouraged to color. Coloring is not only a worthwhile creative arts experience but also helps to develop the fine motor control necessary to write. As children become increasingly aware of the differences between their drawing and real writing, they begin to experiment with controlled marks and lines. Even before they can physically control their written marks, they are cognitively aware that their writing does not look like the writing of adults. To conform to what they perceive as real writing, they begin to scribble in rows that increasingly travel from left to right much like conventional print (Feldgus and Cardonick 1999).

With gains in alphabet knowledge, children make the developmental leap to including real letters in their writing. At first, children's writing will include both letters and letterlike marks in random order. Typically children most often use and reuse the letters in their name, since those are the first they learn confidently. As a result, name writing is an extremely meaningful and authentic first writing task for children. Children learning the letters and their sounds begin to apply this knowledge in their writing, representing whole words first by including a letter to represent the first sound in the word. From beginning sound writing, children progress to including letters to represent both beginning and ending sounds in words. Since vowels are much trickier to spell correctly, children will initially leave them out, then begin to include a letter which may or may not be correct, before eventually learning the correct short- and long-vowel patterns (Bear et al. 2011).

At this stage in their writing development, children have had enough experience to begin writing more. The volume of their writing increases. They sound out words to spell just like they do while reading. They also spell more and more high-frequency sight words correctly as they are introduced during reading instruction. Writing instruction can help children focus on organizing their writing into paragraphs, including elements required by certain genres and the mechanics of grammar and punctuation. Figure 7.1 summarizes eight developmental writing stages defined by Feldgus and Cardonick (1999).

| Writing Stage | Characteristics |
|---|---|
| **Emerging** | • writes in scribbles<br>• makes unidentifiable markings |
| **Pictorial** | • draws semi-recognizable pictures<br>• tells about pictures when asked |
| **Precommunicative** | • writes to communicate ideas<br>• begins to use random letters |
| **Semiphonetic** | • relies on beginning sound in words to match letters<br>• writes in left-to-right format |
| **Phonetic** | • includes beginning and ending sounds in words<br>• begins to use sight words |

**Figure 7.1** Developmental Writing Stages
Adapted from Feldgus and Cardonick (1999)

| Writing Stage | Characteristics |
|---|---|
| Transitional | • spells many sight words correctly<br>• uses vowels in words<br>• includes punctuation |
| Conventional | • uses larger vocabulary<br>• includes capitalization, punctuation, and spacing |
| Advanced | • organizes writing into paragraphs<br>• uses advanced punctuation and grammar<br>• incorporates elements of genre |

**Figure 7.1 (continued)** Developmental Writing Stages
Adapted from Feldgus and Cardonick (1999)

# What Does Instruction Look Like?

Figure 7.2 provides a preview of instructional methods described in this chapter for fostering children's writing. In the sections that follow, each instructional method will be developed and explained so that you can begin implementing the strategies in your own classroom.

| Instructional Method | Format | Characteristics | Strengths |
|---|---|---|---|
| Modeled Writing | Whole class or small groups | The teacher models writing in front of the class, thinking aloud as she writes. | • Provides a model for how writers think as they write<br>• Models that the teacher is a writer too |
| Interactive Writing | Whole class or small groups | The teacher models writing, sharing the pen with students for certain parts of the writing activity. | • Slowly releases responsibility to students, engaging them in the act of writing while still scaffolding the process |
| Kid Writing | Individuals | • Beginning writers are taught to use invented spelling to sound out the words they are trying to write.<br>• Later the teacher helps children to see the conventional spelling of words under their invented spelling. | • Helps beginning writers learning to apply their knowledge of letter-sound correspondence to the writing process |

**Figure 7.2** Preview of Instructional Methods in This Chapter

| Instructional Method | Format | Characteristics | Strengths |
|---|---|---|---|
| **Writing Workshop** | Small Groups or Individuals | • Students work independently on a piece of writing, taking it through the steps of prewriting, drafting, revising, editing, and publishing.<br>• Teachers teach mini-lessons on elements of writing and meet individually with students to conference about their writing. | • Allows for high level of individualized writing instruction<br>• Highly motivating for children to see a piece of writing to completion by working at their own pace |
| **Genre Writing** | Small Groups or Individuals | Students read multiple examples of a target genre, critique the characteristics and elements of quality for the specific genre, and write their own examples of the genre. | • Integrates the reading and writing processes<br>• Actively involves students in exploring elements of genre that they will be reading and writing |
| **Writing in Context** | Small Groups or Individuals | Students work independently or in small groups to write in meaningful, play-based contexts. | • Highly motivating<br>• Models purposes for writing<br>• Allows for daily practice writing |
| **Technology Integration** | Small Groups or Centers | Various websites and apps designed to target writing | • Good review activity<br>• High student engagement<br>• Potential to foster twenty-first-century technology skills |
| **Connecting with Families** | Multiple | Parents reinforce writing in the home. | • Fosters home-school connection<br>• Provides writing practice outside of classroom context |

Figure 7.2 (Continued) Preview of Instructional Methods in This Chapter

# Modeled Writing

Modeled writing is when you write and your students watch. Modeled writing can be done on a variety of surfaces—chalkboard, dry erase board, chart paper, or even Smart Board. When you write in front of students, you are modeling not only how to physically hold a writing utensil and form letters but also how to sound out and spell words, generate and organize ideas, incorporate conventions of genre or writing form, and revise or edit draft versions of writing. As the expert writer in the classroom, you serve as the model for the entire writing process. A critical element of effective modeled writing is your ability to make the process transparent to your students by thinking aloud as you write.

It may not come naturally to you to think aloud and verbalize all the thoughts that go through your mind as you are writing. In fact, it is pretty awkward for everyone when they first try it! However, in order for children to learn how to write well, thinking aloud is an extremely important learning tool. Depending on the grade level that you teach, you may focus on thinking aloud different aspects of writing (see Figure 7.3). For example, a kindergarten teacher might target letter-sound correspondence by thinking aloud as she sounds out the sounds in words she is writing. Working with more experienced writers, a second-grade teacher may target writing conventions by thinking aloud the required elements of letter writing. We recommend thinking carefully about your instructional goals for each modeled writing activity and focusing on one or two skills at a time so as not to overwhelm beginning writers.

| Writing Skill or Concept | Example Think-Aloud |
|---|---|
| **Letter-Sound Correspondence** | "Next, I want to say that we are going to play in centers today. I am going to write the word *play*. /p/ /p/. I hear the /p/ sound at the word *play*. I know the letter *P* makes the /p/ sound, so I am going to begin the word *play* here with the letter *P*. What sound do I hear next in the word *play*? /l/ /l/ that's the letter *L*!" |
| **Punctuation** | "I just wrote a question in our letter to Mrs. Smith. I asked her if she is feeling better now. I know that a question is different than a statement, so I need to use different punctuation at the end of my question. I am going to put a question mark here so that my reader knows I am asking her a question about how she is feeling." |
| **Ideas** | "Today I want to write a thank-you note to Officer Sporer, who visited our classroom yesterday. Before I start writing, I like to make a list of things that I want to include in my writing. I know I want to tell her thank you for taking time to come to talk to us. I also want to talk about a few things that we enjoyed. I know many of you were impressed with her uniform and badge. Let's include that in our note. Also, you liked it when she let us see her police car. Let's put that in our note too." |
| **Organization** | "OK, after my topic sentence in this paragraph I want to add some detail sentences to support my topic. I just wrote that the main character is scared a lot. One of the ways I know she is scared is that the author tells us she will not go into the dark room alone. I am going to write a sentence about that here to support my topic sentence above." |
| **Genre Conventions** | "I am writing a friendly letter today. Normally a letter begins with a greeting, such as dear and the friend's name. So, I am going to start by writing Dear Andrea, now I am going to move down to the next line of text and begin my message." |

Figure 7.3 Examples of Modeled Writing Think-Alouds

Modeled writing is a versatile instructional method and can be integrated across content areas and instructional purposes. Modeled writing can be used in classroom routines to maintain lists, introduce the day's schedule, welcome students with a morning message, or reflect on the day with an afternoon good-bye (Whyte 2004). In your language arts instruction, you can use modeled writing to respond to literature, introduce new vocabulary words, teach a mini-lesson on grammar, or apply comprehension strategies. Modeled writing can be used in science to make predictions, record observations, or chart data. During social studies instruction, modeled writing can be used to prepare for field trips, write class thank-you notes to guest speakers, or learn about new cultures through pen pal communication. Because writing is an essential learning tool, modeling it can easily occur throughout the classroom day.

## Interactive Writing

Like modeled writing, interactive writing is an instructional method in which the teacher serves as the primary model for writing (McCarrier, Pinnell, and Fountas 2000). However, in interactive writing, the teacher releases more responsibility by sharing the pen with students to involve them in the writing process. You can use interactive writing in all the same content areas we suggested for modeled writing with more active participation from students. During interactive writing, a great idea is to have students try to think aloud and explain their thought process as they are writing. You can share the pen in different ways depending on the grade level you teach. For example, interactive writing in kindergarten could be sharing the pen to have a student come up to write a letter or a sight word. In second grade, sharing the pen could mean having a student come up to write an entire sentence in a letter the class is writing together. The amount of text shared should depend on the abilities of your writers.

## Kid Writing

Kid writing (Feldgus and Cardonick 1999) is an approach especially suited for beginning writers. As children develop their understanding of letter-sound correspondence in reading, they can also apply this understanding to their own writing. Kid writing encourages students to use invented spelling or unconventional spelling that uses letters to represent the sounds children hear in words. Because children's writing will not all be spelled correctly in kid writing, it may be useful to explain the instructional purposes of the strategy to parents ahead of time to ward off any questions about how you are teaching spelling.

The primary goal of kid writing is to get children writing. Sometimes students become blocked as beginning writers when they know that they do not know how to spell a word

## Classroom Vignette: Whole-Class Interactive Writing

Let's listen in to a classroom example of interactive writing. Mrs. Ruble is a kindergarten teacher with several years of experience working in her public school. She has two half-day programs each day, one in the morning and one in the afternoon, with twenty children in each class. Rather than have a morning message prewritten for her students, Mrs. Ruble uses interactive writing to begin her morning meeting so that children have a model of her writing. She uses the morning message to remind students of events occurring during the day, especially if there is anything out of the ordinary. This morning is a crisp fall day in October.

"Good morning, friends! I hope you are well today. We have a lot of exciting things today. Let's begin with our morning message." She grabs a marker and positions her body so she is not blocking the chart paper as she writes. She knows it is crucial for children to be able to see her form the letters of her writing.

Mrs. Ruble is very good at thinking aloud everything she does: "What is the date today? Let's look over at our calendar. Calendar helper? What is the date today? That's right, Eloise, today is October 19, 2014. So, I am going to begin by writing 'Today is.' *Is*—that is one of our sight words. I am going to write a line here for the word *is* and ask a friend to come up and write the word *is*. Michael, can you come share the pen to write the word *is* in our sentence? Let's look. Michael spelled *is* with two letters—*i* and *s*. Exactly right! OK, so far we have 'Today is.' Next I want to write the month. October. That is a long word! *October*. What sound do we hear at the beginning of *October*? /o/ /o/ /o/, short vowel *O*. So, I am going to write the letter *O* to begin this word. I am going to use our calendar as a resource to write the rest of the word. OK, Eloise told us it is the nineteenth, so I am going to write a line here for the number and ask Eloise to come up to write in the date for us. Nice work writing the number 19, Eloise. OK, whenever we write the date, we need a comma in between the day and the year. Now I will write the year, 2014, and a period for the end of our sentence.

"Next, I want to say that we have a special trip to the Pumpkin Patch. I will begin the sentence with *we*; that is another one of our sight words, isn't it? OK, I will draw a line here and ask Caitlin to come up and write the word *we*. Since this is at the beginning of the sentence, Caitlin is going to begin the word with a capital letter. Friends, Caitlin spelled the word *we* with two letters, *W* and *e*. Good work, Caitlin! Now, I am going to write *have*. The next word is a sight word we learned a long time ago. It is just one letter. 'We have a.' I will draw a line and ask John to come up and write our sight word *a*. Very nice, John, you wrote the lowercase *a* here in our sentence. I'm going to reread what we have so far: 'We have a.' Next, I am going to write 'special trip.' Then, listen two more sight words that we know! I am going to write a line for *to* and a line for the word *the*. Madison, can you come up and write the first word for us, *to*? Very nice—*t* and *o* spells the word *to*. Ryan, can you come up and write the word *the*? Good, Ryan spelled our sight word the—*t, h, e*."

"OK, friends, I am going to sound out the next word: *Pumpkin*. What sounds do we hear in the word pumpkin? /p/ /p/, *P*. So I am going to begin by writing a *P*. /u/ /u/ I hear a short vowel *u* next. /m/ /m/, *M*.

## Classroom Vignette: Whole-Class Interactive Writing (continued)

Listen carefully, I hear /p/ again. Next, I hear a /k/ sound, which sometimes is spelled with *K* and sometimes with a *C*. I know *pumpkin* has a *K* in it, so I am going to write that next. OK, then I hear an /i/, short-vowel *I* sound. Last, I hear /n/, /n/, *N*. OK, so we spelled *P-U-M-P-K-I-N*, *pumpkin*. The last word in our sentence is *Patch*. Help me sound that out. /p/ /p/, *P*. /a/ /a/, *A*. /ch/, /ch/, sometimes that sound is spelled *ch* and sometimes it is spelled *tch*. The word *patch* ends with a *tch*. Now let's reread our sentence together. 'Today we have a special trip to the Pumpkin Patch.' Let's end our sentence with some punctuation. Did we write a statement sentence or a question sentence? A statement! I am going to draw a line here for our punctuation and ask Melissa to come up to write a period for our statement sentence's ending."

Mrs. Ruble keeps the writing in her morning message relatively short—two sentences. However, she makes the most of her time writing it by engaging students in review of sight words they already know and practice using their letter-sound knowledge to sound out difficult words. She models herself tackling these tasks so students can see and hear how to sound out in their own writing. Mrs. Ruble is a master at making the invisible visible for her beginning writers.

"correctly." This knowledge can lead to fear and even a refusal to write in some beginner writers. Thus, when you use kid writing you encourage students to sound out words they are unsure how to spell. To make this process concrete for children, teach them to listen for sounds in words and write a line for each sound they hear on their paper. Students can then use these concrete lines to write a letter or letter combination to represent the sounds they hear in the word. If they do not know how to represent a sound, then they can also leave their line blank. Just the simple act of recording the sound with a line helps get children to move past one unknown word in order to write more text.

An important piece of kid writing is for the teacher to spend one-on-one time with each writer to discuss work. The teacher asks the writer to read what he or she has written. Then, the teacher can model any mistakes in conventional spelling by writing the correct spelling of words underneath the student's writing on the same page. This helps to acknowledge the student's effort, provide a correct model, and offer encouragement without stifling the writer's creativity and writing fluency.

Kid writing is a good way to help nonwriters become confident beginning writers. As new high-frequency words, word patterns, and letter combinations are introduced in reading instruction, students can slowly transition from total kid writing to a mix of conventional spelling and kid writing for multisyllabic words. See Figure 7.4 for an example of kid writing.

# Writing Workshop

The writing workshop model (Calkins 2003; Fletcher and Portalupi 2001; Graves 2003) encourages teachers and children to think of writing as a process. The writing process, according to this model, includes several steps. First, the prewriting step involves getting students to generate ideas for their writing. Teachers can introduce children in the prewriting stage to multiple ways writers generate ideas, including brainstorming, webbing, outlining, mapping, and keeping idea notes. Once writers have ideas, they begin the second step, drafting. Drafting usually includes large amounts of uninterrupted time set aside for writing the first draft of a piece (see Figure 7.5). This stage may take the longest for young writers to complete. Next, with a first draft completed, writers engage in a revision process, looking at the ideas, con-

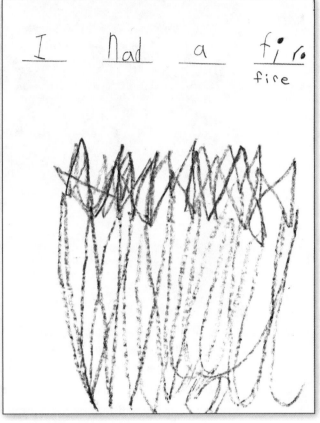

**Figure 7.4** Kid Writing Sample

cepts, organization, and flow of their writing for changes and improvements. After making revisions, writers go into more specific editing and look for mistakes in the writing conventions, such as spelling, grammar, punctuation, and capitalization. Finally, writers take their piece to completion by publishing it. Publication can be informal—typed and printed on a computer—or formal—included on a bulletin board, in a classroom newspaper, or in a portfolio.

Teachers have been using the writing workshop model successfully for years with young children. To work effectively, the model requires an established routine. An important element of the model is that students have choice over what they write and that they have time to work at their own pace on each of the stages in the writing process. Therefore, the instructional routine typically used in the writing workshop takes about an hour and involves much independence on the part of the students. At the beginning of the lesson, the teacher will offer a mini-lesson on a particular aspect of writing that he or she has noticed in students' writing. For example, a mini-lesson could focus on writing better hooks or using commas in punctuation. A mini-lesson could involve any aspect of the writing process itself or any traits of writing.

**Figure 7.5  A Third Grader Participating in Writing Workshop**

After the brief mini-lesson, teachers release students to work on their writing at whichever stage of the process they are currently in. To keep track of where students are, teachers will often use progress charts for students to indicate if they are prewriting, drafting, revising, editing, or publishing. As students are working on their pieces, the teacher's role is to conduct conferences with writers about their work. A good rule of thumb is to review the student's progress since the last meeting, discuss one or two positives, discuss one or two ways to improve the writing, and create a plan for the student's next steps. Informal notes on students' writing can provide valuable progress and assessment information as well as help you plan for needed mini-lesson topics. During the writing time, students can also meet together in partners or with a small group to conduct peer revising or peer editing. Writing workshop not only offers independent writing time but also includes opportunities for students to participate in the social aspect of writing by encouraging peer feedback for improvement.

The writing workshop ends with the group of students coming back together to share. The final reflection period can involve an author's chair where students can share their published writing or a piece in process for feedback. Again, we encourage you to allow students to share only if they feel comfortable doing so at that time. Writing is a highly personal experience, and depending on the nature of the writing, not all writers will want to share in front of the whole class. The ending reflection can also involve you, as their teacher, sharing general observations on the class's progress after conducting individual conferences. The final piece of the writing workshop is important for generating closure before moving on to the next instructional activity.

# Genre Writing

Genre writing engages students in writing in different genres by first carefully exploring text set models (Coker and Ritchey 2015). The premise behind this approach is that you cannot expect children to be able to write like a mystery writer without having read mysteries. Therefore, the first step in using this approach is to gather multiple examples, representing a range of quality, of the genre you are focusing on with students. Figure 7.6 provides some examples of our favorite genre text sets. You can find examples across many formats, including children's books, magazines, newspapers, and former student samples. Occasionally you may also want to write your own samples for students to explore.

| | |
|---|---|
| **Fantasy** | *Where the Wild Things Are* by Maurice Sendak<br>*Flotsam* by David Wiesner<br>*Jumanji* by Chris Van Allsburg<br>*Doctor De Soto* by William Steig |
| **Poetry** | *A Kick in the Head* by Paul Janeczko<br>*Be Glad Your Nose is on Your Face* by Jack Prelutsky<br>*Where the Sidewalk Ends* by Shel Silverstein<br>*Poems to Learn by Heart* by Caroline Kennedy |
| **Informational** | *It's Raining* by Gail Gibbons<br>*Clouds* by Anne Rockwell<br>*The Shortest Day* by Wendy Pfeffer<br>*Wolves* by Seymour Simon |
| **Persuasive** | *The Best Town in the World* by Byrd Baylor<br>*Should There be Zoos?* by Tony Stead<br>*The True Story of the 3 Little Pigs* by Jon Scieszka<br>*Dear Mrs. LaRue* by Mark Teague |

**Figure 7.6**  Model Text Sets

The second step is to allow children to explore the models. Children will need time to read and digest samples individually, as a large group, or both. Once students have read the samples, the teacher and students discuss what they are seeing in them in terms of characteristics of the genre and elements of quality. The goal of this discussion is for students to come to an understanding of what makes a good piece of writing in the particular genre under study. For instance, if students are studying letter writing, you want them to be able to explain what makes a good letter based on their critique of sample letters. It may be helpful to capture students' understanding by recording ideas on chart paper for future reference as they begin writing themselves.

The final step in the genre approach to writing is releasing students to compose their own examples of the target genre (see Figure 7.7). Having viewed samples and discussed elements of quality with one another, students are now theoretically equipped with the skills necessary to write with greater understanding. The genre approach is extremely versatile, working with every genre from poetry to essay writing. In addition, the approach can be implemented within the larger framework of the writing workshop model.

**Figure 7.7 Sample of Second-Grade Informational Writing**

# Writing in Context

In order to improve as writers, children need daily opportunities to write. They also need contexts to write within that are meaningful to them. Think about your own writing. Do you ever write just for the sake of writing? For most of us, writing tends to have a clear purpose. For young children, this can be writing during dramatic play. For older children, this can be writing letters to communicate ideas or seek information. Here are some ideas for providing children with meaningful writing in the classroom.

## *Writing in Dramatic Play Center*

The dramatic play center provides an ideal context for writing, as so much of writing is specific to the social context (Vukelich and Christie 2009). Children see different kinds of writing in different environments around them. They know that nurses and doctors write on clipboards during visits to the pediatrician. They also know that parents write lists to go to the grocery store. The first step in getting children to write during play is to provide paper, writing utensils, and other writing props such as clipboards or ordering pads. An additional step is to model writing in context through coplay. When you take on a play role in the dramatic play center, model appropriate writing behavior so that children see you writing while pretending to be a doctor or a customer at the store. Another important step is to think about preparing the play environment by including children in the creation of environmental print. For example, children can help create the play materials by helping to write any appropriate signs or labels. Figure 7.8 provides examples of writing props and tasks in several common dramatic play themes. Figure 7.9 illustrates an example of a writing prompt added to the Fall Harvest dramatic play area.

## *The Writing Center*

Children need a quiet area in the preschool classroom to write. For some children, a quiet place to write will be their favorite play center; for others, the writing center will be completely uninteresting. To draw all children into the writing center, consider carefully the materials you add. Children need a range of writing utensils—pencils, pens, crayons, markers, colored pencils, alphabet stamps, and dot stampers. They also need a variety of materials to write on—white unlined paper, lined paper, construction paper, different-sized paper, dry erase boards, stationary, postcards, and envelopes. You can also include a variety of props that aid students' writing—alphabet stencils, vocabulary cards, alphabet strips, tactile letters, and alphabet puzzles. We also recommend changing the types of supplies in the writing center periodically so children have new things to discover and explore.

| Dramatic Play Theme | Writing Props | Writing Tasks |
|---|---|---|
| Doctor's Office | Clipboards<br>Patient Forms<br>Prescription Pads<br>Appointment Reminder Cards<br>Doctor's Instructions | Office Hours Sign<br>Doctor's Door Sign<br>Patient Room Sign<br>Waiting Room Sign<br>Information Posters on Staying Healthy |
| Grocery Store | List Pads<br>Check Books<br>Receipts<br>Inventory Lists | Food Labels<br>Store Hours<br>Store Sign<br>Store Labels—Deli, Meat, Dairy |
| Restaurant | Order Pads<br>Menus<br>Receipts<br>Placemats for Kids | Restaurant Sign<br>Restaurant Hours<br>Menus<br>Recipes |
| Train Station | Tickets<br>Timetables<br>Checks and Credit Cards | Departures Schedule<br>Arrivals Schedule<br>Destination Charts |

Figure 7.8 Integrating Writing into Dramatic Play

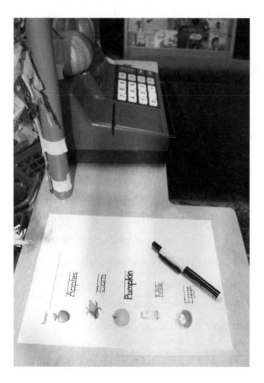

For older children in the elementary school classroom, a writing center is typically one center choice among several to frequent independently or in small groups. There are many tasks that children can do at a writing center; Figure 7.10 lists a few possibilities. We encourage you to provide a range of choices, so that children can self-select a task that motivates them to do their best writing. A primary purpose of the writing center should be to give students daily practice writing (see Figure 7.11). A secondary purpose can be to build skills within writing, such as organization, style, grammar, and format.

Figure 7.9 Writing Tools Incorporated into Dramatic Play

| Center Activity | Description |
|---|---|
| **Journal Writing** | • Students maintain a personal journal on a regular basis throughout the school year.<br>• Students choose what to write about for each entry.<br>• The teacher monitors the student's writing, providing encouragement and constructive feedback. |
| **Creative Prompt Writing** | • Students write to a self-selected prompt from a list provided by the teacher.<br>• This writing can reinforce genre and format knowledge.<br>• This mimics the process used on many standardized assessments. |
| **Response Writing** | Students write in response to:<br>1. a text that they have read—a review, a character portrait, a story element's retelling, a summary, a report, a creative response;<br>2. an intriguing photograph—writing a caption, writing a description, or writing a story based on the picture; or<br>3. an event—a field trip, a holiday, a science experiment, a geography project, a classroom activity. |
| **Writing Workshop** | • Students write in the center, taking an original piece through the process of prewriting, drafting, revising, editing, and publishing.<br>• Students can revise and edit in peer groups at the writing center. |
| **Grammar Games** | • Students participate in hands-on activities and file folder games, or practice tasks to gain extra experience working on skills such as spelling, grammar, or writing quality. |

Figure 7.10 Sample Activities at a Writing Center

## *Writing in the Block Center*

In the early childhood classroom, the block center also provides a meaningful context in which to draw and write. Just as designers and architects plan before they build, children can be encouraged to plan on paper before building with blocks. To facilitate this process, discuss with children the process that builders go through in the real world. There are several great children's books about the building process, such as *Building a Road* (Macken 2008) and *Building with Dad* (Nevius 2006). Of course, you will also need to make writing utensils accessible in the block area. Try including clipboards, drafting paper, tracing paper, and pencils close to the blocks themselves. You can also include sample blueprints or simple shape patterns to encourage student writing.

Figure 7.11  A Preschooler Journal Writing at the Writing Center

## Writing in the Science Center

Real scientists use writing every day to record their experimental procedures, data, and findings. Teaching young children the connection between science and writing serves as a perfect model for the authentic purposes of writing. A good science center should include journals for children to record scientific observations through drawing or writing. For example, one classroom in which we worked completed a theme on farms and hatched chicks right in the classroom. As part of the learning experience, the teacher asked children to maintain a journal of their observations of the eggs, and eventually the chicks, each day. At the end of the unit the children really enjoyed looking back over their journals to see how the eggs changed over time.

In addition to individual science journals, the science center is also an ideal place for modeled or interactive writing. When conducting an experiment or observation as a class, you can use chart paper to record students' predictions about what might happen. You can also record what actually happened after the experiment has been completed. You can write down the steps or procedures to follow, much like a recipe. It is also helpful to record data by using modeled writing to create a graph, table, or chart to capture the findings.

## Writing in the Classroom Library

The classroom library also provides meaningful opportunities for students to write. We know that sometimes students struggle to come up with ideas to write about. If children can connect writing to what they are reading, then they will always have something to write about. Writing as a response activity to reading develops comprehension and writing simultaneously—a win-win for teachers!

For young children, the classroom library can be stocked with books that encourage student creativity and writing. For older students, the library can also be a place to include model text sets of high-quality writing that exemplifies defining characteristics of genre and format and that students can try in their own writing. Figure 7.12 provides examples of picture books that encourage positive feelings about writing.

| Writing Concept | Example Children's Books |
|---|---|
| **Purposes of Writing** | *Dear Mrs. LaRue* by Mark Teague<br>*Diary of a Worm* by Doreen Cronin<br>*The Jolly Postman: Or Other People's Letters* by Janet and Allan Ahlberg |
| **Ideas** | *Never Take a Shark to the Dentist* by Judi Barrett<br>*Tuesday* by David Wiesner<br>*What Do You Do with an Idea?* by Kobi Yamada |
| **Perspective** | *Owl Moon* by Jane Yolen<br>*The True Story of the 3 Little Pigs* by Jon Scieszka<br>*Voices in the Park* by Anthony Browne |
| **Word Choice** | *I Know a Librarian Who Chewed on a Word* by Laurie Knowlton<br>*Max's Words* by Kate Banks<br>*The Seashore Book* by Charlotte Zolotow |

**Figure 7.12** Children's Books Encouraging Writing

A natural writing task in the classroom library is the book review (Coker and Ritchey 2015). At the heart of any book review is a gut reaction—either you liked the book or you did not. Even preschool students can form an opinion about whether they like a book given instruction and scaffolding. For these young students, a book review may be a simple drawing. For older kindergarten students, a book review can consist of a sentence or two.

While the format of the text can vary depending on the grade level you teach, the purpose of the book review is to communicate ideas about a book to others. Therefore, we strongly recommend creating a classroom system for sharing book reviews. One teacher with whom we worked had an interactive bulletin board in her classroom where students wrote brief book reviews on sticky notes and added their thoughts, whether they were for or against recommending a book to other students. A first-grade teacher we know uses her author's chair time to invite children to share their book reviews with the whole class. This teacher reports that often the shared book reviews create the most engaging conversations, with students taking sides either for or against a particular book. A great consequence of this discussion is that other students read the reviewed book to see whether they agree or disagree with their friend's review.

# Technology Integration

There are many great websites and applications that foster students' writing development. In Figure 7.13 we have included a variety of technology that enables students to publish their writing in safe, controlled environments. While there are plenty of applications and websites that offer students practice with writing skills such as grammar review, handwriting, or typing, we believe the greatest role for technology in student writing is in its capacity to help children publish and, ultimately, share their writing with others. Before using any technology with students, it is important to know where students' writing is stored (within the program or on the Internet) and what its accessibility to viewers is (inside and outside the classroom). For young children, we recommend avoiding programs in which outside reviewers on the Internet are able to write comments in response to students' writing. There is simply too much chance of harming a young writer's self-esteem with ill-minded comments.

| Website or App | Description |
| --- | --- |
| **Story Lines**<br>**(App)** | A social writing activity in which one student begins a story, passes it on to a friend who writes the next piece, and so on. Students can also illustrate their story and write captions for their illustrations. |
| **Strip Designer**<br>**(App)** | • Program enables students to create and illustrate their own comic strips; students can use photographs within their comics as well.<br>• Using speech bubbles helps students think about conventions of dialogue. |
| **Comic Life**<br>**(App)** | • Program helps students create, illustrate, and edit their own comic strips.<br>• Use of templates, speech bubbles, and graphics help encourage students to think about conventions of their writing. |
| **Story Builder**<br>**(App)** | Students record their responses to a series of related questions and the program links the responses together in order to create a narrative. |

Figure 7.13  Popular Technology for Targeting Writing

| Website or App | Description |
|---|---|
| **Writing Prompts for Kids**<br>**(App)** | This writing prompt generator creates hundreds of creative writing prompts for students who need ideas of what to write about. |
| **Kidblog**<br>**(Website and App)** | • Available on Kidblog.org<br>• A safe online environment for students to create and write content for their own blog<br>• Program includes settings for teachers to insert comments and to moderate posts from classmates |
| **The Saurus**<br>**(App)** | Interactive thesaurus that generates synonym webs and visuals to describe words |
| **Sago Mini Doodlecast**<br>**(App)** | • For young writers learning to link drawing and print<br>• Students draw a picture and record their voice describing or telling a story about their picture. |

**Figure 7.13 (continued)** Popular Technology for Targeting Writing

# Connections with Families

Since writing can be a time-intensive activity, asking students to write at home is a viable way to give them more uninterrupted time to compose, reflect on, and revise their writing. We also know that students need practice writing every day in order to improve, so connecting this daily writing task with homework makes sense. Here are some ideas for engaging families in writing at home.

## *Classroom Mascot Journal*

One creative teacher with whom we worked had a classroom puppet mascot that helped with morning meeting and various other content areas throughout the day. One year she decided to capitalize on the puppet's popularity by sending it home with students. She chose a special student each week, rotating through the class so that everyone got a chance to take home the puppet in a backpack. She included a writing journal in the backpack for families to record what the puppet did while they were at home with them. In a preschool classroom, the writing can be a drawing or parents can write with their children. Older students can take more ownership of the actual writing, using their parents for support. It is important to include the opportunity for students to share their writing with the class when they return the classroom mascot. This enables them to develop pride in their writing and to build community by teaching the class a little bit about their families.

## *Family Weekend Journal*

My son's second-grade teacher implemented a brilliant idea in her classroom this year. On Fridays she has the students reflect on all the things they learned and explored during the week. This forms the basis of a discussion that encourages students to reflect on their own learning. Then, students are asked to write a letter to someone at home explaining their impressions of the week at school. For each student this writing is highly personal, focusing on the aspects of the week that had the most impact on him or her. Once the writing goes home, parents are encouraged to write a letter back to their children in the same notebook. Students are given time on Monday to read their caregivers' letter privately in class. This exchange of letters between student and parent encourages reflection, writing, communicating ideas, and personal relationship building among family members. We love it!

## *Weekly Writing Prompt*

We know that as young children grow and move into the upper grades they will be asked to write in response to certain writing prompts in class and on assessments. Young children can begin practicing this skill by responding to writing prompts as part of their weekly work at home. We highly recommend sending a writing prompt home no more than once a week. We also believe in giving students a choice about what they write. A great idea for providing children with a choice in their writing is to organize a calendar of writing prompts and give students the opportunity to choose any they want to write to within that month. If children have a choice among many creative ideas, it is much more likely that they can identify something that engages them. Being forced to write about something that is uninteresting is a quick way to dampen children's motivation to write. This is especially true for reluctant or struggling writers.

As young children begin to write, it is important to consider how intimidating a blank piece of paper can be. Children may feel a lot of pressure to fill an entire page, even if they are just beginning to write. This pressure can quickly turn an enjoyable experience to a nightmare for some children. Therefore, we recommend making conscious decisions about space allocations in home writing activities. For young kindergarten and first-grade students, try using a sheet of paper divided in half, with the top half blank for drawing a picture and the bottom half including three or four lines where students can write one or two sentences. For older students, limiting lined paper to a certain number of pages can be comforting to reluctant writers who prefer set boundaries to the otherwise limitless writing task.

## Connecting Reading and Writing

You can also capitalize on the close connection between reading and writing in home writing tasks. Elsewhere in this book we have recommended that families read together to foster multiple literacy skills. Whether parents are reading to young students or beginning readers are reading to their parents, children can also write about their reading at home. A reader's journal can be used on a weekly basis for students to reflect on and respond to what they have read. The response can take a variety of forms, including a retelling or a book review. Within a reader's journal, children can begin to recognize which types of books and authors they enjoy reading.

# Assessment

There are many effective methods to assess student writing, and most include using some sort of a rubric, scale, or checklist. These can involve teachers assessing, students working in small groups or pairs to offer feedback, or students working by themselves to assess their own writing. In each case, the assessment tool should provide opportunities for both compliments and praise as well as suggestions for improvement. Teachers and students should be actively involved in setting goals for future writing pieces in order to meet personal and academic standards. Here, we provide various types of writing assessments and discuss their respective purposes.

## Writing Rubrics

Writing rubrics are effective tools for both teachers and students as they clearly define expectations and organize them on a point-level scale. Teachers introduce the rubric, explain the components of it, and model effective writing for each component during writing mini-lessons. In effect, the model demonstrates what good writing looks like. Teachers can use the rubric as a form of assessment since it provides a point value for the writing piece, and, more important, as an opportunity for "praises and polishes." Some categories outlined in a writing rubric can include ideas, organization, voice, word choice, sentence fluency, conventions, and presentation. An ideal place to start when designing your writing rubrics is 6+1 Trait Rubrics, available at http://educationnorthwest.org/traits/traits-rubrics.

## Writing Conferences

For classrooms that use the writer's workshop model, writing conferences serve as the primary way to provide individualized writing instruction. The teacher plays a facilitative role by listening, asking questions, and prompting, all in an effort to guide students toward becoming powerful writers. Some helpful tips when conducting writing conferences include: (1) Don't try to solve all the problems at once. Prioritize the goals and choose one or two writing conventions as a focus. (2) Offer students both "glows" (strengths) and "grows" (elements that need improvement). A rule of thumb is one glow to every two grows addressed in the conference. (3) Use some sort of conference checklists—one for the teacher and one for the student. These checklists typically include the dates of the conference and a recording of evidence of the glows and the grows that students can use to make edits and revisions and teachers can use as a reference when grading. Figure 7.14 provides a template for a possible writing conference checklist (also in the appendix).

Name _____

| Date | Revising Teaching Points<br>*How Can We Make It Sound Better?* | Editing Teaching Points<br>*How Can We Make It Look Better?* |
|------|------|------|
|      |      |      |
|      |      |      |
|      |      |      |

**Figure 7.14** Example Writing Conference Checklist
Adapted from WriteSteps (www.WriteStepsWriting.com)

## *Peer Editing*

Peer editing involves partners or small groups working together to help improve, revise, or edit their writing. It's important that teachers clearly explain the expectations of peer editing and model a sample peer editing exchange scenario so that the process is a worthwhile and effective use of instructional time. Some helpful tips when setting parameters during peer editing conferences include: (1) Glows—Students should stay positive and offer at least two glows. They need to remember that they are editing someone else's writing and should be kind and respectful. A good idea is to give peers a list of sentence starters so that they are offering specific praise. (2) Grows—Students should also be ready to offer at least two grows for student writing. A good idea is to give peers a topic list for the grows so that they are offering specific feedback. Topics can include topic clarity, word choice, using details, sentence fluency, and organization. (3) Corrections—Peers should engage in actual peer editing of the writing piece. Students can use the peer editing and proofreading marks directly on the paper so that students can make the necessary edits including grammar, punctuation, and spelling. Figure 7.15 outlines three helpful tips for successful peer editing (also in the appendix).

| Tip #1: Give some Glows! | Peer editor should stay positive and provide at least two glows. What specific things did the writer do well in the writing piece? |
|---|---|
| Tip #2: Give some Grows! | Peer editor should offer at least two grows. What specific feedback can you provide to the writer to improve the writing piece? |
| Tip #3: Give some Corrections! | Peer editor should edit the writing piece using proofreading marks. |

Figure 7.15 Tips for Peer Editing

### Student Self-Assessment

Students should be offered the opportunity to review the writing piece themselves before it is considered finished. This is a valuable process for self-reflection and continued self-improvement. A helpful tip is to provide students with a self-assessment checklist. It is often a student-friendly version of the same writing rubric the teacher will use to assess their writing. Oftentimes, students attach this rubric to their finished product that teachers can use as another form of assessment documentation and student feedback.

# Summary

Writing is closely connected to reading, for as students make decisions about the words they write they are constantly applying the word recognition skills they use when reading. We can use this natural connection to support students' development in both reading and writing simultaneously. When writing instruction is integrated within a social context at any grade level, students see its importance and value. For example, while second graders may find writing to a writing prompt less motivating, they can find a clear purpose in writing a letter to a friend or pen pal. The same is true for young students who will delight in writing for different purposes when it is embedded in their dramatic play with friends. As you plan for writing instruction in your classroom, think about how its social contexts and purposes will engage students.

The writing process also opens up many opportunities in the classroom to integrate technology. There are multiple platforms appropriate for young children to use in order to publish their work. Whether you experiment with podcasting, short animated films, professional presentations, or blogs, students will be excited to use technology in meaningful ways in the classroom. Taking the first steps of writing high-quality drafts and then revising and editing prior to publishing with technology will show students the value of the writing process. No matter what format your students' writing takes, remember that students need practice every day to become better writers.

# Chapter 8

# Putting It All Together

$O$ ne day after conducting an undergraduate class in literacy methods, a student with a look of grave concern on her face approached me. When I asked her what was wrong, she took a deep breath and said she was not sure she was going to be able to be a teacher after all. I asked her why, and she explained that she had no clue how she was going to fit everything that needs to be taught to develop students' literacy in the course of a day, let alone in a language arts block. I know exactly how she felt!

Even though elementary schools today devote a lot of time to literacy, especially when compared to content areas such as social studies and science, we still struggle as teachers to fit everything in because we know it is all essential. We cannot make a decision to skimp on vocabulary in order to boost comprehension skills—that choice makes no sense because of the relationship between the literacy components. In the area of literacy where the foundational skills build on one another, there is no way to leave anything out.

Therefore, it is essential that preschool and primary grade teachers think carefully about how we use our time. Since we are limited by the framework of the school day, including the specials, recess, lunch, and school assemblies, we must use the instructional time we do have to maximize efficiency. We must work smarter, not harder. In this chapter we discuss the global routines and strategies we have found indispensable in our work to develop students' total literacy.

# Scheduling Classroom Time

The biggest decision you can make about your literacy instruction is the decision about what to teach during whole-group versus small-group formats. Luckily, research by Walpole and McKenna (2007, 2009) helps shed light on this by suggesting the components of literacy that work best for each format. One of the major factors in making this decision is the grade level you teach.

The whole-group format is attractive because it enables you to ensure that every student receives the same message at the same time. However, the downside is that you are limited in the amount of time you can reasonably expect students to pay attention. The younger the students you are working with, the shorter their attention span will be, especially with the social distractions that occur when they are seated in close proximity on the rug or at their desks (Boushey and Moser 2014). The read-aloud method is best suited for whole-group instruction. You can control the length of time, ensuring you maintain more of the students' attention, by carefully selecting the text you are reading aloud and the number of literacy activities you are targeting. As we have previously discussed, the read-aloud can meaningfully develop all the literacy skills. For preschool and kindergarten classrooms, the whole-group read-aloud can introduce the alphabet, phonological awareness, and concepts of print. For pre-K through second grade, the read-aloud offers the most authentic context for vocabulary and comprehension instruction.

The whole-group format is also important for introductions to new skills and strategies. When beginning a new comprehension strategy, introducing the concept by modeling it to the whole group is an effective use of time. Similarly, using your basal reader or core reading-program curriculum materials to introduce a new letter of the alphabet or phonics concept to the whole group can be done effectively. However, with all literacy skills, students will need repetition and practice that can be best done in small-group formats.

The small-group format allows you to provide targeted instruction to address the needs of the students with whom you are meeting. The best differentiated instruction can occur in small groups, where you can plan the specific literacy targets and materials to meet the needs of the students you have grouped together. Small groups also allow for more attention and focus from the teacher, whose attention is divided among five or six students rather than twenty-five. Walpole and McKenna (2007, 2009) recommend planning your small-group instruction to target two literacy skills at a time. For example, when working with kindergartners, you may have one small group that practices the new letter of the week that was introduced in whole group and then practices segmenting and blending sounds in words. In the same classroom, you may also have a small group of students who are a little bit below grade level and need to review letters they have not yet mastered from past instruction and continued work in rhyming words. Finally, you may have a third small group of students who have already mastered all the letters of the alphabet; literacy targets with this group can be more advanced—working with new sight words and decoding words in the same word family. Thus, small groups enable you to meet the students where they are in their literacy development and move them forward toward grade-level goals. Figure 8.1 provides an example of managing differentiated small-group instruction in a literacy block with one teacher.

| Rotation | Group A | Group B | Group C |
|----------|---------|---------|---------|
| 1 | Teacher-led Group | Centers | Centers |
| 2 | Centers | Teacher-led Group | Centers |
| 3 | Centers | Centers | Teacher-led Group |

Figure 8.1 Example of Small-Group Rotational Schedule

There are several factors to consider when making the whole-group versus small-group decision. First, consider the literacy skill. As we have seen, some literacy skills are more suited for whole group or small group. Knowledge of your grade-level expectations and data from literacy assessments can help you group students and plan instruction for their needs. Second, the purpose of the instruction—introduction versus time for deliberate practice—is another important factor to consider. Sometimes you are introducing a brand-new concept; other times you are planning review and targeted practice for students to develop mastery. Time is also an important factor. We cannot reasonably expect young students to focus for long periods of time in the same instructional format. Finally, your role as the teacher also varies by format. If your goal is to work with all, then whole group is perfectly acceptable. If your goal is to help advance struggling students or further challenge students already at grade level, then small group makes more instructional sense.

# Global Literacy Routines

In addition to whole-group versus small-group decisions, there are times during the classroom day and global literacy routines that can help you target multiple literacy skills simultaneously and efficiently. We describe some of these briefly. While this list is not meant to be exhaustive, it represents routines that we have tried with success in our classrooms.

## Morning Work

Many primary grade teachers we work with have time at the very beginning of their day called morning work. During this transitional time when students are arriving from cars or buses, several administrative duties must be completed, such as attendance and lunch counts, and the front office may be making announcements. Rather than waste this precious time, why not use it for extra literacy work? morning work can be time spent independently reading with very little prep work; the only thing that needs to be in place is a classroom system for quickly identifying interesting books. Young students can look at books with interesting pictures even if they cannot yet read. This time can also be used for extra time writing in writing notebooks or continuing pieces begun in writing workshop. An important element for ensuring students' independent success is providing writing resources such as student dictionaries, lists of commonly missed words, editing and revising checklists, and choices of engaging writing prompts. Because readers and writers need time to practice, morning work can be used for this practice.

## Morning Meeting

Morning meeting typically is the first whole-group time of the elementary classroom day. This is the perfect time for targeting students' oral language development by planning a question of the day or building in a routine such as show-and-tell. This whole-group time is also ideal for an additional read-aloud, modeling the joy of reading, new vocabulary words, and fluent reading. Morning meeting can be used to introduce students to new genres, such as poetry, newspaper articles, and quotations. This time can also be used for modeling writing in a morning message to students about the day. Clearly, morning meeting is a versatile time to target several different literacy skills depending on your need.

## Literacy Centers

Literacy centers provide practice for students to work on developing the skills that have been introduced in whole group. Literacy centers require some work up front to get them running smoothly. You will want to think about them ahead of time and have a plan for management. For example, how will students know what group they are in? How will the groups know when and where to rotate? How will materials for each center be stored? How will centers work be differentiated for different groups of students? We strongly recommend creating a handful of centers that remain consistent (Diller 2003). Of course, the materials and activities at the centers can change with time, but if the actual centers remain constant you can save a lot of time planning. A list of traditional literacy centers in the primary grades may include a library/reading center for practice with independent reading, a word work center for practice with high-frequency words, phonics, and word recognition skills, a writing center for practice writing in multiple genres, and a computer center using technology as a resource to practice reading, word recognition, vocabulary, or writing. In the preschool classroom, centers may be more play based, including a dramatic play center for oral language development; a sensory center for vocabulary and writing; a writing center with a variety of writing materials; a classroom library with soft materials, books, and puppets to encourage oral storytelling and comprehension; and a manipulatives center with alphabet puzzles, word games, and rhyming sorts.

In each chapter of this book we recommend literacy centers to target each of the literacy skills necessary for developing readers and writers. It can be tempting to turn literacy centers into a series of worksheets; it certainly is simpler to plan a worksheet-based center, and every once in a while a well-intentioned worksheet is effective. However, we strongly discourage making worksheets your go-to literacy center activity. When we think of the overall goal of motivating young readers and writers to love literacy, using worksheets alone each and every day is a surefire way to diminish motivation. We encourage you to make your centers active and hands-on whenever possible to engage students in the important practice they need to develop their literacy skills.

## Integrated Content-Area Instruction

With different curriculum resources and teacher's guidebooks, sometimes it is easy to lose sight of the fact that literacy is embedded in all content areas. You cannot learn science or math or social studies without knowing how to read and write. Therefore, we encourage you to think outside the box of your curriculum. Think about ways in which it makes sense to incorporate literacy across all of your content areas. For example, read a great picture book connected to the social studies idea you are studying. There are some fantastic children's picture books and biographies designed to engage children in learning about the past. Similarly, there are high-quality informational texts that create effective introductions for new units in math and science.

Writing can be a good way to cement student learning in the content area while at the same time giving students opportunities to practice writing. There are many ways to meaningfully connect writing and content learning. In science, students can maintain a science notebook, a place for recording observations, descriptions of experiments, and data. In social studies, end-of-unit assessments can sometimes be written projects that combine social studies learning, reading, writing, and creativity. One example of this in geography is a pen pal project in which students read and write letters to one another from different geographic locations. Other end-of-unit projects may ask students to create a travel brochure, scrapbook, playlist, and CD cover; write a biography of a real or fictional character; compose a diary of a real or fictional character; construct a poster board display; give an oral or a visual technology-based presentation; or respond to a creative writing prompt. The possibilities are endless!

## Author Study

Once or twice a year, taking time out of your curriculum to devote to an author study can be extremely rewarding in terms of its effects on students' motivation and literacy skill development. An author study can be done at any grade level. We have seen successful author studies in preschool with Eric Carle, in kindergarten with Lois Ehlert, in first grade with Mo Willems, and in second grade with Roald Dahl. Of course, you can use any author for an author study. We recommend choosing authors that you and your students enjoy reading. A sure sign is if, after reading one book by an author, the class begs you to read something else by the same author!

In order to orchestrate an author study, you will need multiple books by the same author. You will need to plan time within the study to read several examples of the author's work and time to discuss with students what they see as similar and different in the various books you read. Creating big charts together for display across the study can be useful for keeping track of all the observations students will make. An author study can also include online research on the author's life and website, which can be interesting in showing students how authors work and fruitful in introducing research strategies or using technology tools.

Lastly, an author study gives you the perfect writing connection. After reading multiple examples of writing by the same author, students can apply what they observe about that writer's style in their own writing. For example, works by Chris Van Allsburg provide masterful mentor texts for learning the elements of fantasy writing. It is natural in the course of reading multiple works by the same author that students will want to try out the writer's style and technique.

## The Reading/Writing Workshop

In previous chapters, we discussed using a reading workshop model for developing students' word recognition and comprehension and the writing workshop model for fostering students' writing. While it is certainly possible to use the two instructional routines separately, we also wanted to take a moment to point out the obvious connection between the two. In a reading workshop, students read and discuss the same texts in small groups, sometimes with and sometimes without the teacher. In the writing workshop model, students work independently to take a piece of writing through the writing process. Why not combine the two to get that much more instructional power?

Teachers who use a reading/writing workshop plan a comprehensive unit around a literature theme, topic, genre, or specific author. During the reading portion of the workshop, students read and discuss multiple books connected by a common thread. Then, during the writing portion of the workshop, students apply their new understandings based on the reading to their own writing, typically writing in a format or style or on a topic related to the texts read. By taking advantage of the natural connection between reading and writing, teachers who use a combined reading/writing workshop model create authentic experiences for their students.

## Literature Circles

A literature circle (Daniels 2002) is an instructional approach that also combines reading and writing in a natural context. Much like adult book clubs, a literature circle in the classroom occurs when students are given a choice of text to read and discuss together in small groups. You can scaffold literature circles by prechoosing books that are related by theme or topic that vary by reading level. Thus, all readers, regardless of ability, will find themselves with a real choice of what to read that is related to what others in the same class are reading. For example, a second-grade teacher created a literature circle on the theme of friendship and gave her students the choice to read *Ivy and Bean* (Barrows 2006), *Bink and Gollie* (DiCamillo and McGhee 2010), *Frog and Toad Together* (Lobel 1979), or *Best Friends: The True Story of Owen and Mzee* (Edwards 2007). The teacher's careful selection included multiple choices, varying reading levels and text difficulty, and both fiction and informational text to appeal to different readers' interests.

Once students have selected the text for their literature circle and formed a small group of students reading the same book, you can support the groups as they make decisions about how much to read before the next class session. During the class session, students meet as a group to discuss their thoughts and reflections about the part of the book that the group read. To help support this discussion, many teachers will assign roles to the group members (Daniels 2002). Figure 8.2 provides a list of possible roles students can enact during the literature circle. For example, a discussion leader is in charge of keeping the discussion going and making sure every student gets a chance to talk. A questioner may come to the literature circle with a list of questions about the reading. An illustrator can visually depict his or her favorite scene in the reading and share the illustration to the group for discussion. The summarizer may write a short summary of the plot to help remind the group members about what happened in the reading. Through their participation in the reading, preparation for their role, and in-class discussion, students can build fluency, comprehension, and enjoyment of reading.

| Role | Description |
|------|-------------|
| Discussion Leader | Leads the group's overall productivity by ensuring that each member of the group contributes his or her role. A good leader makes sure everyone has a chance to share his or her responses to the discussion questions. A good leader keeps an eye on the time so that the group moves through every role. |
| Questioner | Generates a list of thoughtful questions to ask and discuss with the group. A good questioner includes a variety of questions to engage the group in discussion. |
| Summarizer | Composes a summary of the section of reading in his or her own words in order to help remind the group about what happened in the selection prior to discussion. |
| Illustrator | Designs an original composition from any medium to depict a memorable scene, character, event, or turning point. Shares the illustration with the group and discusses its significance. |
| Connector | Creates a list of connections he or she had with the text, including text-to-text, text-to-self, and text-to-world connections. This role may require additional research to strengthen the connections. |

**Figure 8.2** Literature Circle Roles
Adapted from Daniels (2002)

To integrate writing into the literature circle process, we recommend ending the circle with a culminating project. We see these projects as an effective way of assessing students' comprehension, piquing other students' interest in a book to read in the future, and incorporating writing into the reading process. Culminating writing projects may ask each literature circle group to write a book review to share with the class. After sharing example book reviews with students, they quickly see the authentic purpose for book reviews and the common characteristics of the book review format. The beauty of having students write a book review is that their writing can be shared and posted for their peers, either to recommend or dissuade them from reading the book. Culminating projects can also take on many other forms, including creative writing, creative book report formats, and informative writing pieces.

## Transitions

No matter how much we plan as teachers, there are always some transitional times in the classroom day when we are waiting for someone or to go somewhere. We hate to waste these precious times! There are many ways we can make these transitions into literacy gold mines.

A great idea for any grade level is to have a few tried-and-true books to read aloud during down times. I cannot tell you how many times my undergraduate students speak fondly of teachers who read aloud to them in elementary school. The benefits are numerous, including modeling fluent reading, spurring conversation and oral language, introducing students to new vocabulary, and simply demonstrating a love of reading. Consider chapter books that students in your classroom cannot read aloud yet themselves. Classic choices for classroom read-alouds include *Matilda* (Dahl 2007), *Charlotte's Web* (White 2012), *Lemonade War* (Davies 2009), *Flora and Ulysses* (DiCamillo 2015), *Superfudge* (Blume 2007), and *Harry Potter and the Sorcerer's Stone* (Rowling 1999). Poetry can also be fantastic for short transitions because of its length and rarer appearance in other parts of the classroom day. Offering children's poetry anthologies by Shel Silverstein, Jack Prelutsky, and Langston Hughes can be a productive use of two minutes between a bathroom break and the next special.

In addition, transitions can give you time for needed review of concrete literacy skills. In a kindergarten classroom, a transition may give you three or four minutes to review trickier letters of the alphabet that some students are still struggling to master. In a first-grade classroom, a quick transition could let you review a phonics concept, such as the bossy *R* or that the /ch/ pattern makes one sound. While in second grade, you could use a transition as a meaningful extension to a vocabulary word introduced during an earlier read-aloud. The best transitions take very few materials and little setup; rather, they maximize our effectiveness by using time wisely.

### Afternoon Meeting

Just as morning meeting begins the day with literacy activities that engage students in the classroom community, the afternoon meeting can also be a time to develop your students' literacy skills. Take advantage of the five or ten minutes at the end of the day before students pack up for dismissal to review what students learned that day. This can be a way to engage students in oral conversation, developing pragmatics and vocabulary knowledge. You could also choose to conduct this review in writing by modeling an afternoon message on the board for students to read and discuss. This quick review helps to cement learning, reviews important skills and concepts, and sets students up to successfully answer the inevitable question, "What did you learn in school today?"

## The Reflective Practitioner

We felt strongly about including a section in our book about scheduling time in your teaching routine to reflect on your own practice. Sometimes as teachers we get so involved with the day-to-day planning cycle that we forget to take a step back to reflect on our own work. We truly believe that this reflection is the component that makes for successful, effective teaching.

When we make time in our day to reflect on what went well in our literacy instruction and what did not go as well, it helps us to learn about ourselves and grow as educators. This type of reflection requires brutal honesty. If you need help being honest with yourself, consider using a camera to record your teaching to view later. It is hard to deny what is on a screen right in front of your face. Other teachers we know also enjoy periodically inviting a colleague into their classroom for some honest, objective feedback. No matter which method you choose, find a format that allows you to reflect honestly on what went well and what bombed that day. Personally, we like to reflect as soon as possible after we have taught a lesson so that our memories do not fade or begin to gloss over what we did.

It is also helpful to reflect on student learning in order to plan for instruction the next day. If you can identify which students got it and which students did not, then you have helpful information for planning your lesson the next day to include targeted review of concepts for specific students. In this way, our own reflection becomes an informal assessment of student learning and can help to catch students who are falling behind before it is too late. Figure 8.3 provides a listing of effective teacher reflection questions.

- Did students achieve the objectives? How do you know?
- What went well? What did not go as planned?
- How did this lesson support the required standards?
- How did this lesson reflect academic rigor?
- How did this lesson cognitively engage students?
- What will you do to address student learning in the next lesson?

**Figure 8.3** Reflection Questions

While reflection adds to our duties and responsibilities as teachers, we believe it is an essential element for ensuring our literacy instruction meets students' needs, remains engaging, and is effective at developing students into lifelong readers and writers. As you make decisions about how to incorporate all the literacy instruction necessary in your day, please make sure to include time for your own professional reflection.

## Summary

As my undergraduate student found out, it can be absolutely overwhelming to be responsible for teaching a classroom full of children to read and write. Since we cannot make decisions about what to leave out of our literacy instruction, we push ourselves and the teachers we work with to ask, "How do I do more in the time that I have?" While we would always welcome more instructional time, we all know that is not going to happen. Indeed, every year brings new demands on our time within the classroom. Thus, we must work within the confines we are given.

In this chapter, we have described several global literacy routines that can help you work smarter, not harder. The key to making these routines work for you is integration. Global literacy routines such as morning meeting, literature circles, small-group instruction, and writing workshop can cover several literacy objectives at the same time, saving time and strengthening the instruction itself. Obviously a literacy routine that targets multiple literacy skills simultaneously maximizes your use of time. Additionally, we know that young students' understanding thrives when new information is connected to prior knowledge.

One strength of the global literacy routines we describe here lies in the potential for you to connect learning across literacy skills and content knowledge. For example, you could plan a writing workshop unit to include having students research multiple rain forest animals and working through the writing process to publish and present a final oral presentation using technology. In this one unit, you would be covering multiple literacy skills—reading, researching, vocabulary, speaking and listening—as well as science and technology content knowledge. This is working smarter, not harder. We find this way of thinking liberating as literacy educators, freeing us from the pressure of scheduling discrete skills and covering everything we need to in the course of a day.

Teaching literacy is an incredibly important job. It is not an easy job. It comes with many challenges and hurdles to overcome. Therefore, it is crucial to stop every once in a while and reflect on your teaching. Reflection will most certainly benefit your students as you think about what went well in your teaching, what did not go so well, and what you would do differently next time. Taking this time benefits both your students and you. Because teaching reading is challenging, it is easy to burn out sometimes. Reflecting on your own health as a literacy teacher can help to rejuvenate you by reminding you what you love—about reading and writing, about your students, and about teaching in general—and is essential to your mental well-being as a teacher. Remember, the work you are doing is important, and we join your students in thanking you.

# Appendix

| Behavior | Description | Example |
|----------|-------------|---------|
| **Model Rich Language** | Add rich language by describing the illustrations or adding more sophisticated vocabulary to describe what is in the text. | "When I look at the cover of this book, I see three children holding pumpkins. There is a large pumpkin, a medium-sized pumpkin, and a small pumpkin. I think this book is going to be about comparing these three pumpkins." |
| **Ask Open-Ended Questions** | Ask questions that do not have a correct answer and require more than a one-word response. | "Why do you think the largest pumpkin will have the most seeds?" |
| **Repeat and Expand** | When a child answers a question, repeat his or her response and add language by rephrasing the response using correct grammar or more sophisticated vocabulary. | Child: "I have ate seeds before." Teacher: "Oh good, Sam has eaten pumpkin seeds at home before. You can toast pumpkin seeds in the oven and eat them as a healthy snack." |
| **Ask Follow-Up Prompts** | Stay with the same child for more than one question if a follow-up question is appropriate to get a more detailed response. | Teacher: "Which pumpkin do you think has the most seeds inside?" Child: "The small one." Teacher: "Why do you think the smallest pumpkin has the most seeds?" |
| **Actively Listen** | Listen to children's responses so that you can phrase appropriate follow-ups and repeat what they said. | "I just heard Mary say that she thinks the medium-sized pumpkin will have the most seeds. That is an interesting prediction. Let's keep reading to see if Mary is correct." |

## Let's Take a Book Picture Walk

A picture walk helps develop your children's
language and pre-reading skills.

- Have a conversation with your child
  around a book before you read it.
- A picture walk is not reading the book. It's
  talking about the pictures - getting to
  know the book together.
- Speak in the language that is most
  comfortable for YOU!

**What to do:**
- Look at the cover.
- Point to and say name of author and title.
- Looking at the cover, ask your child what
  he thinks the book will be about.
- Without reading the words in the book,
  encourage your child to turn the pages
  one at a time.
- Allow time for your child to respond to
  what you say - 5 seconds.
- Point to a picture and ask "what" questions-
  "What's this?" "What do you think is happening?"
- Follow your child's lead.
- Repeat what your child says and wait. This
  is one good way to encourage them to
  speak more.
- Remember to take turns talking.
- Ask questions to discuss what your child
  thinks is happening. Examples:
    - What is happening on this page?
    - Where do you think they are going?
    - What might happen next?
    - What do you think . . . ?
    - I wonder what would happen if . . .
- Acknowledge what your child says.
- Introduce or explain words and what they mean.
- Add a bit more information to what the
  child says.
- Help your child make connections to past
  experiences and future events.
  **Examples:**
    - When did you . . . ?
    - How did you feel when. . . ?
    - How would you feel if . . . ?

# patient

## Waiting for something or someone without getting upset.

*Starting Strong: Evidence-Based Early Literacy Practices* by Katrin Blamey and Katherine Beauchat.

188

Copyright © 2016. Stenhouse Publishers.

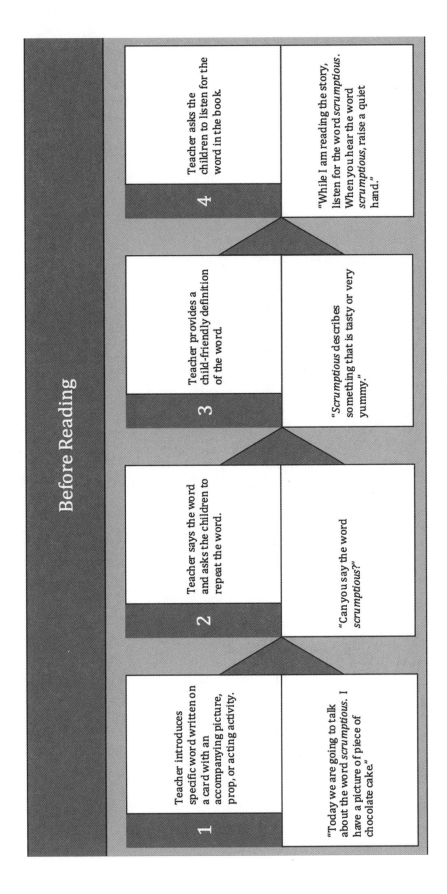

## Before Reading

**1**

Teacher introduces specific word written on a card with an accompanying picture, prop, or acting activity.

"Today we are going to talk about the word *scrumptious*. I have a picture of piece of chocolate cake."

**2**

Teacher says the word and asks the children to repeat the word.

"Can you say the word *scrumptious?*"

**3**

Teacher provides a child-friendly definition of the word.

"*Scrumptious* describes something that is tasty or very yummy."

**4**

Teacher asks the children to listen for the word in the book.

"While I am reading the story, listen for the word *scrumptious*. When you hear the word *scrumptious*, raise a quiet hand."

# Scrumptious

## Something that is very tasty or yummy.

*Starting Strong: Evidence-Based Early Literacy Practices* by Katrin Blamey and Katherine Beauchat.

190

Copyright © 2016. Stenhouse Publishers.

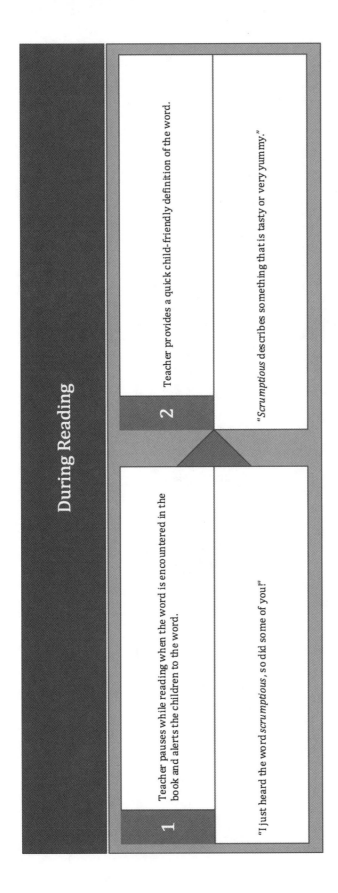

## During Reading

**1**

Teacher pauses while reading when the word is encountered in the book and alerts the children to the word.

"I just heard the word *scrumptious*, so did some of you!"

**2**

Teacher provides a quick child-friendly definition of the word.

"*Scrumptious* describes something that is tasty or very yummy."

# After Reading

**1**
Teacher reintroduces the word using the picture, prop, or acting activity.

"Remember, today we are talking about the word *scrumptious*. The chocolate cake is *scrumptious*."

**2**
Teacher asks the children to repeat the word.

"Can you say the word *scrumptious*?"

**3**
Teacher provides a child-friendly definition of the word.

"*Scrumptious* describes something that is tasty or very yummy."

**4**
Teacher physically goes back into the pages of the book to talk about how the word was used in the context of the story.

"Let's go back into the book to see where the word *scrumptious* is used. Oh, here it is...the wolf made a stack of 100 *scrumptious* pancakes."

**5**
Teacher provides examples of using the word outside of the context of the story.

"Other things can be *scrumptious too.* Thanksgiving dinner is very *scrumptious.* Ice cream cones are *scrumptious.*"

**6**
Teacher asks the children to say the word they have been learning.

"What word have we been learning? Say *scrumptious*."

## Before Reading

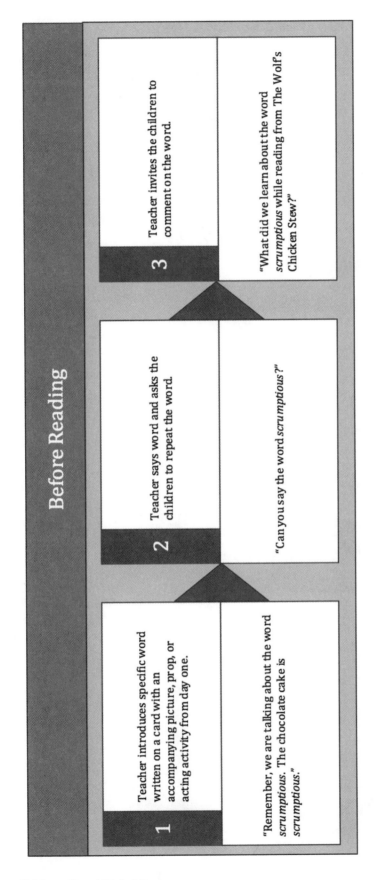

**1** Teacher introduces specific word written on a card with an accompanying picture, prop, or acting activity from day one.

"Remember, we are talking about the word *scrumptious*. The chocolate cake is *scrumptious*."

**2** Teacher says word and asks the children to repeat the word.

"Can you say the word *scrumptious*?"

**3** Teacher invites the children to comment on the word.

"What did we learn about the word *scrumptious* while reading from The Wolf's Chicken Stew?"

# During Reading

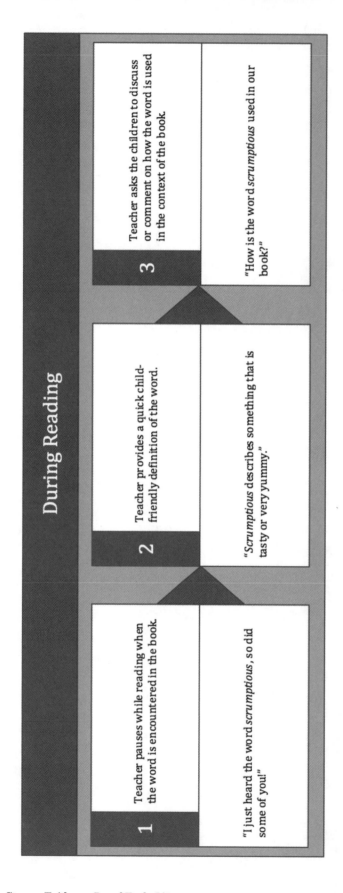

**1**

Teacher pauses while reading when the word is encountered in the book.

"I just heard the word *scrumptious*, so did some of you!"

**2**

Teacher provides a quick child-friendly definition of the word.

"*Scrumptious* describes something that is tasty or very yummy."

**3**

Teacher asks the children to discuss or comment on how the word is used in the context of the book.

"How is the word *scrumptious* used in our book?"

# After Reading

**1** Teacher reintroduces the word written on card with accompanying picture, prop, or acting activity.

"Remember, today we are talking about the word *scrumptious*. This chocolate cake is very *scrumptious*."

**2** Teacher asks the children to repeat the word.

"Can you say the word *scrumptious*?"

**3** Teacher provides a child-friendly definition of the word.

"*Scrumptious* describes something that is tasty or very yummy."

**4** Teacher physically goes back into the pages of the book and asks the children how the word was used in the context of

"Let's go back into the book to see where the word *scrumptious* is used. Oh, here it is. Can you tell me why these pancakes are *scrumptious*?"

**5** Teacher invites the children to think of examples of using the word outside the context of the book.

"Can you think of other things that are *scrumptious*?"

**6** Teacher asks the children to say the word they have been learning.

"What word have we been learning? Say *scrumptious*."

*Starting Strong: Evidence-Based Early Literacy Practices* by Katrin Blamey and Katherine Beauchat.

195

Copyright © 2016. Stenhouse Publishers.

DIRECTIONS: Each night please select one activity from the menu to complete using your Word Work words. Ask your caregiver to initial and date the box to indicate which activity you completed each night. Please return your menu on Friday of week.

| | | | |
|---|---|---|---|
| Write your words once in red. Then trace over the words a second time in green and a third time in purple. | Put some rice or flour on a baking sheet. Write your words by moving your finger through the rice or flour. | Use letter tiles or magnetic letters to write your words on a table or refrigerator. | Write a poem or short story using as many of your words as you can appropriately. For an extra challenge, illustrate your poem or story. |
| Go outside and write your words in chalk on a sidewalk or driveway. | Draw a picture and hide your words in it. See if someone else can find your hidden words. | Ask a caregiver if you can use a computer to type your words. | Choose four words and write a sentence using each one. Make sure to underline your target word in its sentence. For an extra challenge, see if you can use two words appropriately in one sentence. |
| Put some shaving cream in a tray or on a piece of wax paper on the table. Write your words in the shaving cream. | Look through a magazine or newspaper. Circle any of your words you find with a pencil or crayon. | Write your words in alphabetical order from A–Z or backward from Z–A. | Ask a caregiver to download the Spelling City app (www. spellingcity.com) on an electronic device to play games with your words. |

| Acronym | Type of Question | Example |
|---|---|---|
| C | **C**ompletion Questions | "Whenever Kitten saw Splat, she pulled his ears and poked his belly, tied his tail and called him _____." |
| R | **R**ecall Questions | "Who gave a valentine first? Second? Last?" |
| O | **O**pen-Ended Questions | "Why do you think Splat gets tongue tied every time he sees Kitten?" |
| W | **W**h- Questions | "Where are Splat and Kitten?" |
| D | **D**istancing Questions | "Have you ever sent or received a valentine? What did it say?" |

### Predicting

When I guess what will happen next in the story using text clues

### Text Connections

When I make connections to the book that I am reading to other things

(text-to-text, text-to-self, text-to-world)

### Retelling

When I explain what happened in the text using story elements (characters, setting, lesson, problem, solution, and purpose)

### Visualizing

When I create a mental image in my mind using the details in the story to help me better understand

### Questioning

When I ask myself questions BEFORE, DURING, and AFTER reading the text

### Inferring

When I look for clues to try and figure out what the author is trying to say, but doesn't

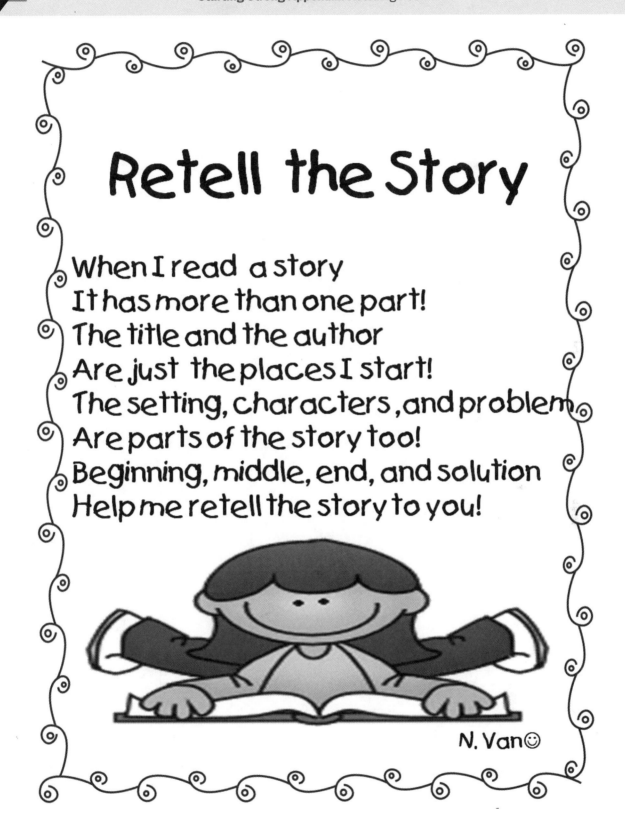

# Retell the Story

When I read a story
It has more than one part!
The title and the author
Are just the places I start!
The setting, characters, and problem
Are parts of the story too!
Beginning, middle, end, and solution
Help me retell the story to you!

N. Van☺

Child's Name: _____

Parent's Signature: _____

# Home Reading Record Log

Please help your child with this shared reading record.

| Date | Title of Book* Shared... | ✓ Read By<br>Child | ✓ Read To<br>Child | Comments... |
|---|---|---|---|---|
|  |  |  |  |  |
|  |  |  |  |  |
|  |  |  |  |  |
|  |  |  |  |  |
|  |  |  |  |  |

\* "Books" can be: books, magazines, news articles, recipes, menus, cereal boxes, etc. that are read together.

*Thank you for your support of your child's growth.*

# Reading Log

| | Book Title — Please have your child write the book title...it is good practice. | Parent's Initials — Read for 20 minutes and read each word on their word ring 1 time. |
|---|---|---|
| Monday | | ☐ Read for 20 min ☐ Practiced word ring |
| Tuesday | | ☐ Read for 20 min ☐ Practiced word ring |
| Wednesday | | ☐ Read for 20 min ☐ Practiced word ring |
| Thursday | | ☐ Read for 20 min ☐ Practiced word ring |

Dear Parents,
This reading log will go home with your child on Monday. Your child should keep it in their reading bag and I will collect it each Friday.

201

# My Reading Log

S – Someone else read this book to me
H – I read it to someone with HELP
M – I read it to someone all by MYSELF

| Title | S | H | M | How many stars does this book get? | Parent's Initials |
|-------|---|---|---|-----------------------------------|-------------------|
| 1. | | | | ☆☆☆☆☆ | |
| 2. | | | | ☆☆☆☆☆ | |
| 3. | | | | ☆☆☆☆☆ | |
| 4. | | | | ☆☆☆☆☆ | |
| 5. | | | | ☆☆☆☆☆ | |
| 6. | | | | ☆☆☆☆☆ | |
| 7. | | | | ☆☆☆☆☆ | |
| 8. | | | | ☆☆☆☆☆ | |
| 9. | | | | ☆☆☆☆☆ | |
| 10. | | | | ☆☆☆☆☆ | |
| 11. | | | | ☆☆☆☆☆ | |
| 12. | | | | ☆☆☆☆☆ | |
| 13. | | | | ☆☆☆☆☆ | |
| 14. | | | | ☆☆☆☆☆ | |
| 15. | | | | ☆☆☆☆☆ | |

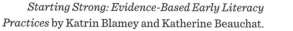

# Readers are Thinkers!

What lesson could someone learn from this story?
Use details from the story to support your thinking.

*Starting Strong: Evidence-Based Early Literacy Practices* by Katrin Blamey and Katherine Beauchat.

203

Copyright © 2016. Stenhouse Publishers.

**BOOK BUDDIES** | Week of 10/1 - 10/5

Dear Parents,

This week your Book Buddies selection is *Mrs. Wishy Washy's Farm*. This is a fictional story with an engaging rhyming text. You and your child are sure to love this story!

## DAY 1

This month, we are working on asking questions before, during, and after reading. Good readers ask questions! Please read the book aloud to your child and ask the following questions before you begin reading, while you are reading, and after you've finished the story:

### Before:

1. After reading title and looking at the cover: What do you think this story will be about? Why?

2. Have you ever visited a farm? What kind of animals live on a farm?

### During:

1. Was your prediction correct?

2. Why do the farm animals call her "Mrs. Wishy Washy?"

3. Do you like to take a bath?

4. Should the animals live in the city or on the farm? Why?

### After:

1. What was your favorite part of the story?

2. Can you tell me 3 things that happened in the story?

## DAY 2

Reread the story and ask questions!

We are also working on retelling a story in our own words and completing story maps. Using the character sticks, prompt your child to retell the story. Be sure to provide help or to go back into the book to help them retell the story in the correct order. After they've retold the story have him/her complete the "Beginning, Middle, and End" story map. Provide assistance as needed.

## Retelling Checklist

Student's Name: _____  Date: _____

Title: _____  Author: _____

| | |
|---|---|
| ☐ Recalls main characters | ☐ Makes comparisons/connections with other stories and own experiences |
| ☐ Recalls supporting characters | ☐ Retells fluently |
| ☐ Summarizes main points | ☐ Uses author's language in retelling (including vocabulary) |
| ☐ Identifies setting | ☐ Distinguishes between fact/fiction |
| ☐ Identifies problem & resolution | ☐ Distinguishes between fact/opinion |
| ☐ States appropriate theme of story | |

Comments:

*Starting Strong: Evidence-Based Early Literacy Practices* by Katrin Blamey and Katherine Beauchat.

 205

Name _____

| Date | Revising Teaching Points<br>*How Can We Make It Sound Better?* | Editing Teaching Points<br>*How Can We Make It Look Better?* |
|---|---|---|
|  |  |  |
|  |  |  |
|  |  |  |

| | |
|---|---|
| **Tip #1:**<br>**Give some Glows!** | Peer editor should stay positive and provide at least two glows. What specific things did the writer do well in the writing piece? |
| **Tip #2:**<br>**Give some Grows!** | Peer editor should offer at least two grows. What specific feedback can you provide to the writer to improve the writing piece? |
| **Tip #3:**<br>**Give some Corrections!** | Peer editor should complete an edit of the writing piece using proofreading marks. |

# Bibliography

Adams, M. J. 1990. *Beginning to Read: Thinking and Learning About Print.* Cambridge, MA: MIT Press.

Aram, D. 2006. "Early Literacy Interventions: The Relative Roles of Storybook Reading, Alphabetic Activities, and Their Combination." *Reading and Writing: An Interdisciplinary Journal* 19: 489-515.

Bardige, B. 2009. *Talk to Me, Baby! How You Can Support Young Children's Language Development.* Baltimore, MD: Brookes.

Bear, D. R., M. A. Invernizzi, S. Templeton, and F. A. Johnston. 2011. *Words Their Way: Word Study for Phonics, Vocabulary, and Spelling Instruction.* 5th ed. New York: Pearson.

Beck, I. J., and M. G. McKeown. 2007. "Increasing Young Low-Income Children's Oral Vocabulary Repertoires Through Rich and Focused Instruction." *Elementary School Journal* 107 (3): 251–71.

Beck, I. J., M. G. McKeown, and L. Kucan. 2002. *Bringing Words to Life: Robust Vocabulary Instruction.* New York: Guilford Press.

Berk, L. 2012. *Child Development.* 9th ed. New York: Pearson.

Biemiller, A. 2001. "Teaching Vocabulary: Early, Direct, and Sequential." *American Educator* 25: 24–28.

Biemiller, A., and N. Slonim. 2001. "Estimating Root Word Vocabulary Growth in Normative and Advantaged Populations: Evidence for a Common Sequence of Vocabulary Acquisition." *Journal of Educational Psychology* 93: 498–520.

Blamey, K. L., and K. A. Beauchat. 2011. "Word Walk: Vocabulary Instruction for Young Children." *The Reading Teacher* 65 (1): 71-75.

Bodrova, E., and D. J. Leong. 2003. "Chopsticks and Counting Chips: Do Play and Foundational Skills Need to Compete for the Teacher's Attention in an Early Childhood Classroom?" *Beyond the Journal: Young Children on the Web*. https://www.naeyc.org/files/yc/file/200305/Chopsticks_Bodrova.pdf.

Boushey, G., and J. Moser. 2006. *The Daily 5*. Portland, ME: Stenhouse.

———. 2014. *The Daily 5: Fostering Literacy in the Elementary Grades*. 2d ed. Portland, ME: Stenhouse.

Calkins, L. 2003. *Launching the Writing Workshop*. Portsmouth, NH: Heinemann.

Clay, M. M. 1991. *Becoming Literate: The Construction of Inner Control*. Portsmouth, NH: Heinemann.

Coker, D. L., and K. D. Ritchey. 2015. *Teaching Beginning Writers*. New York: Guilford.

Collins, M. 2010. "ELL Preschoolers' English Vocabulary Acquisition from Storybook Reading." *Early Childhood Research Quarterly* 25: 84–97.

Cunningham, A. E., and K. E. Stanovich. 1997. "Early Reading Acquisition and Its Relation to Reading Experience and Ability 10 Years Later." *Developmental Psychology* 33 (6): 934–45.

Daniels, H. 2002. *Literature Circles: Voice and Choice in Book Clubs and Reading Groups*. Portland, ME: Stenhouse.

Dickinson, D. K., A. McCabe, and M. J. Essex. 2006. "A Window of Opportunity We Must Open to All: The Case for Preschool with High-Quality Support for Language and Literacy." In *Handbook of Early Literacy Research*, ed. D. K. Dickinson and S. B. Neuman. New York: Guilford.

Dickinson, D. K., A. McCabe, and K. Sprague. 2001. "Teacher Rating of Oral Language and Literacy (TROLL): A Research-Based Tool." Center for the Improvement of Early Reading Achievement. Report #3-016.

Diller, D. 2003. *Literacy Work Stations: Making Centers Work*. Portland, ME: Stenhouse.

———. 2007. *Making the Most of Small Groups: Differentiation for All*. Portland, ME: Stenhouse.

# Bibliography

Education West. "6+1 Trait Rubrics." Retrieved from http://educationnorthwest.org/traits/traits-rubrics.

Elkonin, D. 1971. "Development of Speech." In *The Psychology of Preschool Children*, ed. A.V. Zaporozhets and D. Elkonin. Cambridge, MA: MIT Press.

Enz, B., and J. Christie. 1997. "Teacher Play Interaction Styles: Effects on Play Behavior and Relationships with Teacher Training and Experience." *International Journal of Early Childhood Education* 2: 55-69.

Feldgus, E. G., and I. Cardonick. 1999. *Kid Writing: A Systematic Approach to Phonics, Journals and Writing Workshop*. Columbus, OH: Wright Group.

Fletcher, R., and J. Portalupi. 2001. *Writing Workshop: The Essential Guide*. Portsmouth, NH: Heinemann.

Fountas, I. C., and G. S. Pinnell. 2012. "Guided Reading: The Romance and the Reality." *The Reading Teacher* 66 (4): 268–84.

Fry, E. 2004. *1000 Instant Words: The Most Common Words for Teaching Reading, Writing, and Spelling*. Westminster, CA: Teacher Created Resources.

Gambrell, L. B., and B. Marinak. 2008. "Reading Motivation: What the Research Says." Retrieved from www.readingrockets.org.

Graves, D. H. 2003. *Writing: Teachers and Children at Work, 20th Anniversary Edition*. Portsmouth, NH: Heinemann.

Gray, P. 2011. "The Decline of Play and the Rise of Psychopathology in Children and Adolescents." *American Journal of Play* 3 (4): 443–63.

Hansen, J. 2004. *Tell Me a Story: Developmentally Appropriate Retelling Strategies*. Newark, DE: International Reading Association.

Hart, B., and R. T. Risley. 1995. *Meaningful Differences in the Experience of Young American Children*. Baltimore: Brookes.

Harvey, S., and A. Goudvis. 2007. *Strategies That Work: Teaching Comprehension for Understanding and Engagement*. Portland, ME: Stenhouse.

Harvey, S., and P. D. Pearson. 2005. *What Every Teacher Should Know About Reading Comprehension Instruction*. Portsmouth, NH: Heinemann.

Hasbrouck, J., and G. A. Tindal. 2006. "Oral Reading Fluency Norms: A Valuable Assessment Tool for Reading Teachers." *The Reading Teacher* 59 (7): 636–44.

Hopkins, C. J. 1979. "The Spontaneous Oral Vocabulary of Children in Grade 1." *The Elementary School Journal* 79 (4): 240–49.

Johnson, C. J., and E. Yeates. 2006. "Evidence-Based Vocabulary Instruction for Elementary Students via Storybook Reading." *EBP: A Scholarly Forum for Guiding Evidence-Based Practices in Speech-Language Pathology* 1 (3): 1-23.

Justice, L. M. 2002. "Word Exposure Conditions and Preschoolers' Novel Word Learning During Shared Storybook Reading." *Reading Psychology* 23: 87–106.

Labbo, L., M. S. Love, and T. Ryan. 2007. "A Vocabulary Flood: Making Words 'Sticky' with Computer-Response Activities." *The Reading Teacher* 60 (6): 582–88.

Layne, S. L. (2015). *In Defense of Read-Aloud*. Portland, ME: Stenhouse.

Lonigan, C. J., and G. J. Whitehurst. 1998. "Relative Efficacy of Parent and Teacher Involvement in a Shared-Reading Intervention for Preschool Children from Low-Income Backgrounds." *Early Childhood Research Quarterly* 17: 265-92.

MacDonald, C. and L. Figueredo, L. 2010. "Closing the Gap Early: Implementing a Literacy Intervention for At-Risk Kindergartners in Urban Schools." *The Reading Teacher* 63 (5): 404–19.

McCarrier, A., G. S. Pinnell, and I. C. Fountas. 2000. *Interactive Writing: How Language and Literacy Come Together, K–2*. Portsmouth, NH: Heinemann.

McKenna, M. C., and S. A. Stahl. 2003. *Assessment for Reading Instruction*. New York: Guilford.

Morrow, L. M., and L. B. Gambrell. 2011. *Best Practices in Literacy Instruction*. 4th ed. New York: Guilford.

National Institute of Child Health and Human Development. 2000. *Report of the National Reading Panel: Teaching Children to Read—An Evidence-Based Assessment of the Scientific Research Literature on Reading and Its Implications for Reading Instruction*. NIH Publication No. 00-4769. Washington, DC: US Government Printing Office.

Neuman, S. B. 2006. "The Knowledge Gap: Implications for Early Education." In *Handbook of Early Literacy Research*, ed. D. K. Dickinson and S. B. Neuman. New York: Guilford.

Newcomer, P. L., and D. D. Hammill. 2008. *Test of Language Development: Primary*. 4th ed. Austin, TX: Pro-Ed.

Paris, S. G. 2009. "Constrained Skills—So What?" In *58th Yearbook of the National Reading Conference*, ed. K. M. Leander, D. W. Rowe, D. K. Dickinson, M. K. Handley, R. T. Jimenez, and V. J. Risko. Oak Creek, WI: National Reading Conference.

# Bibliography

Pianta, R. C., K. M. LaParo, and B. K. Hamre. 2008. *Classroom Assessment Scoring System Manual, Pre-K*. Baltimore, MD: Brookes.

RAND Corporation 2002. *Reading for Understanding: Toward a Research and Development Program in Reading Comprehension*. Santa Monica, CA: RAND.

Rasinski, T. V. 2010. *The Fluent Reader: Oral and Silent Reading Strategies for Building Fluency, Word Recognition, and Comprehension*. New York: Scholastic.

Rasinski, T., and C. Blachowicz. 2012. *Fluency Instruction*. 2d ed. New York: Guilford.

Rasinski, T., S. Homan, and M. Biggs. 2009. "Teaching Reading Fluency to Struggling Readers: Method, Materials, and Evidence. *Reading & Writing Quarterly* 25 (2): 192-204.

Reading Rockets. 2013. "Sharing Wordless Picture Books." Retrieved from www.readingrockets.org.

Roskos, K., and J. Christie. 2001. "On Not Pushing Too Hard: A Few Cautionary Remarks About Linking Literacy and Play." *Young Children* 56: 64–66.

Schickedanz, J. A., and R. M. Casbergue. 2009. *Writing in Preschool: Learning to Orchestrate Meaning and Marks*. Newark, DE: International Reading Association.

Schweinhart, L. J., J. Montie, Z. Xiang, W. S. Barnett, C. R. Belfield, and M. Nores. 2005. *Lifetime Effects: The HighScope Perry Preschool Study Through Age 40*. Monographs of the HighScope Educational Research Foundation, 14. Ypsilanti, MI: HighScope Press.

Schweinhart, L. J., and D. P. Weikart. 1997. *Lasting Differences: The HighScope Preschool Curriculum Comparison Study Through Age 23*. Ypsilanti, MI: HighScope Press.

Senechal, M. 1997. "The Differential Effect of Storybook Reading on Preschoolers' Acquisition of Expressive and Receptive Vocabulary." *Journal of Child Language* 24 (1): 123–38.

Silberg, J. 2005. *Reading Games for Young Children*. Beltsville, MD: Gryphon House.

Smith, S. B., D. C. Simmons, and E. J. Kame'enui. 1998. "Phonological Awareness: Instructional and Curricular Basics and Implications." In *What Reading Research Tells Us About Children with Diverse Learning Needs: Bases and Basics*, ed. D. C. Simmons and E. J. Kame'enui. Mahwah, NJ: Lawrence Erlbaum.

Snow, C. E., M. S. Burns, and P. Griffin. 1998. *Preventing Reading Difficulties in Young Children*. Washington, DC: National Academy Press.

Stanovich, K. E. 1986. "Matthew Effects in Reading: Some Consequences of Individual Differences in the Acquisition of Literacy." *Reading Research Quarterly* 21: 360-406.

Stauffer, R. 1970. *The Language Experience Approach to Reading*. New York: Harper.

Vukelich, C., and J. Christie. 2009. *Building a Foundation for Preschool Literacy: Effective Instruction for Children's Reading and Writing Development*. Newark, DE: International Reading Association.

Walpole, S., and M. C. McKenna. 2007. *Differentiated Reading Instruction: Strategies for the Primary Grades*. New York: Guilford.

———. 2009. *How to Plan Differentiated Reading Instruction: Resources for Grades K–3*. New York: Guilford.

Walsh, B., and P. Blewitt. 2006. "The Effect of Questioning Style During Storybook Reading on Novel Vocabulary Acquisition of Preschoolers." *Early Childhood Education Journal* 33 (4): 273–78.

Wasik, B. A., and M. A. Bond. 2001. "Beyond the Pages of a Book: Interactive Book Reading and Language Development in Preschool Classrooms." *Journal of Educational Psychology* 93: 243–50.

Wasik, B. A., M. A. Bond, and A. Hindman. 2006. "The Effects of Language and Literacy Intervention on Head Start Children and Teachers." *Journal of Educational Psychology* 98 (1): 63–74.

Whitehurst, G. J. 1992. "Dialogic Reading: An Effective Way to Read to Preschoolers." Retrieved from www.ldonline.org.

Whyte, D. 2004. *Morning Meeting, Afternoon Wrap-Up: How to Motivate Kids, Teach to Their Strengths, and Meet Your State's Standards*. Peterborough, NH: Crystal Springs Books.

Yopp, H. 1995. "A Test for Assessing Phonemic Awareness in Young Children." *The Reading Teacher* 49(1): 20-29.

## Children's Books

Adamson, H. 2009. *Families in Many Cultures*. North Mankato, MN: Capstone Press.

Adler, D. 2004. *Cam Jansen: Case 24: The Snowy Day Mystery*. New York: Scholastic.

Ahlberg, J., and A. Ahlberg. 1986. *The Jolly Postman: Or Other People's Letters*. New York: Little, Brown.

# Bibliography

Aliki. 1984. *Feelings*. New York: Greenwillow.

Allen, J. 2003. *Are You a Butterfly?* New York: Kingfisher.

Arnold, T. 2012. *There's a Fly Guy in My Soup*. New York: Scholastic.

Atkinson, M. 1998. *Why Can't I Be Happy All the Time?* New York: DK Children.

Baker, K. 2014. *LMNO Peas*. New York: Beach Lane Books.

Bang, M. 1999. *When Sophie Gets Angry—Really, Really Angry*. New York: Scholastic.

Banks, K. 2006. *Max's Words*. New York: Frances Foster Books.

Banyai, I. 1998. *Zoom*. New York: Viking.

Barrett, J. 2008. *Never Take a Shark to the Dentist*. New York: Atheneum Books.

Barrows, A. 2007. *Ivy and Bean*. San Francisco, CA: Chronicle Books.

Baylor, B. 1982. *The Best Town in the World*. New York: Macillan.

Becker, A. 2013. *Journey*. Somerville, MA: Candlewick.

Bingham, K. 2012. *Z Is for Moose*. New York: Greenwillow.

Blume, J. 1980. *Superfudge*. New York: Puffin.

Bossio, P. 2013. *The Line*. Tonawando, NY: Kids Can Press.

Brett, J. 2007. *The Three Snow Bears*. New York: Putnam.

Brown, J. 2013. *Flat Stanley*. New York: HarperCollins.

Browne, A. 2001. *Voices in the Park*. New York: DK.

Burleigh, R. 2014. *One Giant Leap*. New York: Puffin.

Campbell, S. 2010. *Growing Patterns*. Honesdale, PA: Boyds Mill Press.

Carle, E. 2009. *The Tiny Seed*. New York: Little Simon.

Colandro, L. 2012. *There Was an Old Lady Who Swallowed Some Books*. New York: Scholastic.

Cole, H. 2012. *Unspoken: A Story from the Underground Railroad*. New York: Scholastic.

Cooper, E. 2010. *Farm*. London: Orchard Books.

Cowley, J. 2003. *Mrs. Wishy-Washy's Farm*. New York: Puffin.

Crews, D. 1993. *School Bus*. New York: Greenwillow Books.

Cronin, D. 2002. *Giggle, Giggle, Quack*. New York: Atheneum Books.

———. 2003. *Diary of a Worm.* New York: HarperCollins.

———. 2011. *Click, Clack, Moo: Cows That Type.* New York: Little Simon.

Dahl, R. 1973. *James and the Giant Peach.* New York: Puffin.

———. 1989. *Matilda.* New York: Puffin.

Davies, J. 2007. *The Lemonade War.* New York: Sandpiper.

Day, A. 1996. *Good Dog, Carl.* New York: Little Simon.

Dean, J. 2013. *Pete the Cat: Pete at the Beach.* New York: HarperCollins.

———. 2014. *Pete the Cat: Old MacDonald Had a Farm.* New York: HarperCollins.

dePaola, T. 1978. *Pancakes for Breakfast.* New York: HMH Books.

———. 1996. *The Legend of the Indian Paintbrush.* New York: Puffin.

Dewdney, A. 2005. *Llama Llama Red Pajama.* New York: Penguin.

———. 2007. *Llama Llama Mad at Mama.* New York: Scholastic.

DiCamillo, K. 2009. *Mercy Watson to the Rescue.* Somerville, MA: Candlewick Press.

———. 2013. *Flora and Ulysses.* Somerville, MA: Candlewick Press.

DiCamillo, K., and A. McGhee. 2010. *Bink & Gollie.* Somerville, MA: Candlewick Press.

Dickmann, N. 2010. *Farm Animals.* New York: Heinemann.

Downing, J. 2011. *Amazon Alphabet.* New York: Pelican.

Edwards, R. 2007. *Best Friends: The True Story of Owen and Mzee.* New York: Penguin.

Egan, R. 1997. *From Wheat to Pasta.* Chicago, IL: Childrens PR.

Ehlert, L. 1988. *Planting a Rainbow.* San Diego, CA: Red Wagon Books.

———. 2001. *Waiting for Wings.* New York: HMH Books.

Elting, M., and M. Folsom. 2005. *Q Is for Duck: An Alphabet Guessing Game.* New York: HMH Books.

Fleming, D. 1991. *In the Tall, Tall Grass.* New York: Henry Holt.

———. 2002. *Alphabet Under Construction.* New York: Scholastic.

Freedman, R. 2004. *The Voice That Challenged a Nation: Marian Anderson and the Struggle for Equal Rights.* New York: Clarion Books.

Galdone, P. 1985. *The Little Red Hen.* New York: HMH Books.

Galvin, L. 2006. *Alphabet of Space.* Norfolk, CT: Soundprint.

# Bibliography

Gibbons, G. 1990. *Farming.* New York: Holiday House.

———. 1993. *From Seed to Plant.* New York: Holiday House.

———. 2005. *Chicks & Chickens.* New York: Holiday House.

———. 2014. *It's Raining.* New York: Holiday House.

Grant, J. 2008. *Chicken Said, "Cluck!"* New York: Scholastic.

Gustafson, S. 2007. *Favorite Nursery Rhymes from Mother Goose.* Muskogee, OK: Artisan.

Hamilton, K. 2009. *Police Officers on Patrol.* New York: Viking Books.

Harris, R. 2012. *Who's in My Family?* Somerville, MA: Candlewick Press.

Hawksley, G. 2012. *Jake Bakes Cakes: A Silly Rhyming Children's Book.* CreateSpace.

Heide, F. 2011. *Some Things Are Scary.* Somerville, MA: Candlewick.

Henkes, K. 1993. *Owen.* New York: Greenwillow Books.

———. 1995. *Julius: The Baby of the World.* New York: Greenwillow Books.

———. 1996. *Sheila Rae, The Brave.* New York: Greenwillow Books.

———. 2008. *Chrysanthemum.* New York: Mulberry Books.

———. 2010. *Wemberly Worried.* New York: Greenwillow Books.

———. 2014. *Lily's Big Day.* New York: Greenwillow Books.

Herzog, B. 2006. *K Is for Kick: A Soccer Alphabet.* Chelsea, MI: Sleeping Bear Press.

Hubbell, P. 2012. *Firefighters! Speeding! Spraying! Saving!* New York: Two Lions.

Janeczko, P. 2009. *A Kick in the Head: An Everyday Guide to Poetic Forms.* Somerville, MA: Candlewick.

Jeffers, O. 2014. *Once Upon an Alphabet: Short Stories for All the Letters.* New York: Philomel Books.

Jenkins, S. 2011. *Just a Second.* New York: HMH Books.

———. 2014. *Creature Features: Twenty-Five Animals Explain Why They Look the Way They Do.* New York: HMH Books.

Jordan, H. 2000. *How a Seed Grows.* New York: HarperCollins.

Karlin, N. 1996. *The Fat Cat Sat on the Mat.* New York: HarperCollins.

Kasza, K. 1996. *The Wolf's Chicken Stew.* New York: Puffin.

Kelly, D. 2011. *The Fenway Foul-Up.* New York: Random House.

Kennedy, C. 2013. *Poems to Learn by Heart*. New York: Hyperion.

Knowlton, L. 2012. *I Know a Librarian Who Chewed on a Word*. New York: Pelican.

Kontis, A. 2012. *AlphaOops! The Day Z Went First*. Somerville, MA: Candlewick.

Lamia, M. 2010. *Understanding Myself: A Kid's Guide to Intense Emotions and Strong Feelings*. Washington, DC: Magination Press.

Lawton, C. 2011. *Bugs A to Z*. New York: Scholastic.

Layne, S. L., and D. D. Layne. 2007. *T Is for Teachers: A School Alphabet*. Chelsea, MI: Sleeping Bear Press.

Lee, S. 2008. *Wave*. San Francisco, CA: Chronicle Books.

Lehman, B. 2004. *The Red Book*. New York: HMH Books.

———. 2007. *Rainstorm*. New York: HMH Books.

Levenson, G. 2002. *Pumpkin Circle: The Story of a Garden*. Berkeley, CA: Tricycle Press.

Liebman, D. 2000. *I Want to Be a Police Officer*. Ontario, Canada: Firefly Books.

Liu, J. 2002. *Yellow Umbrella*. San Diego, CA: Kane/Miller.

Lobel, A. 1970. *Frog and Toad Are Friends*. New York: HarperCollins.

———. 1971. *Frog and Toad Together*. New York: HarperCollins.

Macken, J. 2008. *Building a Road*. Mankato, MN: Capstone Press.

Maestro, B. 2000. *How Do Apples Grow?* New York: HarperCollins.

Maslen, B. 1987. *Ten Men*. New York: Scholastic.

———. 2006. Bob Books series. New York: Scholastic.

Mattick, L. 2015. *Finding Winnie: The True Story of the World's Most Famous Bear*. New York: Little, Brown.

Mayer, M. 2003. *A Boy, a Dog, and a Frog*. New York: Dial Books.

McDonald, M. 2010. *Judy Moody Was in a Mood*. Somerville, MA: Candlewick.

———. 2013. *Stink: The Incredible Shrinking Kid*. Somerville, MA: Candlewick.

McNamara, M. 2007. *How Many Seeds in a Pumpkin?* New York: Schwartz & Wade Books.

McNaughton, C. 1998. *Suddenly!* A Preston Pig Series Story. New York: HMH Books.

Nevius, C. 2006. *Building with Dad*. New York: Two Lions.

# Bibliography

Novak, P. 2009. *Engineering the ABCs*. Northville, MI: Ferne Press.

Onyefulu, I. 2015. *Deron Goes to Nursery School*. London: Frances Lincoln Children's Books.

Osborne, M. P. 2013. *Hurry Up, Houdini!* New York: Random House.

Owen, A. 2003. *Keeping You Safe*. North Mankato, MN: Picture Window Books.

Pallotta, J. 2006. *The Construction Alphabet Book*. Watertown, MA: Charlesbridge.

Parr, T. 2010. *The Earth Book*. New York: Little, Brown Books.

Penn, A. 1993. *The Kissing Hand*. Terre Haute, IN: Tanglewood Press.

Pfeffer, W. 2004. *From Seed to Pumpkin*. New York: HarperCollins.

_____. 2014. *The Shortest Day*. New York: Puffin.

Pilkey, D. 1999. *Captain Underpants and the Attack of the Talking Toilets*. New York: Scholastic.

Pinkney, J. 2009. *The Lion and the Mouse*. New York: Little, Brown Books.

Pollaco, P. 1998. *My Rotten Redheaded Older Brother*. New York: Simon & Schuster.

Prelutsky, J. 2006. *Scranimals*. New York: Greenwillow Books.

_____. 2008. *Be Glad Your Nose Is on Your Face*. New York: Greenwillow Books.

Raschka, C. 2011. *A Ball for Daisy*. New York: Schwartz & Wade Books.

Rathmann, P. 1995. *Officer Buckle and Gloria*. New York: G. P. Putnam.

Rockwell, A. 1999. *One Bean*. London: Walker Childrens.

_____. 2008. *Clouds*. New York: HarperCollins.

Rotner, S. 2003. *Lots of Feelings*. Minneapolis, MN: Millbrook.

Rowling, J. K. 1999. *Harry Potter and the Sorcerer's Stone*. New York: Scholastic.

Roy, R. 1997. *A–Z Mysteries: The Absent Author*. New York: Random House.

Rylant, C. 1993. *The Relatives Came*. New York: Modern Curriculum Press.

_____. 1994. *Mr. Putter and Tabby Pour the Tea*. New York: HMH Books.

_____. 1995. *Henry and Mudge and the Best Day of All*. New York: Aladdin Books.

Scarry, R. 2004. *A Day at the Police Station*. New York: Golden Books.

Scieszka, J. 1989. *The True Story of the 3 Little Pigs*. New York: Puffin Books.

_____. 1998. *The Time Warp Trio: The Knights of the Kitchen Table*. New York: Puffin Books.

_____. 2004. *Science Verse*. New York: Viking Books.

Scotton, R. 2008. *Love, Splat*. New York: HarperCollins.

Sendak, M. 1963. *Where the Wild Things Are*. New York: HarperCollins.

Seuss, T. G. 1960. *Green Eggs and Ham*. New York: Beginner Books.

Shannon, D. 1998. *No, David!* New York: Blue Sky Press.

_____. 1999. *David Goes to School*. New York: Blue Sky Press.

Sharmat, M. 1977. *Nate the Great*. New York: Yearling.

Showers, P. 2004. *A Drop of Blood*. New York: HarperCollins.

Silverstein, S. 1974. *Where the Sidewalk Ends*. New York: Harper and Row.

Simon, S. 2006. *Lightning*. New York: HarperCollins.

_____. 2009. *Wolves*. New York: HarperCollins.

_____. 2014. *Our Solar System*. New York: HarperCollins.

Skutch, R. 1997. *Who's in a Family?* Berkley, CA: Tricycle Press.

Snicket, L. 2007. *A Series of Unfortunate Events: The Bad Beginning*. New York: HarperCollins.

Stead, T. 2011. *Should There Be Zoos?* New York: Mondo.

Steig, W. 1982. *Doctor De Soto*. New York: Farrar, Strauss and Giroux.

Teague, M. 2002. *Dear Mrs. LaRue*. New York: Scholastic.

Thaler, M. 2008. *The Teacher from the Black Lagoon*. New York: Scholastic.

Thomas, J. 2009. *Rhyming Dust Bunnies*. San Diego, CA: Beach Lane Books.

Thomas, P. 2006. *Do I Have to Go to School?* Hauppauge, NY: Barron's Educational.

Thomson, B. 2010. *Chalk*. New York: Two Lions.

Tryon, L. 1994. *Albert's Alphabet*. New York: Aladdin.

Vamos, S. 2013. *Alphabet Trucks*. Watertown, MA: Charlesbridge.

Van Allsburg, C. 1981. *Jumanji*. New York: Scholastic.

Viorst, J. 1987. *Alexander and the Terrible, Horrible, No Good, Very Bad Day*. New York: Atheneum Books.

Ward, N. 2001. *A Wolf at the Door*. New York: Schoalstic.

White, E. B. 1952. *Charlotte's Web*. New York: Harper & Brothers.

# Bibliography

Wiesner, D. 2006. *Flotsam*. New York: Clarion Books.

_____. 2011. *Tuesday*. New York: HMH Books.

_____. 2013. *Mr. Wuffles*. New York: Clarion Books.

Willems, M. 2007. *My Friend Is Sad*. New York: Hyperion.

_____. 2013. *That Is Not a Good Idea*. New York: Balzer & Bray.

Wilson, K. 2009. *Bear's New Friend*. New York: Little Simon.

Wood, A. 2001. *Alphabet Adventure*. New York: Blue Sky Press.

Yaccarino, D. 2001. *The Lima Bean Monster*. London: Walker Childrens.

Yamada, K. 2014. *What Do You Do with an Idea?* Seattle, WA: Compendium.

Yolen, J. 1987. *Owl Moon*. New York: Philomel Books.

_____. 2003. *Least Things: Poems About Small Natures*. Honesdale, PA: WordSong.

Yolen, J., and H. Stemple. 2003. *Roanoke: The Lost Colony: An Unsolved Mystery from History*. New York: Simon & Schuster.

Zolotow, C. 1994. *The Seashore Book*. New York: HarperCollins.

# Index